DYNASTIES

DYNASTIES

THE 10 G.O.A.T. TEAMS THAT CHANGED THE NBA FOREVER

MARCUS THOMPSON II

Illustrated by Yu-Ming Huang

BLACK DOG
& LEVENTHAL
PUBLISHERS
NEW YORK

Text copyright © 2021 by Marcus Thompson II
Illustrations copyright © 2021 by Yu-Ming Huang

Jacket design by Katie Benezra
Jacket copyright © 2021 by Hachette Book Group, Inc.

Black Dog & Leventhal Publishers
Hachette Book Group
1290 Avenue of the Americas
New York, NY 10104
www.hachettebookgroup.com
www.blackdogandleventhal.com

First edition: October 2021

Black Dog & Leventhal Publishers is an imprint of Perseus Books, LLC, a subsidiary of Hachette Book Group, Inc. The Black Dog & Leventhal Publishers name and logo are trademarks of Hachette Book Group, Inc.

The publisher is not responsible for websites (or their content) that are not owned by the publisher.

The Hachette Speakers Bureau provides a wide range of authors for speaking events. To find out more, go to www.HachetteSpeakersBureau.com or call (866) 376-6591.

Print book interior design by Katie Benezra

Library of Congress Cataloging-in-Publication Data
Names: Thompson, Marcus, II, 1977– author.
Title: Dynasties: the 10 G.O.A.T. NBA teams that changed the NBA forever / Marcus Thompson II.
Description: First edition. | New York, NY: Black Dog & Leventhal, 2021. | Includes index. |
Summary: "Acclaimed sports journalist Marcus Thompson explores the 10 teams that transformed basketball in this illustrated history of the sport"–Provided by publisher.
Identifiers: LCCN 2020046460 (print) | LCCN 2020046461 (ebook) |
ISBN 9780762496297 (hardcover) | ISBN 9780762496280 (ebook)
Subjects: LCSH: National Basketball Association–History. | Basketball teams–United States–History. | Basketball players–United States–Biography.
Classification: LCC GV885.515.N37 T55 2021 (print) | LCC GV885.515.N37 (ebook) |
DDC 796.323/640973–dc23
LC record available at https://lccn.loc.gov/2020046460
LC ebook record available at https://lccn.loc.gov/2020046461

ISBNs: 978-0-7624-9629-7 (hardcover); 978-0-7624-9628-0 (ebook)

Printed in China

1010

10 9 8 7 6 5 4 3 2 1

To my favorite little girl in the whole wide world.

You are an array of brilliant colors, making life
more vivid. You are the rhythm behind my most
random dance. You are the warmth in my laugh,
the happiness healing my jadedness.
You are the perfect princess.

1

DYNASTIES MATTER

The NBA's special sauce is hatred. It's like a dollop of sour cream in pound cake batter, or a pinch of cayenne pepper in a latte.

What? You've never spiced up your joe?

That's what hate is for the NBA. Spice. Admittedly, it might sound ridiculous. People love sports. Heart-in-place-of-the-*o* kind of love. They love their teams. They love the players. They love the games, watching them and playing them. Sports is such a huge industry and so central to American culture because people absolutely love it. They live for it, watch it constantly, talk about it incessantly, dream about it, spend what amounts to the price of a new car on season tickets. This is especially true with the NBA. One of the league's most memorable marketing ploys was the *I Love This Game* campaign that ran from 1992 to 1999. Commercials filled with game highlights and fans having a blast were punctuated with celebrities declaring, "I love this game!" Love propelled the NBA, it would seem. People get team logos tattooed on their calves and have players' likenesses shaved into the backs of their heads by barber artists. They wear hoop jerseys with pride despite revealing hairy shoulders or side boob. They get married at center court during halftime. All for the love of the game.

Yes, love is at the core of fandom, and people across the world love the NBA. But love alone didn't elevate the league over the last forty years from an afterthought in America's psyche to a sports behemoth with the kind of magnetism that can supplant politics as the lead story. It wasn't love alone that pushed the NBA into the mainstream, past baseball in the hearts of many Americans, and made it popular enough to make the NFL pay attention. Love alone is not why the NBA's biggest stars are among the most well-known celebrities in the world.

In the realm of sports, love is a metaphor for passion. A strong accelerant for that passion is hate. Yes. Hate is how the NBA and its story lines grow from a warm campfire enjoyed among hoop heads to a consuming blaze infiltrating society. Hate helps expand the NBA's reach past that of diehards and into the curiosity of those who prefer binge-watching *Ozark* but can't escape the NBA buzz.

Let's explain a little further.

"Hate" is not exactly *hate* in this context. It has become more of an umbrella word used to encompass a host of negative feelings. Dislike. Disrespect. Animosity. Or just good ol'-fashioned jealousy. All of that fits under "hate"—hyperbole for the antagonistic component of fandom. Generally speaking, to be sure. Because sometimes it is actual hate. The real stuff. But that is usually masked, often poorly, behind acceptable sports animus. (More on that later.) In this sense, we're talking about the "*you hatin'*" version of hate. The kind that prompts yelling at the television until the foam builds in the corners of the mouth. The kind that triggers frantic all-caps typing in an argument with a stranger on social media. The kind that finds more joy in ridiculing the loser of the game than celebrating its victor. When the hate rises, clashing with the aforementioned love, it creates a duality that explodes interest.

> **Look at your fists. If you can envision the brass knuckles of Radio Raheem from *Do the Right Thing* (played by the late Bill Nunn) with "LOVE" on the right hand and "HATE" on the left, you are the coolest person reading this.**

It's akin to the Howard Stern Effect, unofficially coined for the radio personality in the 1990s. In his prime, most of his listeners were people who couldn't stand him. They disliked him so much they couldn't help but tune in to the shock jock so he could fuel their rage. They wanted more reasons to clutch their pearls and gasp in horror. So he had those who loved him listening as well as those who hated him, making him incredibly popular. The same happens in the NBA. And when the love is so strong, eventually it spawns hate. And as the hate rises, a phenomenon is created worthy of national attention. Both sides become so consumed, so invested, that casual fans can't help but be drawn in for the spectacle.

It's magnified when the hate is among the players. When the country was locked down in the spring of 2020 due to the COVID-19 pandemic, the airing of the ESPN documentary *The Last Dance* was pushed up two months to April 2020. In the second weekend of the five-week, ten-episode showing, the excitement was really turned up when it covered the rivalry of Michael Jordan's Bulls and Isiah Thomas's Pistons from the late '80s and early '90s. Just seeing Jordan's disdain for Thomas, still after thirty years, instantly reignited the Pistons-Bulls enmity.

The thing about this love-hate dynamic, though, is that it requires a certain level of greatness. It's so much more than just an unlikable star or a team with an irritating style of play. It takes all-time greatness to inspire these ardent levels of emotion.

That's why dynasties have always been good for the NBA.

The entire aura and appeal of the NBA is built on dominant teams with dominant players. The history of the league is segmented into dispensations based on the dynasty that controlled it. It is their collective excellence—usually spearheaded by an elite player whose ability, production, and personality is captivating—that is responsible for pushing the league to new heights.

The modern NBA as we know it began with the birth of the dynasties of Earvin "Magic" Johnson and Larry Bird, who rose to power simultaneously. The two captivated the nation when they were in college and clearly the best players in the land: Magic at Michigan State and Bird at Indiana State. They met in the NCAA title game in 1979 in one of the most anticipated matchups in history, fueled by their contrasting personalities and race relations in America. Magic, the inner-city kid with the boisterous personality and flamboyant game, against Bird, the aw-shucks Midwesterner whose game was fundamental brilliance. They led their respective teams to the tournament championship game, and 40 million people watched these two transcendent stars go at it, marking a 20 percent increase over the 1978 championship game viewership.

People followed their rivalry into the NBA. Magic was selected by the Los Angeles Lakers with the No. 1 pick in the 1979 NBA Draft. The Lakers were already a playoff team, led by Kareem Abdul-Jabbar and featuring exciting, young talents such as Norm Nixon and Jamaal Wilkes. Adding Magic lifted the franchise. The Lakers won the championship in 1980 as Magic famously started at center, in place of an injured Abdul-Jabbar, and played all five positions.

Bird was selected No. 6 overall by the Boston Celtics. The Celtics already had a Hall of Fame–bound point guard in Nate "Tiny" Archibald along with forward Cedric Maxwell and future Hall of Fame center Dave Cowens. But the addition of Bird produced a massive turnaround for the franchise. The Celtics went from 29 wins in 1978–79 to 61 wins in 1979–80 and a trip to the Eastern Conference Finals. A year later, Boston added veteran center Robert Parish and rookie forward Kevin McHale and won the 1981 NBA Championship with Bird leading a loaded Celtics squad.

Magic and Bird ushered the NBA into relevance. Before their arrival, the NBA was all but begging for credibility in the sports landscape. The 1980 NBA Finals featured two popular teams in the Los Angeles Lakers and Philadelphia 76ers. This series was stacked with Hall of Famers in their prime or near it: Kareem, Julius "Dr. J" Erving, Bobby Jones, Jamaal Wilkes, Maurice Cheeks. And the superstar rookie in Magic Johnson. Yet CBS aired three of the games on tape delay.

Game 2 and Game 5 in Los Angeles aired at 11:30 p.m. on the East Coast. The deciding Game 6—when Magic the point guard started at center and led the Lakers to the title—was televised on a two-and-a-half-hour tape delay. NBA ratings were so poor, CBS didn't think the Finals were worthy of bumping ever-popular tv show *Dallas* out of its time slot. And that's not even the craziest part.

In the spring of 1980, season three of *Dallas* ended with J. R. Ewing getting shot and sparking a whodunit mystery. This is especially memorable because fans had to wait until season four in November to find out the answer, and for eight months CBS ran the famous "Who shot J. R.?" commercials. Season three ended on March 21, 1980. Game 6 of the NBA Finals was nearly two months later on May 16. So the clinching Game 6 between the Lakers and Sixers, one of the most legendary performances of Magic's career, was actually tape-delayed in favor of *Dallas* reruns.

Yes, reruns. So disrespectful.

But that's where the NBA ranked in the hierarchy of entertainment. In the 1981 playoffs, seventeen games started at 11:30 p.m. on the East Coast. The last game to air on tape delay was still five years later, in the 1986 Western Conference Finals between the Lakers and Rockets.

Even with that, though, the NBA was percolating as the Lakers' and Celtics' dynasties were building. Bird followed Magic's 1980 title by winning the 1981 championship. Then Magic won again in 1982, beating the 76ers.

The 76ers made it back to the Finals in 1983, beating the Lakers on the third try. Then, in 1984, the Lakers and Celtics met. It was Magic vs. Bird again. The NBA, fifteen years after the first Celtics dynasty ended, shifted to another gear.

FOLLOW THE ANALYTICS: THE RATINGS

In the first five years after Magic and Bird entered the NBA, TV ratings rose. That couldn't be said for any other sports league. After they met in the 1984 and 1985 Finals, CBS went from considering dropping the NBA to re-upping with the league for four years at $173 million. When that deal ended NBC swooped in and agreed to pay the NBA $600 million for four years to air games.

Since then, the fifteen most-watched games in NBA history involve a dynasty or a dynastic player. The absolute highest-viewed game in history was Game 6 of the 1998 NBA Finals featuring Michael Jordan's Bulls, which held an average viewership of 35.89 million. An astounding 72 million people in America watched at least part of the game, which ended with Jordan's last shot as star of the Bulls, his famous game-winning pull-up over Bryon Russell. Game 5 of that series averaged 30.6 million viewers, good for fourth on the list.

The second-highest viewership average was the series-clinching Game 6 in 1993, when Jordan beat Charles Barkley's Phoenix Suns on the road. That game averaged 32.1 million viewers.

Seven of the top ten games with the highest viewer averages include Jordan.

The only other game since Jordan to average at least 30 million viewers was the 2016 winner-take-all in Oakland, when LeBron James completed a comeback from a 3–1 deficit to upset the Warriors. It peaked at 44.8 million and averaged 31 million. That was because the Warriors had risen to dynastic realms.

Golden State came out of nowhere and won the championship in 2015. It was the culmination of a three-year journey in which the Warriors constructed a core group and worked their way up the NBA mountain the earnest way—through the draft, through developing their own young talent and through the

Highest NBA Finals Ratings

AVG. VIEWERS (IN MILLIONS)	SERIES	TEAMS
35.89	1998 Finals, Game 6	Bulls vs. Jazz
32.1	1993 Finals, Game 6	Bulls vs. Suns
31.0	2016 Finals, Game 7	Warriors vs. Cavs
30.6	1998 Finals, Game 5	Bulls vs. Jazz
29.04	1998 Finals, Game 1	Bulls vs. Jazz
28.2	2010 Finals, Game 7	Lakers vs. Celtics
27.2	1993 Finals, Game 1	Bulls vs. Suns
26.7	1998 Finals, Game 2	Bulls vs. Jazz
26.3	1998 Finals, Game 3	Bulls vs. Jazz
26.3	2013 Finals, Game 7	Heat vs. Spurs
26.0	2019 Finals, Game 6	Warriors vs. Raptors*
24.86	1996 Finals, Game 1	Bulls vs. Sonics
24.7	2019 Finals, Game 5	Warriors vs. Raptors*
24.47	2017 Finals, Game 5	Warriors vs. Cavs
24.12	1987 Finals, Game 1	Lakers vs. Celtics
23.88	2011 Finals, Game 6	Heat vs. Mavericks
23.25	2015 Finals, Game 6	Warriors vs. Cavs

*Includes Canadian viewership

acquisition of perfectly fitting veterans complementing their core. Then they hijacked the nation by starting the 2015–16 season 24–0, breaking through the ceiling on their expectations. They started drawing comparisons to Jordan's Bulls as they obliterated the league. Stephen Curry, the league MVP, put together a season like no one had seen before. Eventually, the Warriors broke the Bulls record of 72 regular-season wins, which Chicago set in 1996, a record nobody thought would ever be touched. In the process, the Warriors went from the sexy sleeper to the NBA's beloved and, wait for it, behated franchise.

Indeed, all the fanfare developed a seething contempt, heightening their fame and the NBA's along with them. The truth is, and it was true even for Jordan, that when anything gets too popular in the NBA, it inspires a contrary reaction. Add in the cultural elements these players and teams come to embody and the intensity gets real. Because of their visibility and how few of them there are, NBA players have a unique connection with the fan base. They become representations of ideals, beliefs, and perspectives. Fans get entrenched. In 2016, the Warriors had fans on both sides dug in about their greatness or overrated-ness. Then the Finals came around, and the Warriors earned the ire of the enormous and loyal fan base LeBron James has cultivated over his stellar career. Casual fans were like moths drawn to the flame of the heated beef between the warring factions dueling on social media, at proverbial water coolers and between pick-up hoop games across the nation.

The celebration of LeBron's historic victory was short-lived for his faithful, likewise for the heartache of Warriors fans. The Warriors' rebuttal was signing Kevin Durant, arguably the best player in the NBA. The Warriors went on to win in 2018 and 2019, vanquishing an overwhelmed LeBron. Of course, that only turned up the hate. The validity of the Warriors' status was questioned by a legion of dissenters because of their stacked roster. Durant received the brunt of the discreditation and disrespect.

There is a dope book out about this—*KD: Kevin Durant's Relentless Pursuit to Be the Greatest*. You'll love (or hate) it.

And *then* the Warriors added another All-Star, albeit an injured one, in center DeMarcus Cousins.

It all seemed to break the psyche of the basketball world. No team ever assembled has caused so much dread. Their team was so daunting—five players who are All-Stars in their prime on the same roster—as to render the regular season meaningless. It didn't even matter that Cousins was available because he tore his Achilles and no one knew if he'd ever be the same. The sackcloth, ashes, and wailing commenced nonetheless. The annual question shifted from who would win the title to how easily would the Warriors win it. Fans bemoaned their favorite team not having so much as a pipe dream of a chance. Media and analysts pontificated endlessly about the state of the league with such a dominant team. The hot takes and think pieces churned. Former players and opposing players decried the decisions of Durant and Cousins to even join the Warriors, questioning their competitive spirit and even their character for choosing to win in such a way. The entire time Warriors fans reveled in the glory of their team's preeminence.

Golden State leaned into its new role as NBA bully. At one team party, they erected a series of alphabet balloons that spelled out "Super Villains." Curry, the cornerstone of this sudden behemoth of a franchise, mocked the popular narrative with his Under Armour shoe campaign, which featured the tagline "Ruin the Game" as an inspirational slogan.

The Warriors were bad for basketball, allegedly. For four straight years, they played Cleveland in the NBA Finals. It became a summer tradition. The clashes became decidedly less competitive as the rivalry progressed: The Dubs were seen as the league's big problem. But maybe everyone should have listened to Warriors All-Star Draymond Green.

"Everyone wants to say, 'Ah man, this is boring and this, that, and the other,' but you usually don't appreciate something until you don't have it anymore. And so, I think maybe there's just a lack of appreciation for greatness. But then when you look at a situation, most people have never reached greatness. So maybe there's just not an understanding of what you're watching. I think you've found two great teams, and we've played that way, and maybe people don't appreciate it because of a blowout or because of a sweep. But people may want to be careful, because I think right now you're witnessing greatness."

LeBron eventually left the Cavaliers, dismantling Cleveland's reign in the East and leaving the Warriors without a formidable opponent to get excited about. It ended up being the Toronto Raptors. The Canadian team didn't inspire much excitement in the States, but the series was riveting theater. In Game 5 of the 2019 NBA Finals, Kevin Durant returned from a previous injury and tore his Achilles tendon—and weeks later, he ended a season of speculation about his future when he became a free agent and signed with the Brooklyn Nets. In Game 6, Klay Thompson, who'd already missed a game with a sprained ankle, tore his ACL. Cousins played with a torn thigh muscle on the mend. Kevon Looney played with a broken clavicle. The Raptors beat the hobbled Warriors.

The crash landing of Golden State back to earth coupled with Canada's entire country on tilt over the Raptors ranked as one of the most-watched series as two games landed in the top fifteen most-watched of all time—Durant's return in Game 5 and the Raptors' clinching game.

With Golden State out of the picture, their dissenters had the parity they clamored for during the Warriors' reign. The common refrain was how their dynasty robbed the league of suspense and trivialized the regular season. And now, they'd lost Durant to the Nets and Thompson to injury. Four games into the 2019–20 season, Curry broke his hand and was out four months. The Warriors were off the throne. This was supposed to be a good thing for the NBA.

In October 2019, just before the 2019–20 season began, an article in the *Sports Business Journal* told of how excited networks that air NBA games were for the coming season. LeBron finally got his costar in Los Angeles as Anthony Davis was traded to the Lakers, making them instant title contenders. Then Kawhi Leonard left the Raptors for the Clippers, returning to American households and joining the No. 2 market in the country. He did it because Paul George joined him by forcing a trade out of Oklahoma City, creating a powerhouse out of the already-good Clippers team. The NBA had two contenders in Los Angeles.

The balance of power shifted again when Russell Westbrook asked to be traded from Oklahoma City following George's trade. Westbrook landed with Houston to play with former teammate James Harden, pairing two MVPs. With Milwaukee and Philadelphia already in the mix as contenders, the NBA suddenly had several teams entering the season with legitimate hopes for a title.

In addition to the new powers formed, some good young teams were expecting to be even better. The young Denver Nuggets, which finished No. 2 in the Western Conference in 2018–19, returned with postseason experience. Dallas had a healthy and ready-to-go Kristaps Porziņģis, whom the Mavericks got from New York, to give young superstar Luka Dončić a sidekick.

Then rookie Zion Williamson came out of Duke as the most hyped rookie since LeBron sixteen years earlier, landing with New Orleans.

"I haven't been this excited for an opening day for a long time," Craig Barry, executive vice president and chief content officer for Turner Sports, told the *Sports Business Journal*. "We're coming off one of the most interesting and provocative off seasons, maybe in the history of the NBA—certainly in the thirty years that we've been covering it [on TNT]."

Four months after its first article, the *Sports Business Journal* ran another piece: "NBA's Local Ratings Dip, Matching National Trend."

In the article, it reported TNT's viewership of national NBA games was down 13 percent. Local ratings were also down as thirteen teams posted ratings drops of at least 19 percent. Despite more teams having a chance, and the star power more evenly distributed across the league, the ratings were dropping. The declining ratings was a major point of discourse throughout the 2019–20 season before the COVID-19 pandemic eventually shut down the NBA and all of sports. Then as the season continued in the bubble at Disney World, the ratings suffered even more despite the long wait and supposed appreciation for live games. Even with LeBron, the ratings for the 2020 NBA Finals hit an all-time low. Many factors played into the sharp decline. The pandemic, a recession, and the nation reckoning with race relations were chief among them. Also, the sports calendar was significantly altered. The NBA Finals kicked off four months after its normal time and in a fall cluttered with sports. But undoubtedly, one of the factors was the absence of the Warriors, the magnetic dynasty dethroned by injury and free agency. The bubble produced the Lakers' first title in a decade but it didn't feature a dynasty.

> But undoubtedly, one of the factors was the absence of the Warriors, the magnetic dynasty dethroned by injury and free agency.

History had repeated itself, and it was laid bare for all to see. The NBA thrives on dynasties. So many were in their feelings about the Warriors they forgot what butters the NBA's bread. The league thrives when a superpower is at the top—setting the bar for the rest of the league to clear, giving the divided fan bases a galvanizing force, giving a single market a reason to go all in, sparking the interest of casual fans with something spectacular. The NBA lost that with the collapse of the Warriors. LeBron James, Anthony Davis, and the Lakers might have left the bubble as a potential dynasty in the making but they didn't have a sexy rival to generate enough hate, especially after Kawhi Leonard's Clippers lost early and thwarted the Battle for Los Angeles many wanted to see. It was just the latest and newest example of what makes the NBA arguably the greatest sports league in America: dynasties.

2

WHAT IS A DYNASTY?

"To be able" or "to have power" or "dominion."

That is what the Ancient Greek word *dynastéia* means and where the word "dynasty" has its origins. The concept carried with it this idea of elongated dominion, sustained by bequeathment.

Merriam-Webster defines a dynasty as both a succession of rulers from the same line, in which the power is passed down, and as a powerful group or family that maintains its position for a long time. Dictionary.com adds a dynasty is a family that is distinguishable by its success, wealth, and the like.

The Qing Dynasty is a prime example, ruling for nearly three centuries in what is now China. Familial dynasties also fit the mold, à la the Kennedys, or even in the fictional form like the Ewings of the '80s television show *Dallas* or the Roys of *Succession*.

But sports dynasties? They are much less official, much more metaphorical.

Dynasties aren't familial. Well, except in ownership, such as Lakers' owner Jeanie Buss, whose 2020 championship adds to the legacy of her father, late Lakers owner Jerry Buss. But NBA fans don't care too much about ownership reigns. Neither are dynasties in sports passed down to the next generation.

Sports dynasties are entities that hold on to power for a sustained period. Being labeled a dynasty is the ultimate accomplishment in team sports. NBA fans don't dish out such a label lightly. So though there isn't a tangible bar, it must be cleared.

How long do they have to hold power? How thorough must their dominion be? What are the characteristics that separate dynasties from mere ordinary greatness?

The easiest answer perhaps mirrors the Supreme Court explanation of what makes something pornography. As Justice Potter Stewart put it: "I know it when I see it." The same could apply for whether a team meets the criteria for a dynasty: You just know it when you see one.

But we'll get a little more scientific with hopes to qualify and quantify which teams get the ever-so-important designation. Let's define an NBA dynasty.

DYNASTIES ARE WILDLY SUCCESSFUL

Multiple championships are the bare minimum requirement. Consider it an application fee.

To be classified as a dynasty, a team must go above and beyond multiple championships. Their success needs to be something extra, reach historic levels. Their excellence must be sustained in a way that is memorable and distinguishable.

While at least two titles are required, it helps the case if they are consecutive. A three-peat essentially guarantees a seat at the table. Since it is indeed an incredible feat to make it to the NBA Finals, trips to the championship level are worthy bonus points.

DYNASTIES ARE EVOLUTIONARY

A critical mark of a dynasty is how it raises the level of the NBA and basketball itself.

Dynasties are born of excellence. They are led by players who transcend previous notions of what could and should be done on the court. They dominate with a style of play and scheme that is often revolutionary. As a result, they influence the entire league by becoming the gold standard, forcing opponents to adapt and adjust, even imitate.

So a dynasty should have some kind of pioneering element. Or maybe it went about its success in a different way, a way that forced the game to change. Dynasties should be agents of evolution.

DYNASTIES ARE CULTURALLY RELEVANT

Throughout the life of the NBA, the reigning dynasty has been illustrative of its time. The team is either a microcosm of the society in which it exists or an example of shifting cultural winds. Maybe the team is the one powering the gust. The ability to make such an impact is one of the strengths of the NBA.

Because there are only five players on the court and fifteen players on the team, the audience has always had an intimate relationship with NBA players—especially in the early years, when marketing the game required a level of intimacy. The NBA has been driven by stars from its inception. It has always sold a special kind of access to the best players. When the Lakers moved from Minneapolis to Los Angeles, they'd travel around the city in a truck or van, with a hoop court connected to the back, holding live practices and exhibitions. Jerry West, the inspiration for the future logo of the NBA, was part of pop-up camps in random neighborhoods as part of a grassroots marketing effort.

Central figures of dynasties become spokespeople for an era, ambassadors for causes.

The star of an NBA team, even the second and third star, experiences a relationship with the fan base similar to that of a quarterback on a football team, or a star of an individual sport. They are able to build a bond with viewers because of how much they impact games. The emotions of wins and losses, of moments, get superimposed onto them because they are in the mix and recognizable. Players who directly affect the outcome of games tend to develop a more intense union with fans. Their contributions are tangible. Since basketball has fewer players on the court than other team sports, that relationship is easier to forge.

In baseball, it's been decades since the stud pitcher took the mound every day. The starting pitcher throws once every five days now. Also, nine players take the field at a time, and twenty-five are on a roster. In football, eleven players are on the field at a time for each team, and fifty-three are on every roster. And they're all wearing helmets, which makes it more difficult for fans to recognize and develop a personal vibe with the players. It's why players want to take off their helmets when they do something great, which is now a penalty in the NFL. In sports with more players, it's harder for fans to feel that connection. It takes more for players to stand out.

NBA stars, on the other hand, have been able to supplement their performances with their personalities—because who they are is so much more on display. All of that means more adoration, and more scrutiny, and a stronger individual connection with the diehards. With such comes influence. With such comes the perspective of the basketball player, perspectives shaped by the world from which he comes. Thus, central figures of dynasties become spokespeople for an era, ambassadors for causes, inspirations, prominent voices in culture, setters of trends. Their plights and successes are on the table; their convictions become part of their story. The best players, and thus the best teams, have a relevance that extends even beyond the game.

That was perhaps never more true than in 2020. On March 11, Utah Jazz center Rudy Gobert tested positive for COVID-19, and the NBA responded by suspending play. The league was the first domino in what would be a historic nationwide halting of sports.

Some three months later, the NBA worked out a plan to finish the 2019–20 regular season and hold the playoffs inside a bubble created at Disney World. Initially, many players did not want to participate. Video had surfaced of a Minneapolis police officer killing George Floyd, an unarmed African-American man, by holding his knee on the man's neck for eight minutes, forty-six seconds. People watched him die on social media under the weight of police brutality, and it sparked months of protests around the globe in a plea for the end of racial injustice. Several players voiced a preference to join the marches and protests instead of being isolated from the historic movement that spread into other countries. For some players, playing basketball seemed secondary to the fight for equality. Eventually, play resumed after the National Basketball Players Association and the league reached an agreement. Part of that agreement included the NBA becoming a platform for the players' participation in the movement. Their jerseys had phrases expressing messages of social justice. The courts were emblazoned with "Black Lives Matter." Postgame interviews included monologues about policing and the importance of voting.

The clout of NBA stars and their teams, their cultural relevance, was on full display.

DYNASTIES ARE FOREVER

Perhaps the most significant mark of a team, and an indicator of its dynastic prowess, is the legacy it leaves behind.

Does its impact survive and span the generations? Do we end up talking about the team, using it as a barometer for the future? Does the team still captivate us? Does what it did still impress long after its reign has ended?

For the first month of the pandemic, sports fans went through withdrawals as live games were canceled during the country's shutdown to stop the spread of the novel coronavirus. Accustomed to an unrelenting list of sports options, fans were left with replays of old classic games or binging on Netflix like a recovering addict leans on cigarettes. To appease a desperate fan base, ESPN moved up the date of its ten-part series on Jordan's Bulls, originally scheduled to release in June 2020. For five Sundays straight, an average of nearly six million people tuned in to watch a documentary about the Bulls dynasty featuring behind-the-scenes footage of their final season. It was called *The Last Dance*. All ten episodes topped five million viewers each. Only the NFL Draft, a NASCAR race at Darlington, and a special golf match featuring Tiger Woods and Phil Mickelson drew more viewers during the stoppage of sports in the pandemic. More than two decades after they played, Jordan and the Bulls still mattered. And it wasn't just a thirst for sports because none of the other documentaries that aired in the same window—one about Lance Armstrong, one about the 1998 home run chase between Mark McGwire and Sammy Sosa—got near the amount of viewers as *The Last Dance*. Nor did any of the seeding games once the NBA season resumed in the Orlando bubble.

The Bulls were just that iconic.

There has to be something special about a dynasty. Something we can't explain and just know. Let emotion decide. Let the gut have the final say. You'll know it when you see it.

3

THE GEORGE MIKAN LAKERS

In the locker room pregame, George Mikan took off his glasses while putting on his uniform. He could hardly see without them. So he didn't know what was going on around him. But when he put them back on, his Minneapolis Lakers teammates were in street clothes.

Surprised, he asked what was going on. Slater Martin, the Lakers' rookie guard, told the big man it was about the marquee on the face of Madison Square Garden. It declared the NBA attraction happening inside that night, December 14, 1949: the host New York Knickerbockers vs. George Mikan.

"It says you're playing the Knicks. Go out and play 'em," Mikan told the *New York Times*, recalling Martin's reply. "Slater was the instigator of them giving me the rib. Well, I gave them a few choice words, and we all broke out laughing."

Before Lakers big man Anthony Davis leapt his six-foot-ten frame in the air, extending that seven-foot-six wingspan to catch one of his Inspector Gadget alley-oops, there was Mikan. Every time 76ers seven-foot center Joel Embiid gets the ball down low and goes to work in the post, he is carrying on the legacy of Mikan.

The NBA has an addiction to size. For most of its history, big men have always been the most coveted possession. Some serious draft disasters— Portland passed up on Michael Jordan and Kevin Durant—were born of desperation for a center. The genesis of the NBA's affinity for a big man is Mikan.

And the genesis of George Mikan is Ray Meyer.

Meyer—the son of a candy wholesaler from Chicago who passed on his plans to be a priest—became a coach after graduating from Notre Dame, where he played for famed basketball coach George Keogan. Meyer ended up working as an assistant under Keogan before an opportunity to be the head man at DePaul opened up. When he got there, he came across Mikan and had a great idea.

Mikan was six foot eight when he graduated high school. He hated being tall. He described himself as round-shouldered because he spent so much time hunching over to hide his height. He was gangly and clumsy. He was so near-sighted, he wore glasses thick like a Coke bottle. He was the walking definition of why basketball was not a sport for big men. He didn't play in high school,

just recreationally in the summer. He wanted to go to Notre Dame, but Keogan thought he was too clumsy.

But Meyer, the rookie coach, had a vision. And he was quite the taskmaster, with a temper to boot. One of his former players, Jim Marino, told the *Chicago Tribune* that when he played for Meyer at DePaul they'd race to the locker room at halftime to get the seat farthest from Meyer.

"We were terrified of him at times," Marino said. "When I signed with DePaul, people came to me and told me what a mistake I had made. 'He's a maniac,' they said. I couldn't understand what they meant. Here was this nice man who came to our house and ate with us and seemed so jolly. Then I got here and knew what they meant."

That same energy is what pushed Mikan, who was willing to put in the work. Meyer worked on the clumsiness. He had Mikan jumping rope, shadowboxing, punching a speed bag, and taking dancing lessons. Meyer even developed

Mikan's touch. He taught him the hook shot with both hands, which became Mikan's trademark. He built his foundation with a drill still used today, even at the NBA level. Stand under the basket and convert a layup on the right side with the right hand. Get the rebound (without the ball touching the ground) and convert a left-handed layup on the left side. Then back to the right side, and back to the left side. It's called the Mikan Drill. Meyer had Mikan doing hundreds of them. He'd put a towel under Mikan's armpit on the off hand to keep his form tight.

He was developing not only Mikan's basketball skills but also his confidence. The not-so-clumsy Mikan was a different breed. He went from Clark Kent to Superman. He went from averaging 11.3 points as a freshman to 23.3 points as a junior. He was named All-American three times.

What Meyer produced was the greatest work of his storied career: the first NBA superstar.

Mikan started with the Chicago American Gears of the National Basketball League in 1946 and led them to the title. His team folded in 1947, so he was signed by the Minneapolis Lakers the following season. In 1948, the Lakers and three other NBL teams joined the new Basketball Association of America and won the title that year, too. In 1949, the BAA became the NBA.

Mikan was instantly dominant, professional basketball's first superstar. He averaged 28.3 points in his debut season with the Lakers. He upped that to 31.3 in the playoffs as Minneapolis won the first-ever NBA title.

His height and touch made him a terror around the basket. He would park right outside the lane, his teammate would dump the ball down to him, and he was one simple turn from being at the rim. In 1950, the Fort Wayne Pistons developed a unique strategy to counter Mikan: keep away. The NBA didn't have a twenty-four-second shot clock then, so the Pistons just held the ball. Forever. Fort Wayne won 19–18. Yes, two teams combined to score just 37 points in a forty-eight-minute game. Mikan had 15 of the Lakers' 18 points.

That regular season, he averaged a career-best 28.4 points. Before the 1951–52 season, the NBA changed the rules to keep Mikan from being able to post so close to the rim. The painted area was widened from six feet to twelve feet, pushing Mikan farther away from the basket.

He responded by leading the Lakers to the next three NBA titles. He won five total, including the first one in the BAA. He made four All-Stars and won three scoring titles.

Mikan turned the giants of the land into coveted basketball commodities. Height became the most precious of metals. In a game where the goal was ten feet high, the humans closest to the rim turned out to be the most valuable. For Mikan, that value translated to confidence, a comfort in his own skin. And because of it, the extremely tall had a new career option.

NBA Finals Appearances

1949 (W)	1950 (W)	1952 (W)
1953 (W)	1954 (W)	1956 (L)

THE ORIGIN STORY

King Boring was a middle-class accountant in the city of Dearborn, Michigan. His business partner, Maury Winston, was the owner of Winston Jewelers, also in Dearborn. Both sports fans, and looking to get into this new pro sport called basketball, they created the Detroit Gems. Winston came up with the Gems nickname, for obvious reasons.

The Gems entered the National Basketball League for the 1946–47 season, the league's second season. The Detroit Falcons started the same season in the Basketball Association of America.

The Detroit Gems were easily the worst team in the league, and pretty much one of the worst teams in pro basketball history. They went 4–40. While the Falcons played at Olympia Stadium, the cool home of the Red Wings dubbed the Old Red Barn, the Gems didn't even have a home court. They were hoping to play at the Dearborn Forum that was under construction, but it was never finished. So the Gems started at Ferndale High School. They eventually down-graded to the smaller Holy Redeemer High School and averaged about three hundred fans per game.

With a debt that got as high as $25,000, Boring and Winston sold the team in 1947. Ben Berger paid $15,000 for the Gems, which calculates to be more than $174,000 today with inflation. Berger owned a bunch of theaters, a big restaurant, and multiple real estate properties. He got his start as a promoter in the early 1900s who dabbled in boxing and wrestling.

Pro basketball was far from a sure thing. College, high school, and even AAU basketball was more popular. But basketball was gaining in popularity after World War II and Berger had a vision, so he brought the NBL to Minneapolis.

"I have been in contact with professional basketball people for more than a year," he told the *Minneapolis Star Tribune* in its June 5, 1947, issue. "They have convinced me that professional basketball will be a successful operation in the future even though it is not balancing the books in several spots now. I think professional basketball will be something that is good for Minneapolis. I intend to eventually make this a home-grown team that Minneapolis will call its own. As big league basketball prospers, it will be a credit to Minneapolis to have a team."

He called them the Lakers since they were playing in "the land of 10,000 lakes." One of Berger's first moves was to sign Jim Pollard. The Oakland, California, native and former Stanford star, who left school to join the war, starred for the Coast Guard basketball team in Alameda, California. Pollard took to the AAU circuit after the war. He played a year for the San Diego Dons and a year for his hometown Oakland Bittners, making the national championship game with both teams. Pollard was one of the most coveted amateur players in the country. In September 1947, Berger got him. Even the mayor of Oakland tried to get Pollard to stay with the Bittners, but to no avail. Pollard was the Lakers' new center.

Two months later, the Chicago Gears squad featuring Mikan disbanded when its league was dissolved. The players were dispersed among NBL teams in an expansion draft. And the newest team, the Minneapolis Lakers, had the top pick.

So Berger, in a span of five months, bought the Lakers and signed Pollard and drafted Mikan. Minneapolis was 3–1 when they finally landed Mikan. They really took off once he came aboard and moved Pollard to his natural position, a small forward. In April 1948, the Lakers played in the *Chicago Herald-American* world championships, a three-game tournament that drew forty-four thousand total fans. They beat the New York Renaissance—"a Negro touring aggregation"

known as the NY Rens—75–71 in front of 16,982 fans. Mikan had 40 points, setting the tournament record. The Rens got 24 points from Nathaniel "Sweetwater" Clifton, who would become the first Black player to sign with the NBA. The Lakers then resumed the NBL season and won the title that year. Mikan averaged 24.4 points in the playoffs.

In May 1948, the Lakers made the jump to the Basketball Association of America, along with Indianapolis and Fort Wayne. The BAA was an upgrade over the NBL, which operated in small cities. The BAA played in major cities and in larger arenas.

The Lakers drew nearly eleven thousand in the 1949 championship game in St. Paul, beating Red Auerbach's Washington Capitols as Mikan dominated with a broken wrist. In the crowd watching the game was Vern Mikkelsen, a star at nearby Hamline University. Watching the Lakers win the title made him eager to join Minneapolis.

On August 3, 1949, the NBL and BAA merged to form the National Basketball Association. The Lakers made it to the first-ever NBA Finals, in 1950, against the Syracuse Nationals. The Lakers played the first two home games in the St. Paul Auditorium, getting 10,288 fans in Game 3 and a St. Paul record 10,512 in Game 4. The Lakers clinched the title at the Minneapolis Auditorium before 9,812 fans, a venue record.

Three leagues, three championships, and record crowds. Berger's gamble paid off. The Lakers were the hottest thing in basketball.

When This Dynasty Reigned

- In the heart of the five-championships-in-six-years run by the Minneapolis Lakers, the United States got involved in the Korean War. Data shows 1.5 million men were drafted to support South Korea in its war against North Korea, backed by China and Russia.

- The "Golden Age of Television" kicked off with shows like *The Lone Ranger*, *I Love Lucy*, *Dragnet*, *Lassie*, *Gunsmoke*, and *The Honeymooners*.

- The Blues, migrating from the deep south to places like Memphis and Chicago, were creeping into the mainstream. Blues legends like Muddy Waters and Howlin' Wolf paved the way for 1950s stars like Bo Diddley and Chuck Berry, which planted the seeds for Rock 'N' Roll.

THE FORGOTTEN STAR

The opening slate of games for the NBA's inaugural season included the Minneapolis Lakers at the Philadelphia Warriors. Mikan, who starred in the BAA before the merger, was the main attraction, but the key matchup was between two leapers. Joe Fulks, a six-foot-five small forward from Birmingham, Kentucky, was the star of Philadelphia and had also been dominant in the BAA. He was known for jumping on his shot, which was uncommon then as most players took set shots. But Minneapolis had a rookie from the West Coast, a six-foot-four forward who was so springy they called him the Kangaroo Kid. Jim Pollard was known for how high he could get up.

Jumpin' Joe against Jumpin' Jim.

Pollard cooked Fulks for 30 points. From the *Star Tribune*, November 3, 1949, edition:

Pollard, driving and cutting by Mikan, rolled in 30 points in a spectacular performance that had the 4,784 fans standing and cheering when he left the game late in the fourth period.

Pollard's leaping ability was legendary. He entertained his teammates with his dunks. He was known for taking off from the free throw line and dunking during down moments in Lakers practices. His bouncy athleticism made him a tough cover. He played above the rim, which was rare for a non-center in his day. But he was also quick, zipping around the court and getting where he wanted. Coach John Kundla designed a two-man offense with Mikan and Pollard. The Lakers would get the ball to Mikan, and Pollard would work to get free off the ball. Mikan, so tall no one could take the ball, would pass to an open Pollard for the score.

Washington Capitols star Horace "Bones" McKinney was once quoted saying: "We knew when Pollard had been in the building. The tops of the backboards would be clean where he raked them."

Pollard gained his national fame at Stanford. He was a sophomore when the school made its run to its only championship in 1942.

"I remember one game where one of our passes was intercepted by the other team and this fella went dribbling toward the other basket," Leo McCaffrey, who played at a rival high school of Pollard's in Oakland, told the *Chicago Tribune*. "Jim raced after him, and as the guy was putting the ball up, Jim leapt and pressed the ball against the backboard. He wasn't called for interference. It was just tremendous timing."

Yes, Jumpin' Jim was doing chase-down blocks before LeBron James.

Pollard missed the title game because of the flu. A temperature over one hundred degrees relegated him to the sideline as Stanford handled Dartmouth. But he still led the tournament in scoring.

Pollard went on to become a four-time All-Star at the pro level and won five championships with the Minneapolis Lakers.

THE NBA'S FIRST POWER FORWARD

They called him the Great Dane. He was six foot seven and 230 pounds, and he made his opponents feel every bit of him.

Vern Mikkelsen, the NBA's first bruising power forward.

"I can remember playing against Bill Russell, and I must have knocked his arms so much, he felt like he had a couple of bloody stubs," Mikkelsen told the *Minneapolis Star Tribune* back in 1995.

After the game, Russell came to the Lakers locker room and asked Mikkelsen to come meet his family. The Lakers forward took it as a big sign of respect. The great Bill Russell wanted his family to meet him.

Mikkelsen starred at Hamline University in St. Paul. He was a territorial rights selection by the Lakers in the 1949 BAA draft. He played center in college, winning the NAIA championship. But moving next to Mikan forced him to change his game. He'd scarcely play with his back to the basket and had to develop a set shot.

But his real impact was on defense. He drew the assignment of the best opposing player. Dolph Schayes. Bob Pettit. Paul Arizin. Mikkelsen hounded them all. The six-time All-Star also averaged double figures every year of his career and at least ten rebounds per game four times.

HOW THE DYNASTY ALMOST ENDED EARLY

After staring at DePaul, Mikan signed a five-year, $60,000 deal with the Gears in March 1946. Nine months later, Mikan sued the Gears to get out of his contract because they hadn't paid him and he had no opt outs. But they later settled and he was locked up through 1951.

After Mikan led the Chicago American Gears to the 1947 NBL champion-ship, the owner, Maurice White, withdrew from the National Basketball League. In August it was announced he was the new president of a new league: the Professional Basketball League of America. Mikan and the Gears were the big draw, and White spearheaded a new idea to capitalize with a twenty-four-team league centered on Mikan. Commercial Sports Advertisers bankrolled the league.

The initial plan was for six teams in four divisions, they would play a sixty-six-game schedule, half at home. But eight teams ended up dropping out and the league was down to sixteen teams when it started.

If it had worked, Mikan would've never been available for the Lakers to get.

But in November 1947, two months after the grand announcement, the league dissolved. The costs were too much and the crowds weren't pouring in. The Gears were 9–0 and Mikan was an attraction. But that was when the drama began. The fate of the NBA, in some ways, hung in the balance unbeknownst to anyone involved.

Days after the announcement, the National Basketball League met to deter-mine if it would let Mikan's Gears back into the NBL. All the Gears needed was a new sponsor.

"There is room for them and we shortly will be able to make an announcement," NBL president Paul Walk was quoted saying in the *Chicago Tribune* in 1947.

The eleven members were to put it to a vote. *Tribune* reporter Maurice Shelvin reported he spoke with eight clubs, and they were unanimous in voting the Gears back into the fold of the NBL. It only made sense to do so. The NBL needed the attention and Mikan could deliver.

But shockingly, in a meeting to decide the fate of the Gears, the application to readmit Mikan's team was unanimously rejected. The Gears had multiple suit-ors interested in sponsoring the team; all thought the road was clear to a reunit-ing of the Gears and the NBL. But something happened and the league said no, leaving room to reconsider their application in a year. In the meantime, the Gears players were dispersed among the NBL in an expansion draft.

Even though the Lakers received the draft rights to Mikan, his signing wasn't for sure. While playing in Chicago, Mikan had enrolled in law school at DePaul. There were concerns Mikan wouldn't leave law school and move to Minneapolis as he planned to take the Illinois state bar. As one of the biggest names in basketball, he could've feasibly signed with an independent team nearby and remained in law school—including a proposed barnstorming tour put on by a Chicago company.

But Mikan, who even considered transferring to the University of Minnesota for law school, eventually worked out a plan with DePaul to complete law school in the off-seasons. The Lakers offered Mikan a contract of $15,000 a year—more than the $12,000 a year the Gears paid him—and it was finally a done deal. The path to Kareem Abdul-Jabbar and Magic Johnson, Kobe Bryant and Shaquille O'Neal, LeBron James and Anthony Davis, was set.

THE VILLAIN

The road.

Modern NBA players fly on charter planes with first-class quality seats and an onboard chef. They are contractually obligated to stay in at least four-star hotels, but five-star digs are more common. And, barring emergencies, they never travel on the day of the game.

But back when the NBA began, when its ancestor leagues were creating the foundation, things were much different. Uncomfortable overnight bus rides. Meager accommodations. Travel was brutal.

Each of the Lakers' first six seasons began with a road trip of at least five games. And in every case, the road trip included but a few off days. In 1951, they opened the season with a seven-game road trip—and it was completed in ten days. The trip began with a back-to-back in Rochester and Syracuse, followed by a five-day break. Then it was five games in five days: Philadelphia, New York, Boston, Baltimore, and Indianapolis.

Such taxing travels were par for the course in those days. On top of that was style of play. Games back in the Minneapolis Lakers days were called cages, and players were called cagers, because basketball was initially played in a cage. That mindset survived once the fences came down. Basketball, then a predominantly slow and grounded game, was physical and taxing.

Now imagine playing a game, then taking a three-hour bus ride in the middle of the night, staying at a cheap hotel, and doing it all again the next day.

THE CRAZIEST STAT

When *Forbes* released its annual team valuations in 2020, the Lakers' franchise was listed as worth an estimated $4.4 billion. They were the second most valuable franchise in the NBA, behind only the New York Knicks, and the fourth most valuable sports franchise in the world. That valuation might actually be light, as it doesn't even account for the panache of owning the Lakers and how that might prompt someone to go way above that for such a distinction.

That reality only makes this stat insane to comprehend: $150,000.

That's how much the Lakers sold for in 1957. Factoring in inflation, that was equivalent to $1,389,395 in 2020. For that price, one could own 0.0003 percent of the Lakers. There is no better illustration of how far the NBA has come, how far basketball has come, than the growth of the Lakers from the NBA's first dynasty to the juggernaut it is today.

Let's take those inflation rates in the opposite direction. The Lakers would have had to be sold for $475 million in 1957 to be worth the equivalent of $4.4 billion in 2020.

As it stands, $150,000 was a big enough purchase price to land them in Los Angeles.

It was the beginning of the end for Minnesota when the Lakers completed their three-peat in 1954, surviving a seven-game series against the Dolph Schayes–led Syracuse Nationals. Mikan was just 2-for-10 shooting in the deciding game with 11 points. It was Jim Pollard who led the way to the Game 7 win. Five months later, out of nowhere, Mikan retired. The Lakers had won six titles in seven years—including one in the NBL and one in the BAA—and Mikan wanted to move on to other interests. He said he wanted to quit while he was still physically able and desired to shift his focus to the law. He also had his eye on running for Congress.

$150,000. That's how much the Lakers sold for in 1957.

The thirty-year-old had slowed a bit. Clyde Lovellette was a promising young big man learning under Mikan, who became general manager of the

Lakers following his retirement after buying some ownership shares from owner Max Winter.

But Mikan's departure hurt. Attendance was dropping, and the team was losing. In January 1956, he came back, halfway through the 1955–56 season. He averaged just 20.7 minutes and was a shell of himself. The Lakers lost in the semifinals to the St. Louis Hawks.

Mikan retired for good after that. The Lakers' decline continued. They had a losing record in February 1957 when Berger announced he'd agreed to sell the Lakers for $150,000. Marty Marion, the former Chicago White Sox skipper, and Milton Fischman, a St. Louis businessman, made an offer, and Berger jumped on it after the Lakers had been in the red for a couple of years and were spiraling.

Minneapolis responded with a push to keep the Lakers. Berger agreed to give the city some time to come up with $200,000—to match the sale price and have $50,000 operating costs. Berger said he was willing to retain $20,000 worth of ownership in the team if Minneapolis came through, so the technical goal was $180,000. Local businesses, with the help of even the mayor, launched a city-wide fund-raiser to procure the funds. Mikan even offered to buy the team on a payment plan. He was going to mortgage his house for a $25,000 down payment and pay that amount every year until he footed the whole bill.

On the March 13, 1957, deadline, Berger received a check for $150,000 and called the prospective buyers from St. Louis to tell them thanks but no thanks. Minneapolis saved the Lakers by raising the money. Bob Short was named chairman of the 117-person ownership group.

But the push to keep the Lakers didn't produce greater support at the gate. Even another trip to the Finals in 1959, led by the spectacular rookie Elgin Baylor and Mikkelsen, didn't revive the fervor Minneapolis had had in Mikan's days.

In 1960, looking for a chance to make the franchise financially viable, the new owners announced the Lakers would move to Los Angeles. The investment has been increasing exponentially ever since.

4

THE BILL RUSSELL CELTICS

Bill Russell showed up to the Trinity Church in Boston in 2019. So did Tom "Satch" Sanders. John Havlicek was there in spirit.

All that was missing were K. C. and Sam Jones. That's how close the Celtics were to having all five players back together again. Some fifty-four years earlier, they were on the court for the most memorable moment of this Celtics dynasty: Game 7 of the 1965 Eastern Division Finals. It was undoubtedly the most memorable call in basketball history.

The Celtics, winners of six straight championships, were in danger of being eliminated. They led by a point with five seconds remaining on their home court. Russell took the ball out because he trusted himself the most to make the right pass. But his inbounds toss hit the wiring connected to the basket, and the Celtics turned the ball over. The 76ers had new life. And their star center, Wilt Chamberlain, was in a groove. He had scored 10 straight points and was about to get the ball near his own basket. The fans worried about their Celtics.

On the ensuing inbounds pass, Philadelphia's Hal Greer was trying to throw the ball in to Chet Walker. With Russell fronting Chamberlain, and Sam Jones and Satch Sanders pressing up on the 76ers' wings, Havlicek saw Greer had but one place to go with the ball. So Havlicek jumped into the passing lane. He deflected the ball, Sam Jones scooped it up, and the Celtics survived. So did the call, for ages.

> **And Havlicek steals it**
> **Over to Sam Jones**
> **Havlicek stole the ball**
> **It's all over**
> **It's all over**
> **Johnny Havlicek is being mobbed by the fans**
> **It's all over**
> **Johnny Havlicek stole the ball**
> **Ohhhhh boy what a play by Havlicek at the end of this ball game**
> **Bill Russell wants to grab Havlicek**
> **He hugs him**

He squeezes John Havlicek
Havlicek saved this ball game

The call was by the late broadcaster Johnny Most. He punctuated the iconic moment with his conveyance of just how riveting and relieving that victory was for the Celtics, who went on to win their seventh consecutive championship. He turned Havlicek into a household name. So when Hondo—what they called Havlicek because of his resemblance to John Wayne—died on April 25, 2019, a central part of Celtics lore was lost.

Russell might have been the centerpiece of the Celtics dynasty. But one could argue Havlicek was its heart. He most fit their aesthetic, with his humility and reliable production. He was a thirteen-time All-Star who made eleven All-NBA teams and eight All-Defensive teams. He won eight championships and was the 1973–74 Finals MVP.

But also they rooted for him because he was hardworking and down-to-earth. Havlicek was one of those guys you never heard a bad word about. So when he died of Parkinson's disease, his clout in the green and white was quite the draw. As family, friends, and teammates gathered at Trinity Church, not all five players from the "Havlicek Stole the Ball!" game were there. But with Bob Cousy and Tom Heinsohn in attendance, there were five key players from the 1963 championship.

What was evident then, as they gathered to honor their friend, was how the grains of sand in their hourglasses were dwindling. Cousy was 90 at the time of the funeral. Russell was 85. Tom Heinsohn 84. Sanders 80. Havlicek, who'd just turned 79 before his death, was the youngest of the bunch. K. C. Jones, who died Christmas Day in 2020, was 87 and Sam Jones 85.

They are the last of the NBA's winningest dynasty. They paved the way for so much of what came after them. But these Celtics already get disrespected with dismissive criticisms of their era—the league had fewer teams, fewer Black players, and the offensive game wasn't as polished. The memory of their greatness keeps fading, deeper and deeper into the past. One can only wonder: What happens to the reverence of those Celtics teams when the players are no longer here to command it?

NBA Finals Appearances

1957 (W)	1958 (L)	1959 (W)
1960 (W)	1961 (W)	1962 (W)
1963 (W)	1964 (W)	1965 (L)
1966 (W)	1968 (W)	1969 (W)

THE FACE OF THE DYNASTY

Check out this passage about Bill Russell from the December 31, 1956, edition of the *Boston Globe*, written by Jack Barry:

> Big Red Kerr went the way of all other rival pivot men who have opposed the ex-collegiate star when he tried his hook shot from a pivot position in the game's early moments.
>
> Russell nonchalantly rose in the air to bat down Kerr's intended basket and Coach Paul Seymour was finally obliged to remove Kerr, who stands 6-9 himself, from action. Kerr gathered but two baskets for the day, both when Russell was on the bench.

Imagine how demoralizing Russell must have been. Before facing Russell, Kerr had already won a championship and was an All-Star the previous season. He was beginning a string of eight consecutive seasons averaging a double-double, which would land him two more All-Star bids. The night before, on December 29, the Syracuse Nationals played the Philadelphia Warriors, featuring Hall of Fame big man Neil Johnston. Kerr had 15 points on 16 shots with 22 rebounds. Yet against Russell, Kerr was so overwhelmed his coach pulled him. He finished with 4 points on 6 shots.

Russell was so novel a sight, so unique a specimen, it probably did look nonchalant the way he rose in the air, like a floating, swatting barricade in front of the rim. And this was just his sixth pro game. Russell finished with 20 points and 32 rebounds against Kerr.

It was a bright idea that set Russell on the path to legendary status. The path to eleven rings began with a teenage hunch that made him a defensive wonder, a freak of nature. Yes, it was an open violation of the fundamentals taught by practically every coach since the sport was invented. But Russell, who started playing basketball in Oakland, California, for McClymonds High School, had this revolutionary concept for his approach to defense.

Jump.

Back in those days, one fundamental principle of defense was to stay grounded. Keeping your balance, having active feet, was critical to keeping the ball handler in front. Leaving your feet was a sin. But Russell, a special athlete, figured he could be even more disruptive if he used athleticism to contest shots. He was right.

It made him a star at the University of San Francisco, which he guided to back-to-back national championships. It made him the star of the 1956 Olympic team, which won the gold medal at the Melbourne Games. It made him the winningest player in NBA history.

When Russell arrived, the Celtics were automatically different. With his defensive prowess and the Celtics' pace, they were instantly an innovation. His athleticism was a game-changer as he blocked shots, pressured the ball, and cleaned up the rebounds. Russell could dribble well enough to push the ball once he got the board. And while he wasn't great offensively, he could handle himself around the rim. It is widely believed the NCAA banned offensive goaltending in 1957 as a counter to Russell, who could easily catch the pass over the rim and drop it in, or tap in a rebound while it was still above the rim. As a rookie with the Celtics, Russell averaged 14.7 points on 42.7 percent and a league-best 19.6 rebounds. In the playoffs, his offensive numbers dropped—13.9 points on 36.5 percent shooting—but he went up to 24.4 rebounds.

In his first playoff game, Russell had 16 points and 31 rebounds and tormented Red Kerr again. The Syracuse big man, who started the Eastern Semifinals against the Philadelphia Warriors, was switched to a reserve against Boston. He went 5-for-18 from the field off the bench. Syracuse's starting center, Hall of Famer Dolph Schayes, didn't do much better. He went 3-for-13, getting 15 of his 21 points from the free throw line.

In Game 7 of the NBA Finals against the St. Louis Hawks, the Celtics were locked in a double-overtime thriller before a capacity crowd of more than thirteen thousand fans at Boston Garden. The Celtics were up 122–121 inside of two minutes left. Russell blocked Med Park's shot to get Boston the ball back, and Frank Ramsey hit a twenty-footer to seal the win as the arena went crazy. The Celtics won its first NBA title and, unbeknownst to everyone, a dynasty was born. Russell, who finished with 19 points and 32 rebounds in that Game 7, was its center.

In 165 playoff games, Russell averaged 16.2 points, 24.9 rebounds, and 4.7 assists. He actually finished in the top thirteen in the NBA in assists in eleven of his thirteen seasons, including four times in the top ten. He had forty rebounds twice in Game 7s.

The league didn't start counting blocks until after Russell retired. The first Finals MVP was in 1969—and won by Jerry West, even though the Lakers lost the series to the Celtics. If they had been counting, Russell likely would've had the record for blocks and perhaps ten Finals MVPs. Those would have greatly helped translate his dominance of the era.

When This Dynasty Reigned

- The Vietnam War and the Civil Rights Movement dominated the political landscape. The NBA's political bent began in this era as players, along with other Black athletes in other sports, used their platforms to speak on these issues.

- John F. Kennedy, Malcolm X, and Martin Luther King Jr. were all assassinated during this Boston dynasty.

- Some of the most profound musical influences emerged in these times. Elvis Presley became a giant star in the mid- to late '50s. Berry Gordy started Motown in the late '50s. The Beatles rose to prominence in the mid-'60s.

- The sexual revolution of the '60s also coincided with this dynasty, challenging societal norms regarding orientation, monogamy, and eroticism. The advent of the birth control pill, the overturning of banned erotic books, and the popularization of *Playboy* magazine made sex a staple in the time of the Celtics.

- McDonald's became a thing.

THE ARCHITECT

As the story goes, Walter A. Brown, the original owner of the Celtics, was looking for a new leader to get Boston out of the doldrums. The Celtics went 22–46 in their first season in the NBA—after coming over from the Basketball Association of America, the first professional basketball league. He asked reporters for a coach he should go after. They said Red Auerbach, who was nine years into his coaching career and had already coached Navy, coached the Washington Capitols to the BAA Finals, and served as an assistant coach and heir apparent at Duke. So on April 27, 1950, the Celtics hired Auerbach for $10,000 a year and gave him the reins. They won 57 percent of their games over the next six seasons, making the playoffs but never making the Finals.

Russell, out of the University of San Francisco, was the most dominant player in college and assuredly the No. 1 pick in the 1956 NBA Draft. But Boston—owners of the second-best record in the league in 1955–56, behind the Philadelphia Warriors—didn't have a first-round pick. Back then, the league had what was known as "territorial picks." It allowed for a team to cash in its first-round pick to draft a local college star within fifty miles. This was meant to benefit the franchise and help them to get the players in the area who were already a draw. That year, Tom Heinsohn was a star at Holy Cross in Worcester, Massachusetts. So Boston chose to use the territorial pick on him, meaning they had no pick to get Russell.

But Auerbach coveted Russell. So he and the Celtics owner started making moves behind the scenes.

The Rochester Royals had the No. 1 pick that year. The franchise was struggling financially, so the Celtics offered to secure them an influx of cash. How? Brown had a stake in the Ice Capades, a traveling show of figure-skaters that drew bigger crowds than most sports teams as it toured the nation. The Celtics made a deal to get some Ice Capades dates in Rochester in exchange for the Royals passing on Russell. So instead of the best player in college, Rochester got figure-skating legend Donna Atwood and Duquesne guard Si Green.

Auerbach and the Celtics went to work on the owners of the No. 2 pick, the St. Louis Hawks. Auerbach offered up his starting center Ed Macauley and threw in Cliff Hagan. It was enough to get Russell and proved to be one of the worst trades in NBA history. The Hawks said they agreed because Macauley was a local who played college ball at St. Louis. But the whispers were that

St. Louis, which had an all-White team, was too racist a town for a Black player. Russell agreed.

"St. Louis was overwhelmingly racist," Russell said in an interview on NBA TV. "If I would've gotten drafted by St. Louis, I wouldn't have been in the NBA."

So the Celtics got Heinsohn and Russell. And then with their second-round pick, they selected K. C. Jones, Russell's costar at the University of San Francisco.

The Celtics had been the highest-scoring team in the NBA for the previous five years, led by Bob Cousy and Bill Sharman. What they needed was defense, and they now had it in Russell. They became a complete team and won their first championship in Russell's rookie season. And Auerbach was not just orchestrating a champion, but the dynasty of dynasties. He was also inventing.

Red, as he was called, has been credited with a number of pioneering contributions to basketball.

NBA Fast Break: Auerbach didn't invent the fast break. But his Celtics popularized it in the NBA by using it on one of basketball's biggest stages, led by their crafty ball handler in Cousy. At a time when the game was played slow, half court to half court, Auerbach encouraged his team to get the ball up the court quickly.

Transition Offense: Taking full advantage of Russell anchoring the middle of the paint, Auerbach emphasized using defense to create offense. He taught Russell to keep the shots he blocked in bounds so they could start what was known as the "Celtics fast break." The blocked shot would essentially serve as an outlet pass. Once the Celtics got the rebound, they took off before the defense could set.

Sixth Man: From the time Auerbach took over the Celtics, Cousy and Sharman were the starting guards. But in 1954, Auerbach drafted Frank Ramsey out of Kentucky with the No. 5 overall pick. Auerbach used Ramsey to give a breather to his guards and inject some life into the game. He was a six-foot-three guard who could shoot and defend. He was so good Auerbach had him on the court at the end of a lot of games. Auerbach sold it as saving Ramsey by not starting him, as he wrote in his 1977 autobiography. He ended up doing the same with John Havlicek after drafting him in 1962.

"On a lot of teams they make a big deal out of the starting five," he wrote. "If you don't start, it implies you're not as good or as valuable as the next guy.

"That's not the way we looked at the men on our bench in Boston. Psychologically, as soon as you pull one of your starters out of the game, the other team is going to let down just a bit. That's when I wanted a guy like Ramsey or Havlicek to get out there and run them into the ground."

The Victory Cigar: Technically, Auerbach didn't invent this concept either. It predates the Celtics by more than a half a century. In the early 1900s, cigars were given out as prizes at carnivals. Even the 1902 book *The Night Side of London* mentions cigars as prizes. Most figure this practice to be the genesis of the saying "close but no cigar"—which was used in the 1935 film *Annie Oakley*. But Red took it to another level when he created the tradition of firing up a cigar on the bench, even when the game would still be going on. When he knew there was no chance his Celtics would lose, right there on the bench, he pulled out his stogie and lit it up. The smoke was an epic taunt.

"It all boils down to this," Auerbach told *Cigar Aficionado*. "I used to hate these college coaches or any coach that was 25 points ahead with three minutes left to go, and they're up there yellin' and coachin' because they're on TV, and they want their picture on, and they get recognition. To me, the game was over. The day's work is done. Worry about the next game. This game is over. So I would light a cigar and sit on the bench and just watch it. The game was over, for all intents and purposes. I didn't want to rub anything in or show anybody what a great coach I was when I was 25 points ahead. Why? I gotta win by 30? What the hell difference does it make?"

THE CULTURAL IMPACT

On June 12, 1963, Civil Rights activist Medgar Evers was shot and killed as he got out of his car in Jackson, Mississippi. Russell, who'd been fighting against racism all his life, called the Evers family to ask what he could do to help. The answer required him going to Mississippi.

Shortly thereafter, at the request of Evers's brother Charles, Russell held an integrated basketball camp for youth. The death threats poured in as Mississippi was racially charged following the death of Evers. Members of the Ku Klux Klan showed up and watched from across the street. Armed Black leaders known as the "Deacons Defense" protected Russell. Even Charles Evers slept in Russell's room in a chair, a shotgun in his lap pointed at the door.

Still, Black kids and White kids were learning about basketball together, providing a much-needed picture of racial harmony, and the Boston Celtics were at the center of it.

"We had a few White kids come to that camp," Evers told the *Seattle Times*. "That's the kind of respect even some of the White folks had for Bill Russell. The camp was a success.

"My good friend B. B. King once told me there were only two things that brought Whites and Blacks together. Blues and sports."

The reputation of Boston might be one with racism issues. But the legacy of the first Boston Celtics dynasty is as a pioneer in race relations. The athlete activism that is celebrated among today's NBA players can be traced back to the Celtics, whose willingness to support and promote African-Americans is the foundation of an NBA that is considered the most progressive league. When it wasn't popular to do so, the Celtics were sports' leaders in antiracism.

The legacy of the first Boston Celtics dynasty is as a pioneer in race relations.

In 1950, Celtics owner Walter Brown stood up among the group at an owners meeting and announced he was drafting Chuck Cooper, a six-foot-five forward out of Duquesne. Another person in the meeting intervened. Cousy, in an interview with NBC Sports Boston, said it was Philadelphia head coach and general manager Eddie Gottlieb.

"Walter, don't you know he's a Negro?"

Boston Globe reporter George Sullivan reported that Brown responded: "I don't give a damn if he's striped, plaid, or polka dot! Boston takes Chuck Cooper of Duquesne!"

And just like that, the first Black player was drafted into the NBA, and it was by the Celtics.

Russell became a grandfather of sports and activism, with his willingness to speak out and participate in the struggle for equality and Black progress, as the Celtics' dominance of the NBA coincided with the Civil Rights Movement. Russell partnered with the likes of Muhammad Ali, Kareem Abdul-Jabbar, and Jim Brown to effect change and be a voice for the oppressed. In June 1963, President Kennedy introduced the Civil Rights Bill banning discrimination. Two months later, Russell participated in the March on Washington. He said he met with Dr. Martin Luther King Jr. the night before and was invited to stand with him onstage, but declined out of respect for the organizers.

In September 1963, the Celtics purchased the contract of Willie Naulls from the San Francisco Warriors. That set up the Celtics' next historic move: becoming the first team to start five African-Americans at a time. Tom Heinsohn was the only non-Black starter, and when he rested, Naulls would spell him. So when Heinsohn was injured, it was natural for Naulls to replace him in the starting lineup. And on December 26, 1964, Naulls joined K. C. Jones, Tom Sanders, Sam Jones, and Russell to become the NBA's first all-Black starting lineup. Oddly enough, they played in St. Louis, beating the same Hawks franchise that had traded Russell to the Celtics in 1956.

The first Black coach? That was an Auerbach move, too. In April 1966, he stepped aside and named Russell the head coach. Russell led the Celtics for three years as a player-coach and won two championships.

The currents of America were changing. The country was grappling with race and discrimination, confronted with the injustices permeating society. Citizens were challenging the government and digesting the ideals of equality. And the Boston Celtics represented the transition the country was undergoing—in a sense, they were even ahead of the country.

THE FORGOTTEN STAR

Auerbach was unimpressed with the players coming out of college for the 1957 NBA draft. The previous draft, he landed Russell, Heinsohn, and K. C. Jones. So maybe Auerbach was feeling pretty secure. The Celtics, who had just won their first title, had the No. 8 and final pick of the first round. Auerbach was over it. So over it, indeed, he went with the advice of a college coach on whom he should pick.

Sam Jones was the choice. Few had ever heard of Jones. He was a six-foot-four wing from North Carolina Central, a historically black university in Durham, North Carolina. He had been offered a job to teach and coach basketball at West Charlotte High School. And he was ready to take it and give up on basketball. That was how distraught he was over being drafted by the Celtics.

The Celtics were defending champions and returned eleven players. Boston was pretty set at wing with Bill Sharman, Frank Ramsey, Jim Loscutoff, and Lou Tsioropoulos. Jones thought his basketball career was over.

"I never felt so miserable in my life when I got the news," he was quoted saying. "I really thought it was the end of my basketball career. Sure, I was thrilled with the honor . . . I never thought I'd be able to break into the game, let alone the lineup."

Jones tried to negotiate an extra $500 in salary from the school. If they had said yes, he would've been a teacher and not a Celtic. The school couldn't come up with the money, though.

It turned out Jones was a perfect fit for Boston. He played college ball for John McLendon at North Carolina Central. McLendon was a protege of James Naismith. Naismith was the athletic director at the University of Kansas, where McLendon transferred after a year at junior college in Kansas City, Kansas. McLendon wasn't allowed to play for the segregated Jayhawks, but Naismith taught McLendon the game. He took the essence of what the inventor of basketball taught him and created a unique style of play. Perpetual motion. An offense that attacked. Platooning players to keep them fresh so the pace could stay fast as McLendon's teams pushed the ball up the court. Referees would sometimes have to pause the action to catch their breath because McLendon's teams ran so much. His plan was for players to take a shot every eight seconds—some fifty years before the "Seven Seconds or Less" Phoenix Suns.

So when Jones got to the Celtics, he fit right in with their pace. Jones was quick. He was fast getting up and down the court, even with his push dribble, which made him an ideal outlet for Russell. Jones was a bank-shot master who got pretty high on his pull-up jumpers.

When Sharman retired in 1961, Jones saw an increase in minutes and opportunity. He earned his first of five All-Star bids in 1961–62. His postseason production also jumped. The next eight years, he averaged 22.6 points in the playoffs and developed a reputation for his clutchness.

In a showdown with the Philadelphia Warriors in the 1962 Eastern Division Finals playoffs, it was Jones who saved the day. The Warriors had Wilt Chamberlain, who averaged a career-high 50.4 points in the regular season, and Tom Meschery. And the Celtics had Russell and Tom Heinsohn. The difference proved to be Jones. In Game 7 of the series, Jones had a team-high 28 points and hit the game-winning fifteen-footer with two seconds left to send the Celtics to the Finals.

It was his first postseason game winner but not his last. In Game 7 of the 1969 NBA Finals, his off-balance runner off the wrong foot with a second remaining gave the Celtics an 89–88 win over the Lakers, spoiling a 40-point game by Jerry West. Jones's shot tied the series at 2–2, and Boston won in seven games, its eleventh and final championship.

"In the years that I played with the Celtics, in terms of total basketball skills, Sam Jones was the most skillful player that I ever played with," Russell said in an interview with the Celtic Nation website. "At one point, we won a total of eight consecutive NBA championships, and six times during that run we asked Sam to take the shot that meant the season. If he didn't hit the shot we were finished— we were going home empty-handed. He never missed."

THE VILLAIN

The biggest external threat to the Celtics for the longest time was Elgin Baylor and Jerry West, the Lakers All-Stars who were terrors in their day. But the Celtics beat the Lakers five times in the Finals during their eleven-title run. So though they were the biggest threat and kept the Celtics on their toes, they didn't win enough to compete with the real villain in the Celtics' original dynasty.

Racism.

Before he ever played for the Celtics, Bob Cousy had Boston Garden cheering his name. On January 11, 1949, he was a captain and guard for Holy Cross, which played Loyola of Chicago as part of a double-header. With five minutes left, the crowd chanted, "We want Cousy!" and the coach put him in. He scored 11 points in the final five minutes. He capped the performance by whipping the ball around his back and banking in a left-handed hook shot to win it. His local legend status was cemented, especially after Holy Cross ripped off a twenty-six-game win streak.

The Celtics had the No. 1 pick in 1950, the same year Cousy entered the draft. It was a no-brainer. But Auerbach wanted a big man instead of a guard. So he selected six-foot-eleven center Chuck Share out of Bowling Green. The Celtics passed on Cousy.

One of the writers confronted Auerbach about the choice. Bill Russell told the story on the NBA TV documentary *Red and Me: Bill Russell and Red Auerbach*.

"He told me one of the writers said to him, 'You know you've insulted everybody in New England by not taking Bob Cousy. We're going to run you out of town. And besides that, you're a Jew. We don't like Jews either.' And I said, 'Wow.' I said, 'How did you handle that?' He said, 'Oh, I'll just outlive the bastards.' And that was one of the few conversations that we had about race."

The most pervasive foe in this most epic dynasty was racism. And as it pertained to this dynasty, the city of Boston's infection of racism made it the team's greatest villain. The Celtics won 70.5 percent of their games in Russell's thirteen years, including eleven championships. The rest of the league wasn't much of a foe. But the climate was quite the adversary for a team incorporating Black players led by a Jewish coach.

Satch Sanders said the racism in Boston was on par with the rest of the country. He even said Los Angeles was worse. But friction between Russell and the city became a constant rivalry.

The racism made Russell angry and standoffish in Boston. He infamously said he didn't sign autographs for children, and he had a contentious relationship with the media. At the center of it all was the city's feeling about and treatment of Black people. Russell saw it as a foe. Since he was the best player, his foe was the franchise's foe. And they were going at it as much as Russell did with other NBA stars.

He said at home games he was called a baboon, a coon, and the N-word, and was told to go back to Africa. Russell's home was broken into and vandalized with racial epithets. The perpetrators destroyed his trophies and defecated on his bed despite his delivering of six championships.

In his book, *Second Wind*, he described Boston as a "flea market of racism" because it "had all varieties, old and new, and in their most virulent form. The city had corrupt, city hall–crony racists, brick-throwing, send-'em-back-to-Africa racists, and in the university areas phony radical-chic racists."

In August 1965, two months before the Celtics began the pursuit of their eighth-straight championship, Massachusetts passed the Racial Imbalance Act, which made it illegal to segregate public schools. The first such law of its kind, it required the integration of Boston Public Schools. It was met with resistance by the Boston School Committee, which disobeyed state orders to implement desegregation at the risk of losing funding.

It prompted a 1972 lawsuit against the Committee. The District Court of Massachusetts ruled in 1974 that Boston operated with a pattern of racial discrimination and required compliance. Thus sparked the Boston busing crisis—violent protests of school integration that still plague Boston's reputation today. It was also vindication for all the years Russell had kept a healthy distance from the city and fans.

In 1972, the Celtics retired Russell's jersey, raising his No. 6 into the rafters of Boston Garden. But no fans were there. Russell didn't want them.

"He had animosities toward Boston, as most people know," Heinsohn told the *Boston Globe*. "And they were well-founded animosities, I might add."

THE HOME COURT

When the Celtics joined the Basketball Association of America, ahead of the 1946–47 season, owner Walter Brown wanted the floor to be an attraction. He wanted something fancy. The problem was, however, that America had a wood shortage following World War II. And most of the manufactured wood available was reserved for much-needed housing.

"The only way they could do that was getting scraps of wood at lumber yards throughout Boston and put together a floor," Jeff Twiss, the Celtics vice president of media services and alumni relations, told NBC Sports Boston.

So for the Celtics' new hardwood floor, builders had to use a unique method. Parquet, a French artisty of creating geometric designs by cutting and fitting together small pieces of wood, was the best way to create Boston's court. The $11,000 floor was made of short red oak boards of varying lengths and widths. The grains were still showing, and the alternating directions of the wood panels gave it a distinct decorative look. The parquet floor proved to be a gem.

It made its debut in 1946 at Boston Arena, where the Celtics originally played. In 1952, it moved to the Boston Garden, which would become a legendary edifice in NBA lore.

The Boston Garden was created by the same boxing promoter who built Madison Square Garden in New York: Ted Rickard. After the success of the New York arena, he planned to build six more Gardens around the country. Boston was No. 2—it was called Boston Madison Square Garden when it opened in 1928—and proved to be the last because the $10 million price tag was twice that of the New York arena. Then Rickard died in 1929.

The Celtics moved to the Boston Garden in 1955 and made it one of the most noteworthy home court advantages in the league. Over the years, as the boards of natural wood grew apart and warped, it gave the Celtics' home court some actual texture. Uneven surfaces made dribbling tricky on parts of the court. As legend has it, Celtics defenders would guide ball handlers to the dead spots and swipe the ball when it thudded off the dip in the hardwood.

"It makes a nice story, but it's not true," Cousy once said.

The Boston Garden was built for boxing and Rickard wanted the fans close to the action—to see the sweat, as he would say. That proved to be an intimidating scene for visiting teams as the cheering crowds were so close. Also, Boston Garden had no air-conditioning, so it could be hot and daunting inside. To be continued.

THE CRAZIEST STAT

The 1962–63 Celtics had nine Hall of Famers: Russell, Heinsohn, Havlicek, Ramsay, Sanders, Sam Jones, K. C. Jones, Cousy, and Clyde Lovellette. It is the most Hall of Famers on one team in NBA history.

5

THE MAGIC JOHNSON LAKERS

At his core, the late former Lakers owner Dr. Jerry Buss was a creator. Investor in the long game. Endless well of creativity. His first gig out of the University of Southern California—where he got his doctorate—came as a chemist for the then Bureau of Mines. He then got into the aerospace industry before going into real estate. So, it was only right that his next investment was the best one he ever cooked up.

When Buss purchased the Lakers—along with the Los Angeles Kings of the NHL, the Great Western Forum Arena in Inglewood, and a ranch in the Sierra Nevada Mountains—for $67.5 million in 1979, the Lakers were all set up to take off. Back in '76, after being unable to come to terms with the Lakers, star guard Gail Goodrich signed with the New Orleans Jazz. Back then, when teams lost a player in free agency, they were due compensation, usually a first-round pick. When a team tried to keep the player but couldn't, the commissioner determined the proper compensation. But then-commissioner Larry O'Brien told the teams to work it out, and they agreed on a massive trade. The Lakers received two first-round picks and swapped picks in another year. But by the 1978–79 season, Goodrich was thirty-five years old and long from his glory days. He retired after averaging 12.7 points. The Jazz finished with the worst record in the NBA that year, which meant the 1979 pick they traded to the Lakers as compensation for Goodrich turned out to be the No. 1 pick.

The consensus top pick in 1979 was an All-American point guard from Lansing, Michigan, who led Michigan State to the NCAA tournament championship (beating Larry Bird's Indiana State in the title game) and was named Most Outstanding Player of the Final Four. Yes, Magic Johnson.

The Lakers already had Kareem Abdul-Jabbar from a blockbuster trade in 1975, bringing the former UCLA star back to Los Angeles. They finished 47–35 in 1978–79 and lost to eventual-champion Seattle in the Western Conference semis. So the Lakers had a good team. But as much as any owner ever, Buss set out to build a dynasty as the centerpiece of his empire.

The epicenter of it all would be the fast break, and nobody was better at it—at any level—than this kid out of Michigan State. Getting a player who was simply dubbed Magic couldn't be more of a perfect fit for the vision.

The Lakers, who lost repeatedly to the Celtics in the NBA Finals during the days of Bill Russell, were a running team back then, too. Picking up on the Celtics tempo, the Lakers brought the fast-pace game out to the West Coast. While the East Coast largely stuck with the half-court, physical game, the Lakers sped things up in California, and other teams tried to keep pace with the Lakers.

Buss wanted to turn that up a notch with Magic and new coach Jack McKinney, who also believed in running. Buss didn't want the game just to be fast, but to be fast and dazzling. The Lakers had Kareem, but Magic was the engine he needed. Magic was six foot nine, 215 pounds of charisma. His buoyant personality and fun-loving spirit matched the vibe Buss wanted. Magic, and his thousand-watt smile and energetic style of play, was all about a good time. LA was all about a good time. It was a perfect marriage.

The Lakers finished second in the NBA with 115.1 points per game (their offensive rating of 109.5 was the highest ever at the time) and the Lakers won the championship in Buss's first season of ownership, Magic's rookie year. Kareem was dominating the 1980 Finals against Philadelphia, but then he got hurt in Game 5. They won the game, but he left on crutches, which threw the fate of the series in jeopardy. Kareem was averaging 33.4 points and 13.6 rebounds for the series.

But Magic started at center, a position he played some in high school. He was just twenty years old at the time. The Lakers, stunned by the loss of their star, had to go to Philadelphia to close out the series. It was even more daunting than that. Guess who lined up at center for the 76ers? League MVP Moses Malone.

But as the Lakers rookie famously told his teammates, "Have no fear, Magic is here." Johnson's performance was legendary. He played forty-seven minutes. He totaled 42 points and 15 rebounds with seven assists. The Lakers clinched the title. Johnson took the Finals MVP. A star was born. The Lakers rebrand was official.

NBA Finals Appearances

1980 (W)	1982 (W)	1983 (L)
1984 (L)	1985 (W)	1987 (W)
1988 (W)	1989 (L)	1991 (L)

THE FACE OF THE DYNASTY

Back in January 1975, in Jackson, Michigan, a fifteen-year-old point guard for Everett High turned what was expected to be a tough game into a blowout. Those Parkside fellas didn't know what hit them. Some three thousand people watched this kid, named Earvin Johnson, put up 36 points and 18 rebounds on the road, winning the South Central Conference title game. Fred Stabley Jr. was covering for the *Lansing State Journal*. He was so impressed, he went to Johnson after the game.

"This guy walks in," Johnson recalled in a 2018 interview, "and says, 'Man, that was an awesome game! I got to give you a nickname.' He said, 'Somebody is already called Dr. J and Big E was already taken.' And because those two nicknames were already taken, he said, 'I'm going to call you Magic.'"

Stabley Jr.'s article the next day led with Earvin "Magic" Johnson because "he is like a magician every time he gets his hands on the ball." And from that day forth, he was Magic Johnson.

Then, he was a six-foot-five point guard who dazzled with his passing and transition game. He grew to six foot nine. By the time he got to the NBA, he was a specimen unlike anything the game had ever seen. Oscar Robertson was a big point guard at six foot five. But six foot nine? Running the fast break like that?

Before this current age of positionless basketball, when sometimes five guards are on the court, certain guards would be labeled tweeners. And it was a slight. A tweener is a player who is stuck between positions, having attributes from both, but not enough to be firmly defined by either. For a guard, a liminal space between a point guard and a shooting guard.

Michael Jordan is the quintessential shooting guard. So is Kobe Bryant. So is Dwyane Wade. Depending on the era, a shooting guard will come to mind.

But no matter the era, when the idea of a true point guard is contemplated, everyone thinks of Magic Johnson. He could score with any guard. He wasn't a great shooter but he could make shots. He didn't have the snazziest handles, but he could get where he wanted on the court. Plus he produced a career of clutch moments. But his legacy is being the benchmark of point guards, the truest of the true. He had every skill of a floor general: He was a leader, he controlled pace, he saw everything, he energized, he organized, and he passed the ball like he was telepathic. People around him were better for playing next to him. He was willing to be out front, absorbing the pressure and taking the challenge.

And on November 7, 1991, he was the point guard the nation needed.

Magic shocked the world by announcing he was retiring from the NBA because he contracted the human immunodeficiency virus (HIV). He went from leading the fast break to leading the nation in its understanding of a deadly disease.

In 1982, the Centers for Disease Control first called the immune disorder AIDS. In 1984, the cause of AIDS was identified as HIV, and in 1985 the FDA licensed the first commercial blood test for the virus. That same year, actor Rock Hudson died from AIDS, becoming the first high-profile death. The FDA banned gay men from donating blood because at the time it was seen as a disease contracted by homosexuals. The "gay plague," it was called.

By the end of 1985, more than twenty thousand cases of AIDS were reported. In 1987, AZT—the first licensed drug to treat HIV—was made available. It had its side effects, but it extended a person's life span before HIV developed into AIDS. So when Magic announced, a drug was available.

Magic became the face of HIV/AIDS and the inspiration for a more informed nation. He was walking proof it wasn't a "gay" disease. He forced the nation to confront its biases and discriminatory behaviors. He became a voice to a community too ostracized to have a voice. He prompted the NBA to get out front, learn about the disease, and contribute productively to the national dialogue—including by answering the concerns of its players—as well as develop procedures that weren't yet created for workplaces.

The offense Magic was running was science. He started taking AZT and then the game-changing AIDS cocktail that came out in 1996. That his body never deteriorated, that he never looked sick, helped change the perception about HIV and gave hope to many who lived with the virus.

People started suspecting he was given the secret cure because he was rich and famous. That was how well he thrived after his announcement, which at the time felt like a death sentence. He started the Magic Johnson Foundation and raised millions of dollars for research.

"He is the same guy in life that he is when he's pointing at the Great Western Forum," comedian Arsenio Hall said of his friend in the documentary *The Announcement*. "Same guy. He orchestrated victory."

When This Dynasty Reigned

- ESPN launched in 1979, becoming the first twenty-four-hour sports network. This would come to matter a lot.

- Workout fashion became a thing. Before there was Lululemon, there was Jane Fonda in leotards and leg warmers. Before there was Nike Dri-FIT, there was Richard Simmons in an oversized tank top and track shorts.

- Michael Jackson released two albums in the 1980s— *Thriller* in 1982 and *Bad* in 1987. Both releases came while the Lakers were champions. Prince also released *1999* while the Lakers were champions, in 1982. He dropped his biggest album, *Purple Rain*, two weeks after the Lakers lost the 1984 NBA Finals to Boston. No word on whether Prince meant "Purple Rain" as a metaphor for Lakers' tears.

- The NASA space shuttle *Challenger* exploded seventy-three seconds after liftoff on January 28, 1986. One of the seven passengers who died in the tragedy was a New Hampshire teacher named Christa McAuliffe, who would have been the first civilian in space—and was one of the reasons millions watched the launch on live television, even in schools.

- The highest-grossing movie stars of the 1980s were Harrison Ford (*Indiana Jones*), Carrie Fisher (*Star Wars*), Eddie Murphy (*Beverly Hills Cop*, *Coming to America*), Dan Aykroyd (*Ghostbusters*), and Bill Murray (*Ghostbusters*, *Caddyshack*).

- The Nintendo Entertainment System launched in the United States in 1985, selling for $149.99 and changing the video game industry. It featured two games: *Super Mario Bros.* and *Duck Hunt.*

THE MASTERMINDS

The legend of Pat Riley—the former player turned broadcaster in a plaid blazer, and now essentially an NBA deity who oversees the Miami Heat—began with the Showtime Lakers. When Paul Westhead was promoted to interim coach following a bad bike accident by head coach Jack McKinney, Riley became an assistant coach. Westhead was eventually promoted from full-time coach. Then when he was later fired, Riley was tabbed as the new Lakers coach.

Buss initially hired Riley with Jerry West as an offense-focused co-coach. But West nixed that and declared it was Riley's job. By the following season, West was the general manager and Riley was the coach, and the brain trust was off and running.

They inherited Kareem, Magic, and rookie forward James Worthy. West traded for Byron Scott, an explosive rookie guard whom the San Diego Clippers drafted with the No. 4 overall pick in the 1983 draft. In 1985, West drafted A. C. Green out of Oregon State. At the trade deadline in 1987, the Lakers traded for former No. 1 overall pick Mychal Thompson to bolster their bench. The pieces were in place for arguably the greatest team in this dynasty.

The 1986–87 Lakers went 65–17 and won eleven of their first twelve playoff games. Riley had managed to toughen up the Lakers, largely viewed as a finesse team, while not sacrificing their pace and flamboyance. They took on the personality of their coach—tough and willing to mix it up, but attractive enough to inspire imitation. Riley had other teams in the league trying to run like them, and a legion of grown men copying his slicked-back hair and expensive Italian suits. Riley was every bit as cool as the Hollywood ambiance in which he worked. And yet every bit as hard-nosed and unrelenting as it takes to win a championship.

Riley now uses the same balance to win titles as an executive. He's recruited some of the league's best talents to Miami—including LeBron James, Chris Bosh, and Jimmy Butler. He's groomed a coach in Erik Spoelstra, who keeps alive his legacy of tough defense and creative offense, of flowing and stifling flow. Riley has the clout to get any player in the NBA to listen, and his teams still mirror his personality.

And it began with this dynasty. The legend just kept growing.

At the championship parade following the 1987 title, Riley took the microphone, in sunglasses, and flexed in a way that only bolstered his panache.

"And I'm guaranteeing everybody here," Riley told the crowd gathered to celebrate his team, "next year we're going to win it again."

THE CULTURAL IMPACT

Basketball began with a Midwest vibe. Its origins are grassroots. The game was played in YMCAs and high school gyms. There was nothing glamorous about it.

So how did the NBA get to this point? From peach baskets to red carpets?

In the 1986 book *Winnin' Times*, *Los Angeles Times* writers Scott Ostler and Steve Springer told of the inspiration Buss received from a nightclub in Santa Monica called The Horn. It was a happening spot frequented by stars and socialites who took in the vibes and elite camaraderie along with the live entertainment. Every night, the show would start with the lights going low and three singers under a spotlight performing "It's Showtime." Buss wanted his games to be like a basketball version of The Horn.

Buss wasn't just building a championship team. He was building a brand. He had his sights set on an entertainment empire. Buss was a scientist, businessman, and real estate tycoon, but he was also a socialite. When the sale of the Lakers to Buss went down in May 1979, *Los Angeles Times* sports writer Ted Green wrote this description of Buss:

> He likes fast cars, fast women and fast scores in business and does his darnedest to indulge in them. He squires Playboy bunnies around in a Rolls-Royce Camargue . . . or Cadillac limousine . . . or a Lincoln (that limo has a TV).
>
> His tastes run from Kahlúa to California wines and he has an insatiable sweet tooth. His office looks like Willy Wonka's chocolate factory, stocked with M&Ms, candy bars by the hundreds, jelly beans, lollipops and other sweets.
>
> He lives in Bel-Air in a house with seven bathrooms and six fireplaces and has a Japanese houseboy who cooks midnight suppers, plays tennis on his own court and is host to major league parties.
>
> If he isn't weekending in Palm Springs, recuperating in a plush corner of the hotel he owns, he's apt to be living it up in Las Vegas or New York or nearly anywhere he decides to jet on a whim.

As the book detailed, the connection between the Lakers and Hollywood had already been established. Bob Short, who moved them to Los Angeles, comped tickets to Doris Day—a prominent actress known for romantic comedy roles in the '50s and '60s—to bring some glitz to Lakers games. When Jack Kent Cooke bought the team in 1965, he continued along the same path. He made

sure the Lakers had big-name stars. He brought in Wilt Chamberlain to play with Elgin Baylor and Jerry West. He brought in Abdul-Jabbar. Cooke also created an exclusive area for himself and his guests, blocking off thirteen seats at the top of the section, birthing the idea of box seats. He also held exclusive pregame dinners at the Forum Club inside the arena.

When Buss took over, he took it to an even more extravagant level. The boxed seats section expanded to sixty-three, and Buss brought in celebrities and beautiful women. He created the pricing structure that survives today by jacking up the best seats for the rich people and lowering the worst seats for the working people. This way, the common person could go to Lakers games and always expect to see celebrities there. Even today, Lakers games are still an ideal place for celebrity-watching. There were one hundred courtside seats around the floor, dubbed the "golden rectangle," and they were so exclusive that Michael Jackson was declined when he tried to buy season tickets courtside. They were already sold out.

Buss instituted the Lakers Girls, a collection of dancers who performed during timeouts and at halftime. He also moved the press courtside so they could get a good look at the show and report on it. And one of the best shows of the night was outside the arena before the game where you could see the rich and famous arriving.

But it was all connected to the product on the court, and getting Magic was the most fortuitous of bounces. His vision and no-look passes turned fast breaks into gasp-inducing displays that were as spontaneous and unpredictable as they were aesthetically pleasing. That was the greatest complement to the Lakers' half-court offense, which featured the most recognizable trick in basketball—Kareem's skyhook, which never ceased to marvel.

The hoop on the court, the glitz and glamour off it, the fanfare and entertainment—it was indeed showtime. All that was missing was the opening number from The Horn.

Buss pioneered the NBA-as-event-branding, a phenomenon that remains in full force today. He turned the team's NBA games into a permanent extension of its home city's nightlife. He morphed a basketball game into a game-night experience with pregame festivities, halftime shows, and postgame activities. He made it as worthy of a date night as it was a night out for basketball junkies. Other teams can't exactly replicate the Lakers scene, which is always teeming with actors and actresses, musicians, entertainers, and those who just like looking at them. But teams have followed the model of turning their games into nightlife settings. Every franchise has a dance squad. Every team comps seats to celebrities, and once they're in the arena, visiting stars show up on the big screen. The box seats are now a staple.

The Lakers fancied up the NBA.

HOW THE DYNASTY ALMOST ENDED EARLY

On November 8, 1979, Lakers coach Jack McKinney was scheduled to play tennis with assistant coach Paul Westhead. McKinney was an avid player. He got the call from Westhead that the courts were open and headed that way. McKinney's wife had the family car, so he rode his bike. The one witness, Robert N. S. Clark, was in his car in the intersection when he said he saw McKinney on his bike. He said McKinney slowed when he got to the intersection but when he tried to stop "his bicycle went from under him and all of a sudden he fell forward." He sustained a head injury, a concussion, and a broken elbow.

He wound up in a semicoma, spent three weeks in the hospital, and the rest of the season healing.

Westhead, the assistant and longtime friend of McKinney, filled in as the interim coach. In May 1980, McKinney was fired by the Lakers, who eventually hired Westhead as the head coach.

This was significant because the change in coach led to a change in playing style.

Buss hired McKinney four months before the accident. But first, Buss requested permission to speak to five other NBA coaches and all were rejected by the respective teams. He was also turned down by University of Nevada, Las Vegas coach Jerry Tarkanian. Buss had a fallback plan: McKinney. He was an experienced assistant from the coaching tree of Jack Ramsay, who won the title with Portland in 1977, and Buss liked him because they shared a vision on how the game should be played. Fast.

"I'd like to run very much more than we have here," McKinney said in his introductory press conference. "A constant running game. I'd like a moving offense, rather than having everyone standing round watching Kareem all the time and putting pressure on him. I think we can do that. When you have someone like Magic, I think you can do that. We'll run every chance and under every possible situation."

McKinney coached the Lakers for fourteen games before his fall. Westhead picked up the baton, and the Lakers won the 1980 NBA Finals running McKinney's offense. That year, the Lakers ranked No. 8 in the NBA in pace with an average of 104.1 possessions per 48 minutes.

The next year, with Westhead now the head coach, the Lakers pace slowed considerably. In 1980–81, the Lakers averaged 102.7 possessions per 48 minutes. It was the slowest the Lakers played since 1953–54, when the franchise was in Minneapolis. The last time the Lakers had won the title, in 1971–72, they led the league in pace with 116.9 possessions per game.

The Lakers lost in the first round of the 1981 playoffs, which opened the window for Westhead to really change things. He went to a slower style of play. That was problematic for Magic Johnson. Then, after the eleventh game of the 1981–82 season, a November 18 close win at Utah, Magic unleashed a bombshell to reporters after the game.

"I can't play here anymore. I want to be traded. I want to leave. I want to be traded. I can't deal with it no more. . . .

"I haven't been happy all season. I've got to go. . . .

"I've seen certain things happening. I've sat back and haven't said anything, but I've got to go. . . .

"It's nothing towards the guys. I love them and everybody. But I'm not happy. I'm just showing up. I play; I play as hard as I can, but I'm not happy. I'm not having any fun. I just want to go. . . .

"We don't see eye to eye on a lot of things. It's time for me to go. I'm going to go in and talk to the man, hopefully tomorrow, and see if a trade will happen."

It was Westhead whom Magic wasn't seeing eye to eye with. Just like that, the Lakers dynasty was on the ropes. No Magic meant no hub for Showtime. At this point, they'd won one title riding Kareem most of the way and flamed out in the first round the following year. Showtime hadn't even hit its stride yet.

Magic was barely twenty-two years old and, at that time, such a move by a player, asking to be traded, was frowned upon. He was suddenly being cast as a diva. And who knew how Dr. Buss would respond?

Magic had drawn ire from his teammates for being so close with the owner. They hung out together frequently, even partied together. Magic described Buss as a father figure for the young man so far from home. Buss introduced Magic to a new world of celebrity and wealth. And some four months before Magic's public demand to be traded, Buss had inked him to a twenty-five-year, $25 million contract, believed to be the largest in sports at the time. Would Buss feel offended, betrayed, and ship off Magic out of spite?

Westhead was fired the next day. Crisis averted.

The 1985 playoffs was another time the dynasty almost ended early. The Magic-led Lakers already had two championships, in 1980 and 1982. But they'd also lost two NBA Finals, in 1983 and 1984, and the latter was to the Celtics.

Buss introduced Magic to a new world of celebrity and wealth.

But in 1984–85, they looked to be on to something. They won sixty-two games after putting together one of the greatest offensive seasons ever, averaging 118.2 points. They were even more potent in the playoffs. They won seven of their first eight playoff games and averaged more than 131 points in those games. The only loss was Game 4 in Portland in the second round as the Trail

Blazers rallied to stave off a sweep. They won the seven games by an average of 17.6 points per game, including a 139–122 win over Denver.

The Nuggets topped 120 points per game during the regular season and were the only team to score more than the Lakers. And they stunned the top seed in Game 2 in Los Angeles, blitzing the Lakers 136–114. Alex English, the Nuggets' six-foot-seven All-Star forward, put up 40 in Game 2, giving him 70 the first two games.

The Lakers took Game 3 in Denver, essentially putting all the marbles on Game 4. The game was tied at 93 after three quarters. But it was over before the fourth.

Alex English, who had 28 points in 28 minutes, broke his thumb in the third quarter. He had surgery that night to repair multiple fractures. He was done for the series.

Still, Game 4 was tied at 118 in the final seconds without English. A James Worthy putback proved to be the game winner. The Nuggets' last chance was thwarted when Kareem took the ball away from Danny Schayes. The Lakers survived and went up 3–1 in the series. With no English, the Nuggets lost Game 5 in Los Angeles 153–109, and the Lakers advanced to the NBA Finals.

"If I didn't break my thumb, we would've won that series," a smiling English said at the 2019 Hall of Fame announcement in Chicago, like it still bothered him. "Maybe the Lakers never become a dynasty."

THE VILLAIN

Perhaps everyone in a Lakers jersey wanted to punch M. L. Carr, the Celtics towel-waving, trash-talking agitator on the bench. They probably couldn't stand Cedric "Cornbread" Maxwell either. He talked plenty trash and was good enough to back it up on the court. Maxwell was MVP of the 1984 Finals when the Celtics upset the Lakers.

But without question, the most worthy foe, the one whom they feared the most, was Larry Bird. His power to torch the Lakers and get under their skin was perhaps most evident in the 1984 NBA Finals. In Game 4—after Kevin McHale changed the tone of the game by clotheslining Lakers forward Kurt Rambis on a fast break—tensions were boiling. Bird fouled Kareem, who cleared space from the contact by swinging his elbows. Bird took exception and had some words.

Suddenly, Kareem was yelling back at Bird and had to be restrained.

Kareem was an intellectual. He was a thinker. Mostly quiet and reclusive, he was the last person they expected to lose his temper, but he was ready to land a skyhook to Bird's mouth.

"He fouled me," Kareem told reporters after the game. "Then he started to scream abuse at me. I'm the one who got fouled. I went to the line. And he's holding me up as the one who breaks the rules."

Bird's big rivalry was with Magic, dating back to their showdown in college. They are forever linked as the rivalry that catapulted the NBA. It was made possible by Bird's perennial threat to Magic, who was always being compared to Bird and needed to be exceptional to eclipse Bird's high bar.

"I don't want Larry Bird to have nothing over me," Johnson would later say. "Nothing."

THE HOME COURT

The Forum, the design of which was inspired by the Roman Forum, was a $12 million privately funded engineering marvel, not including the $4 million for the land. It was built in a little over a year, opening in 1967. It was the first large-scale arena, more than seventeen thousand seats, to not be supported by major pillars. Even the Boston Garden had columns inside, obstructing some of the views.

The only pillars holding up the Forum were on the court: Elgin Baylor. Jerry West. Wilt Chamberlain. Gail Goodrich. Kareem Abdul-Jabbar. Jamaal Wilkes. Located in Inglewood, it was dubbed "the Fabulous Forum" by legendary announcer Chick Hearn. It was as much part of the dynasty as the games it housed.

One of the main attractions of the Forum was the Forum Club. It was a restaurant/lounge/bar that became a magnet for celebrities because of its exclusivity. It had a special entrance on the side of the arena and was a perennial red carpet, even without the scarlet fabric. The restaurant inside served Dom Perignon and marinated scallops. Only season ticket holders had access, and even they had to pay extra. There was a VIP room inside the Forum Club where Dr. Jerry Buss hosted his pregame dinners with a collection of young mod-elesque women and celebrities. Fans were fabricating passes to try to sneak in.

Guards wouldn't even take bribes. Once, Mickey Rooney was mistakenly turned away. Cameras were not allowed.

When the games began, the attention shifted to the court, where the stars were working. They emphasized the product on the court with a lighting trick to add drama—dimming lights in the crowd to create a spotlight on the court. Buss even had extra lights hung on the edges of the court to essentially turn the hardwood into a stage. It's a trend used around the league now, dark everywhere but the court, but it began as a unique vibe at the Forum.

THE CRAZIEST STAT

The three teams with the highest regular-season field goal percentage were all led by Magic Johnson.

The 1984–85 Lakers as a team shot a whopping 54.5 percent from the field. The top eleven players by minutes per game all averaged above 46.5 percent shooting. Only Michael Cooper, the team's primary three-point shooter, and Jamaal Wilkes averaged below 50 percent. The 1984–85 Lakers also hold the record for most assists per game in the regular season at 31.4.

The 1983–84 Lakers shot 53.2 percent from the field, the second highest for a team ever. The third-best was by the 1979–80 Lakers, who shot 52.9 percent.

The Lakers had seven players average double figures, and six shot above 50 percent. Kareem Abdul-Jabbar led the way with 21.9 points on 56 percent shooting. James Worthy was right behind him with 21.5 points on an astounding 62.2 percent shooting for a wing.

6

THE LARRY BIRD CELTICS

Beat L.A.! Beat L.A.!

The chant is routinely heard by the Los Angeles Lakers, Los Angeles Dodgers, Los Angeles Kings, even now the Los Angeles Clippers, and every other Los Angeles team. The three-syllable refrain is a staple in the sports lexicon.

It actually began in 1982 in Boston, oddly, at a Celtics game that didn't even feature the Lakers.

Boston was playing Philadelphia in the Eastern Conference Finals; the Lakers had already clinched the Western Conference and were awaiting the winner. This was the third straight meeting between the Celtics and 76ers in the East Finals. Philadelphia needed just five games to win the first meeting in 1980. The Celtics won in seven games in 1981, coming back from a 3–1 deficit with 3 consecutive nail-biting wins by a combined total of 5 points.

So by the time 1982 came around, this was a full-scale rivalry. First off, the amount of talent in this matchup was epic. The Hall of Famers alone: Larry Bird, Julius Erving, Kevin McHale, Bobby Jones, Robert Parish, Maurice Cheeks, and Nate "Tiny" Archibald. Throw in All-Star caliber players Andrew Toney and Darryl Dawkins of the 76ers, and Celtics forward Cedric Maxwell.

On top of the talent, this clashing of powers was heated and physical. Celtics vs. 76ers was a bitter feud between two NBA giants from the same region. And it had come down to another Game 7 in Boston in 1982. Philadelphia left the Garden a year earlier being mocked by Celtics fans as chokers for blowing a 3–1 lead. But in '82, they got their revenge, stifling Bird and shutting down Boston.

When Celtics fans realized it was over and their team was going to lose, their beef with Philadelphia and the 76ers took a back seat. They disliked the Lakers more. So the crowd of better than fifteen thousand people started chanting in unison "Beat L.A.! Beat L.A.!" to the victorious 76ers. Philadelphia had just eliminated their beloved Celtics, yet the Boston faithful became fans of Dr. J, Andrew Toney, and Bobby Jones. Because the enemy of my enemy is my friend.

What was so absurd about it was that Magic Johnson's Lakers and Bird's Celtics had yet to actually meet in the Finals at that point. Magic won the 1980 title and Bird won the 1981 title. They were on a collision course in 1982, but the 76ers derailed those plans. Still, the Celtics faithful were fully invested in the Lakers' demise, a Boston tradition dating back to the '50s and '60s when the Celtics beat the Lakers seven times in the Finals.

Plus, since Magic got out of college, where he beat Bird in the national championship game, there had been talk about the resurrection of the Lakers' dynasty. They already had Kareem Abdul-Jabbar, arguably the greatest player ever at the time. Magic instantly made them formidable, which meant the Celtics-Lakers blood feud of yesteryear was fully back on again.

The rivalry that essentially launched the NBA was reborn. It pushed the NBA to levels no one imagined. And it was fueled by the arrogance of Celtics nation, born of unprecedented success. That arrogance, the eternal green flame burning within, produced a sort of tribal hatred—and it was aimed directly at the Lakers. The Lakers were the only franchise that could possibly stake a claim on Boston's basketball superiority, and the Celtics defended that status with a passion hot enough to fuel an entire sport.

"The L.A. Fakers" was what they called them. And Magic was Cheesy Johnson. And nothing thrilled the Celtics more than beating Los Angeles.

Here is an ironic twist: For help doing so, they turned to a kid from Los Angeles.

After losing in the 1982 East Finals, the Celtics were swept by the Bucks in 1983. That disappointment produced sweeping changes. General manager Red Auerbach fired coach Bill Fitch and hired Celtics great K. C. Jones. They had a glutton of guards at the time—Archibald, Quinn Buckner, Gerald Henderson—but they needed an upgrade. And they found it in Dennis Johnson, a kid from Compton.

When Celtics fans realized it was over and their team was going to lose, their beef with Philadelphia and the 76ers took a back seat. They disliked the Lakers more.

DJ, as he was known, was a six-foot-four point guard who had worn out his welcome in Phoenix. He had a reputation as a bit of a malcontent. But he was the 1979 Finals MVP. He was an All-Star and a regular on the NBA All-Defense team. And he was the ideal antidote to Magic Johnson.

Dennis Johnson was physical with long arms. He wasn't especially speedy, but he was athletic enough to complement his size. He was a big guard, so Magic couldn't overpower him, yet he was quick enough to stay in front of ball handlers and lead the Celtics' opportunistic transition game.

Down 2–1 in the 1984 NBA Finals, Johnson put up 22 points and 14 assists in a Game 4 win at Los Angeles. He scored at least 20 points in the final four games of that series as Boston won the championship in seven games against a Lakers team several in the Celtics locker room thought was better.

During the celebration, after the Celtics pulled out Game 7 in Boston, Auerbach used the moment to remind the world his franchise was still undefeated against the Lakers in the Finals.

"Whatever happened to the Los Angeles dynasty?" Auerbach screamed into Brent Musberger's microphone with the Larry O'Brien Trophy in his hand. "You guys were talking about a dynasty. Here is where it is right here. This is the dynasty. We're the best team in the world."

NBA Finals Appearances

1981 (W)	1984 (W)	1985 (L)
1986 (W)		1987 (L)

THE FACE OF THE DYNASTY

One of the most famous brawls in NBA history happened between two of the greatest players of all time: Dr. J and Larry Bird. And it was also one of the highlights of Bird's legendary banter.

November 9, 1984, Philadelphia and Boston—the two Eastern Conference contenders and bitter rivals—faced off in an early regular-season game. The 76ers were 5–0 and the Celtics were 4–0. Dr. J was thirty-four years old, in his thirteenth season and winding down a storied career. And Bird absolutely torched him.

He scored 13 points in the third quarter as the Celtics pulled away. He had 42 points on 17-for-23 shooting, one of the better performances of his career.

Erving, on the other hand, struggled mightily. He was 3-for-13 with 6 points. And Bird let him hear it.

From the tea leaves coming out of that game, Bird was just undressing Erving all night. Danny Ainge said Bird told Dr. J it was time he retired. Others said he was calling out their respective point totals every time he scored.

"He kept on saying to Erving, 'Aren't you gonna guard me? Can't you do any better?'" renowned official Dick Bavetta, in a 2015 interview with the Naismith Hall of Fame, said of Bird, as he recalled refereeing that game. "He was the greatest soft-spoken trash talker I've ever met."

The two started jawing at each other, Bird and Dr. J. Next thing everyone knew, they were literally grabbing each other by the throats. Charles Barkley and Moses Malone grabbed Bird from behind—Barkley said he was trying to break up the fight—but Dr. J got off three punches while Bird was being held back.

You'd never know about any of the verbal jousting by just watching it. Bird's expression scarcely changes. He didn't ever look to be in the throes of trash talk. But he was the best at it. Bird was a cold-blooded killer. He was known for destroying people on the court and calling out how before he did it.

He has a long legacy of epic trash talk that has produced some legendary stories.

In March 1985, the Hawks hosted the Celtics in one of the twelve games they scheduled in New Orleans because of lagging attendance in Atlanta. Bird caught fire in the second half and put on a show en route to a 60-point night. And he was tormenting the Hawks, and their rising star Dominique Wilkins, with his taunts. Bird made everything he threw up.

"Off the glass."

"Who's next?"

"Where you want this from?"

Even the Hawks' bench was cheering him on, drawing the ire and a $500 fine from Atlanta coach Mike Fratello. Glenn "Doc" Rivers, then a point guard with the Hawks, told a story of Bird getting off some ultimate banter on his last shot.

"He said 'in the trainer's lap' coming down the court," Rivers said, "which meant it was going to be a three and it was going to be from deep. Then he said, 'Who wants it?' Then I think Rickey Brown, I'm not sure who it was, ran out after him, he shot this high rainbow, it goes in, Rickey bumps into him—and accidentally knocks him on our trainer's lap. So it was exactly what he said, it was an accident but it was almost fate. They show a shot of our bench, Cliff Levingston and Eddie Johnson are standing up giving each other high fives. It was pretty awesome."

In March 1987, the Celtics went to Chicago to face the Bulls and a young Michael Jordan. Ben Poquette, in his tenth and final season, got the start that night. Legend has it that when Bird saw who was defending him, he turned to then Bulls coach Doug Collins and expressed his disappointment.

"Ben Poquette?" Bird told Collins. "Are you f***ing kidding me?"

Bird had a thing about being defended by White guys. He was so good, and so confident, he wanted the best defender on him. At the time, White players were known for their lack of athleticism and poor defense. So Bird wanted the best Black player to defend him.

"The one thing that always bothered me when I played in the NBA was I really got irritated when they put a White guy on me," Bird told ESPN. "I still don't understand why. A White guy would come out, I would always ask him: 'What, do you have a problem with your coach? Did your coach do this to you?'

And he'd go, 'No,' and I'd say, 'Come on, you got a White guy coming out here to guard me; you got no chance.' . . . For some reason, that always bothered me when I was playing against a White guy. As far as playing, I didn't care who guarded me—red, yellow, Black. I just didn't want a White guy guarding me. Because it's disrespect to my game."

The following season, in November, Bird had 44 points in overtime at Washington with seven seconds left. Earlier in regulation, with twenty-six seconds left, Bird drilled the go-ahead shot but it was waived off as Celtics coach K. C. Jones had called a time-out before Bird got the shot off. But Bird got another chance for the game winner in overtime. He told his teammates he would get the ball in the same place and do it again. Out of the time-out, he even told the Bullets he was getting the ball, ending any suspense.

Bird did get the ball. And he hit the three-pointer at the buzzer to win it.

In the 1987 NBA Finals, the Celtics were down a point in Game 4 and were looking to even the series against the Lakers. The Garden was teeming with anticipation as the Celtics emerged from a time-out. The Lakers were setting up for the inbounds play and discussing their defensive assignments. So Bird helped them out. Byron Scott shared the story on the ESPN *30 for 30* documentary *Celtics/Lakers: Best of Enemies*.

"Larry said, 'Guys. Guys. Listen. I'ma curl around here and I'ma go to this corner. And I'ma catch it and I'ma shoot it and there ain't a damn thing you can do about it.' He told us the play. It's not shit-talking if you can back it up."

Bird drilled the corner three, putting the Celtics up 106–104 with twelve seconds left.

This was who was leading the Celtics dynasty—a merciless superstar who embodied the arrogance, skill, and unselfishness of the era. With his dry wit and impenetrable confidence, Bird was unapologetic about his greatness, and thus the perfect face of the franchise.

This was who was leading the Celtics dynasty—a merciless superstar who embodied the arrogance, skill, and unselfishness of the era.

When This Dynasty Reigned

- MTV launched and birthed the era of music videos, beginning with "Video Killed the Radio Star" by the Buggles. Some of the legendary videos that appeared were "Sledgehammer" by Peter Gabriel, "Every Breath You Take" by the Police, "Walk This Way" by Run-DMC and Aerosmith, and Michael Jackson's "Thriller."

- The '80s was the era of the cult classic blockbuster movie. *The Empire Strikes Back*, *E.T.*, *The Shining*, *A Christmas Story*, *Ghostbusters*, *Back to the Future*, *Die Hard*, and *Do the Right Thing*. The ten highest-grossing actors of the decade: Harrison Ford, Carrie Fisher, Eddie Murphy, Dan Aykroyd, Bill Murray, Judge Reinhold, Tom Cruise, Christopher Lloyd, and John Candy.

- The Cold War between the United States and Russia took a turn when each country boycotted the other country's Olympics. In 1983, President Ronald Reagan dubbed Russia the "Evil Empire" during a speech and escalated the beef between the countries.

- Hip-hop made its way from a grassroots niche genre into the mainstream. LL COOL J, Big Daddy Kane, Queen Latifah, MC Hammer, and Will Smith became stars. In March 1987, while the Celtics were champions, the Beastie Boys record *Licensed to Ill* became the first rap album to hit number one on the *Billboard* charts.

THE MASTERMIND

That Red Auerbach again.

The Celtics won their last championship in 1976, when Jo Jo White, Dave Cowens, Charlie Scott, and Paul Silas helped give John Havlicek one last banner. But from there it was a steady decline. They won 44 games in 1976–77, then 32 in 1977–78. It proved to be one of the best things to ever happen to the Celtics.

Boston had the sixth-worst record that year and, as a result, got the No. 6 pick in the 1978 draft. They used it to select Bird, who was a junior at Indiana State. It was uncommon to select a player still in college. But after his junior season it was clear Bird—who originally went to the prestigious Indiana University before dropping out because he was homesick—was one of the best players in college basketball. After a stint in community college, he transferred to Indiana State and averaged 32.8 in his first year, followed by 30.0 in his second season. He also averaged 12.4 rebounds, 4.1 assists, and 2.6 steals over those first two years. Auerbach had seen enough.

The uncertainty of whether Bird would turn pro or play his senior season at Indiana State helped the Celtics as the teams ahead of them in the draft couldn't afford to wait. Then when Bird announced he was staying in school, he became an even tougher choice. Auerbach, however, had traded Charlie Scott to the Lakers months earlier and got a first-round pick in exchange. With two first-round picks, Auerbach had the luxury of patience. After the draft in which the Celtics selected Bird, *Boston Globe* columnist Bob Ryan penned these words:

> **There are undoubtedly some unhappy Celtic fans this morning, since Larry Bird, the object of Red's affection, will not be available to the Celtics right away. Those who seek instant gratification cannot see the wisdom in drafting a player who won't sign for a year when this team needs so much help. Those people would not feel this way if they had ever seen Larry Bird play. Larry Bird is worth waiting for.**

The Celtics were even worse in 1978–79, Bird was lifting Indiana State to national prominence, leaving Auerbach pretty secure the Celtics had a future star. So he made another big splash by essentially cashing in his 1979 bounty of draft picks.

In January 1979, Auerbach traded away Jo Jo White and Dennis Awtrey, getting a first-round pick for each. That gave him three to work with, including his own 1979 pick—which was a high one as the Celtics won only twenty-nine games. But before the season even ended, Auerbach traded them all to the Knicks for star big man Bob McAdoo.

McAdoo was a noted scorer who averaged 30-plus points in three straight seasons for the Buffalo Braves. He was averaging 26.9 points for the Knicks when Auerbach maneuvered to get him. But McAdoo was quickly disgruntled with his playing time. By the off-season, he wanted a trade. Before training camp to kick off the 1979–80 season, the Celtics traded him to Detroit, the worst team in the league for two first-round picks.

With Bird finally on the Celtics, they went from 29 wins to 61 wins, the greatest jump in wins in NBA history at the time. They ran into the loaded 76ers in the second round of the playoffs, losing in five games, but it was clear they had their centerpiece. So Auerbach went to work building a core around Bird and pulled off one of the greatest draft steals of all time.

Auerbach traded the No. 1 pick and the No. 13 pick to the Warriors for center Robert Parish and the No. 3 pick. The Warriors had drafted him No. 8 overall in 1976. But he was never the franchise center they hoped. He averaged around 17 points and 10.9 rebounds in 1979–80, but the Warriors were still bottom-feeders in the West. Auerbach didn't need a center to anchor his franchise. He had Bird. But he did need a big man to replace Dave Cowens, who was at the end of his line.

This draft had three big men at the top: Joe Barry Carroll from Purdue, Kevin McHale from Minnesota, and Darrell Griffith from Louisville. With the top pick, the Celtics had their choice. But the trade of McAdoo set Auerbach up to get greedy. He could afford to trade down to get Parish and fill two positions, so he did. The Warriors selected Carroll, the Jazz took Griffith, and the Celtics took McHale.

No one knew it at the time, but Auerbach—who orchestrated a front line of Bill Russell, Tommy Heinsohn, and Sam Jones more than twenty years earlier—had just assembled one of the greatest frontcourts in NBA history: Bird, McHale, and Parish. The foundation for the dynasty was set.

THE CULTURAL IMPACT

In 1976, the American Basketball Association—which openly targeted African-Americans and marketed their style of play—merged with the NBA and brought an influx of Black players. The 1978–79 New York Knicks fielded the first All-Black roster. Early in that season, the Knicks faced the Detroit Pistons, and they put on the first NBA game where all the players who participated were African-American.

Some thirty years before the Bird-led dynasty reached its peak, it was the Russell-led Celtics who normalized the inclusion of Black players. But by the 1980s, the league was predominantly Black. The best players were considered to be the African-American ones. For many, even the accomplishments of earlier teams and players were minimized because they weren't going up against the "best players" since the league had few (or no) Black players when stars from earlier eras were on top.

Enter Bird and the Celtics, and the script was flipped. Now, the Celtics were normalizing White players, all while being led by a Black coach.

It was clear early on Bird was a sensation. The next year, in 1980, the Celtics drafted Kevin McHale—a six-foot-ten power forward out of Minnesota. McHale was a skilled big man who was known for his footwork and array of post moves. Like Bird, he wasn't a great leaper or especially fast. But he combined his skill, instinct, and work ethic to become a dominant player.

"God did something to me that opened my eyes to seeing White people can play," Celtics forward Cedric Maxwell said in the *Celtics/Lakers: Best of Enemies* documentary. "As a person I was very biased, very ignorant, and God punished me by putting me on a team with the two greatest White players playing together at one time on one team ever. Ever."

The 1985–86 Celtics was arguably the best of the Bird dynasty. They won sixty-seven games and lost only three times in the playoffs on the way to the championship, beating Houston's twin towers of Ralph Sampson and Hakeem Olajuwon. That Celtics squad was dominant despite being predominantly White. That team had but four Black players (not counting Sly Williams, who was signed as a free agent and waived after playing just six games). Two of them—point guard Dennis Johnson and center Robert Parish—were pivotal, and the other two—David Thirdkill and Sam Vincent—scarcely played outside of blowouts. Cedric Maxwell, Ray Williams, Quinn Buckner, Carlos Clark, and even renowned trash talker M. L. Carr were all gone. They were replaced by Bill Walton, Danny Ainge, Jerry Sichting, Scott Wedman, and Rick Carlisle.

Larry Bird won his third MVP and his second Finals MVP. Bird was the first White player to win MVP since Walton in 1978 and only the fourth since Bob Pettit became the inaugural recipient of the award in 1956. McHale was widely regarded as one of the best players in the league and a force despite being grounded. Walton, the legend and former Great White Hope, got one last ring to close out his career.

> *But these Celtics . . . commanded what was often missing from these dialogues about race and culture: respect.*

There is no disputing the Lakers-Celtics rivalry of the '80s was racially charged. The predominantly White fan base of the NBA gravitated toward the rare dominant White team—much the same way the Black segment of the NBA fan base gravitated toward Black teams and players. It was unofficially cast as a clash between divergent worlds: playground ball vs. fundamental hoop, the urban aesthetic vs. the rural disposition. But at this juncture of NBA history, the White player and his regard was on the decline. Athleticism was becoming a coveted commodity, and the sport was being dubbed a Black man's game.

But these Celtics, however polarizing they were for what they represented, had commanded what was often missing from these dialogues about race and culture: respect. No matter what you felt about the Celtics, there was no denying those White boys could play. They'd been worthy rivals who struck the fear of God in Magic Johnson, Kareem Abdul-Jabbar, Isiah Thomas, Dominique Wilkins, and even a young Michael Jordan—a ringing endorsement of the Celtics' ability. Where it was customary to disregard White players as inherently inferior, Bird, McHale, and the Celtics refuted such a notion and garnered a respect that would be unifying in the sport, from the hardwoods of the NBA to the blacktops in the streets. Some years later, in 1992, a popular basketball movie became a cult classic by addressing these very themes and the resulting embrace of the diverse cultures in basketball: *White Men Can't Jump*.

HOW THE DYNASTY ALMOST ENDED EARLY

In June 1978, the Pacers finished the season tied with the worst record in the Western Conference. Back then, the draft order was set by inverse order of record. The worst record in the West and the worst record in the East would flip a coin for the top pick. That year, Indiana had to win two coin flips—one for the right to represent the East in the coin flip, then the coin flip for the top pick. They won both.

The Pacers wanted Larry Bird. So did Portland, which had three first-round picks, and Philadelphia. But Bird had options, and drafting him came with some risk. He was eligible to enter the NBA because his draft class had graduated. But he still had one year of eligibility at Indiana State. He could enter the draft or he could play his third season in college. A team could draft him then get him after he finished his final college season. But the risk was that if he didn't like who drafted him, he could always refuse to sign and reenter the draft in 1979.

It seemed the Pacers weren't willing to risk it for the hometown guy. They traded the pick to Portland. Philadelphia was heavy in the mix and wanted Bird. But the 76ers deemed Indiana's demands too high. Portland selected Mychal Thompson with the top pick, and the Pacers selected Rick Robey with the No. 3 overall pick. The 76ers didn't pick until No. 8. So Bird fell right to the Celtics.

Still, Boston had to get Bird signed. It wasn't until June 8, 1979, almost exactly a year after he was drafted by the Celtics, that Bird finally inked his deal with the Celtics—for five years, $3.25 million.

That's twice the Celtics almost didn't get Bird.

THE VILLAIN

"Magic's just a great basketball player. He's the best I've ever seen. You know. I . . . Unbelievable. I don't know what to say."

Larry Bird made this bold confession after Game 6 of the 1987 NBA Finals. The Lakers clinched the championship on their home floor, and Magic Johnson had 16 points, 19 assists, and 8 rebounds with 3 steals. This was the same series where Johnson dropped in his famous baby hook shot to win Game 4.

By the end, Magic, the young star who'd learned the ropes of superstardom against the Celtics, had grown into a full-blown, unstoppable force. He went from being dubbed Tragic Johnson in the 1984 NBA Finals because of his costly mistakes to being the dagger in the Celtics' storied run. Bird knew the throne now belonged to Magic. He maintained the integrity of his audacity by being willing to say that aloud. Three years older, Bird was closer to the end than Magic, who was cresting as a dominant NBA star.

In three NBA Finals matchups against Boston, two of them won by the Lakers, Magic averaged 20.7 points on 53.3 percent shooting with 13.5 assists, 7.5 rebounds, and 2.2 steals. For the final showdown with the Celtics, he was more of a scorer. He'd been a floor general who could score in the first two series, his greatest threat being the transition game he ignited. Kareem Abdul-Jabbar was the hub of the offense. But in 1987, Magic led the Lakers in scoring, assists, rebounds, and steals. He was also second in minutes played and field goal percentage.

He tortured the Celtics.

It wasn't just that Magic was so good. It was how he dominated. His style and energy was so contrary to the Celtics' ethos. He was flashy and pretty, an affront to their tough, blue-collar grind. He played fast, in a way that made the Celtics look slow, manipulating the Lakers' wealth of talent like a puppet master. He drove them crazy with his fast breaks and how he set up James Worthy and Byron Scott for dunk after dunk.

And the pointing. Magic loved to point—to direct traffic, to acknowledge a good play by his teammate, to celebrate a moment. Boston fans wanted to break that finger.

Magic's success was an indictment on the Celtics. They lost to other teams in the playoffs. The 76ers twice. Milwaukee. Detroit. But Magic made losing to the Lakers feel like an attack on their way of life.

The worst part: Magic finished with five championships in the 1980s, compared to three for Bird and the Celtics. And that doesn't even count when Magic led Michigan State over Bird and Indiana State in the 1979 NCAA tournament championship.

Insult to injury: Magic's colorway for his signature Converse was better than Bird's.

THE HOME COURT

Back to the Boston Garden. The highlight of the Garden's home-court advantage résumé came on Friday, June 8, 1984.

Boston was ninety-seven degrees at 3 p.m. local time. The previous record for that date was ninety-three, in 1950 and 1976. This matters because Boston Garden, remember, had no air-conditioning. It was as if the Garden sensed the chance for the Celtics to take control of the series in Game 5 and turned up the heat on its invisible thermostat.

"I suggest you go to the local steam bath with all your clothes on," Kareem told reporters after the game, describing the venue. "First, try to do one hundred pushups. Then run back and forth for forty-eight minutes."

By tip-off at 9 p.m., it was still eighty-five degrees in Boston. Inside of the Garden was measured at ninety-seven degrees. That's ninety-seven degrees in a building crowded with tens of thousands of people, no breeze, and no air. It was the opposite of playing in the snow at Soldier Field.

Kareem Abdul-Jabbar wore an oxygen mask on the bench. Referee Hugh Evans left the game at halftime because of dehydration. Parish got a leg cramp and Bird swathed himself in towels on the bench. The Garden shut down the Lakers' fast break. The only player who seemed to thrive was Bird, who made 15 of 20 shots and had 34 points with 17 rebounds.

"You have to give both clubs credit for enduring a forty-eight-minute steam bath," Lakers coach Pat Riley said. "It was extremely hot; both teams were affected. But Boston showed up better than we did. I think the home crowd had something to do with that. It gave them some adrenaline."

Score one for the Garden.

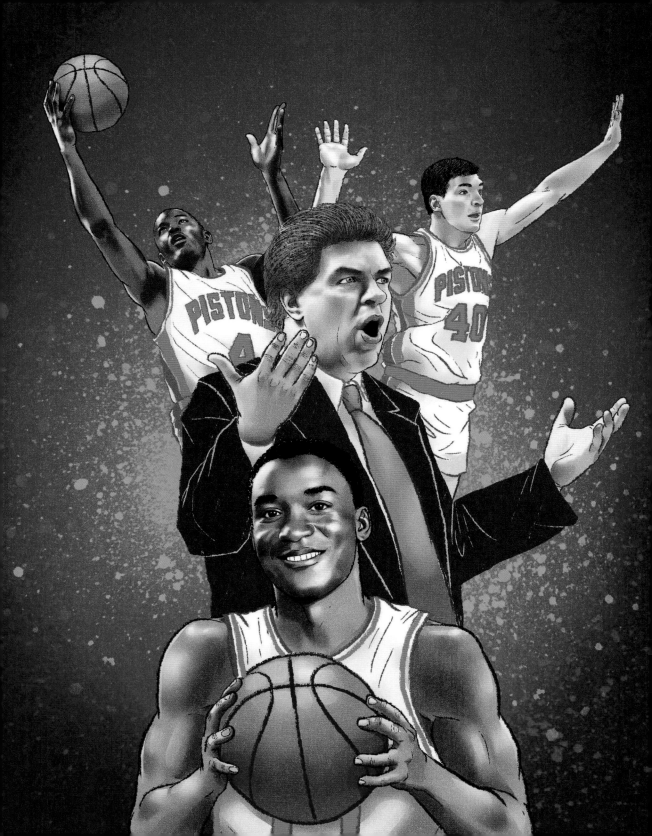

7

THE BAD BOYS
PISTONS

You've got to actually watch some games from the Detroit Pistons dynasty to truly understand. Not edited highlights of their hardest fouls or greatest moments. But games. Not clips inside documentaries with narratives to uphold and messaging to get across. But games.

Do this: Go to YouTube and search "Pistons Blazers 1990 Game 3 full game" and you'll get two hours of the Pistons. The real Pistons. They went into Portland and took control of the series with a huge road win. If you watch it objectively, just take in the game, you know what stands out? They scored 121 points on 53.1 percent shooting. And they did this with just three made three-pointers. Seven players scored in double figures. Portland finished fourth in scoring in the NBA that season and couldn't keep up with Detroit.

The Pistons have been branded as masters of defense. Their legacy in the pantheon of great NBA teams is one of a physically imposing, defensively suffocating collection who bullied opponents with a black-gloved fist.

Indeed, the Pistons are one of the toughest mutha—shut yo' mouth—teams in NBA history. But the revelation evident in the game is how modern their offense was for their era. It gets overshadowed by their punishing defense. No one would be shocked the Bad Boys were a Top 3 defensive team in the NBA from 1987 to 1991. But most would be surprised to know that they were also a Top 10 offensive team from 1983 to 1988, averaging 113 points per game and setting the foundation for their dynasty. Keep in mind, in this era teams attempted an average of 3.7 three-pointers per game. The league average in 2019–20 was 34.1 three-point attempts per game.

What made them such a good offensive team? The same thing that boosted Magic Johnson's Lakers and Larry Bird's Celtics: transition.

The secret potion in this era of the NBA, before the proliferation of the three-pointer, was picking up the pace to increase the number of possessions. For good offenses, more opportunities equal more points. It was outlet passes to fast point guards who could find athletic big men or shooting wings, or even create their own shot. As much as the 1980s are remembered for being a more constricted offensive period, even by those who were there, the footage and stats don't necessarily support the assertion of paltry scoring and grinding paces, at least not among the elite teams. Winning at the highest levels back then required being able to score, and doing so in a variety of ways. A big part of that was the fast break. And the Bad Boys could run the floor with the best of them.

The Pistons had one of the fastest in Isiah Thomas, who was quick and creative with the ball in his hands. His backcourt mate, Joe Dumars, could also get it up the court. Detroit had some potent scorers on the wing in Adrian Dantley and Vinnie Johnson, who came off the bench and was known as "the Microwave" because he could heat up instantly. James "Buddha" Edwards was a big man with an automatic fadeaway jumper below the free throw line. But the sleeper before-his-time player was Bill Laimbeer.

Their legacy in the pantheon of great NBA teams is one of a physically imposing, defensively suffocating collection who bullied opponents with a black-gloved fist.

The six-foot-eleven center could shoot. He wouldn't rise above standing on his tiptoe on his jumpers, but he could knock them down from pretty much anywhere on the court.

In their three straight trips to the Finals, the Bad Boys outscored the Lakers twice (by 25 points in 1988 and by 27 points in 1989), and the Blazers by 18 points in 1990. They out-Showtime'd the Showtime Lakers, who were the masters of the fast break, and then outgunned the Blazers.

"Everybody thinks we're an offensive team; they don't give our defense any credit," Laimbeer said in an ESPN Class doc on the 1989 champions. "So be it, that's to our advantage. Let them keep mumbling to themselves how they're missing open shots and we'll win the series."

The Pistons became a serious title contender when they ramped up their defense. But first they were a bit of an offensive power. They had to become the Bad Boys as a way to get over the hump. They needed to become stalwarts to win a championship, but they were in position because of their offense.

No, the Bad Boys didn't flagrant-foul their way to NBA lore. The NBA is way too smart to be defeated by mere goonery. Just ask the Knicks. With that said, it would be nearly impossible to overwhelm Laimbeer and Rick Mahorn, Edwards and John Salley, a young Dennis Rodman with the energy and athleticism to defend anyone on the floor. Mahorn told Pistons.com columnist Keith Langlois that his rookie season in Washington, going up against Hall of Famers Wes Unseld and Elvin Hayes in practice, taught him everything he needed to know about interior defense. It would be tough to bully the Pistons. But they were as skilled as they were physical. Their basketball IQ was even higher than their shorts.

What made them dynastic was how they complemented that defense and physicality. They had a top-notch offense, one with explosiveness and versatility.

NBA Finals Appearances

1988 (L)	1989 (W)	1990 (W)

THE FACE OF THE DYNASTY

Steph Curry has something to say about it, but many consider Isiah Thomas the second-greatest point guard ever behind Magic Johnson. He's the franchise's all-time leader in points, minutes played, field goals, assists, and eight other statistical categories. But let's talk about the entirety of Isiah Lord Thomas III.

He was the youngest of Mary Thomas's nine children, growing up on the treacherous west side of Chicago. He has spoken frankly about how heroin abuse and violence ravaged his community. Isiah lost two older brothers to drug and alcohol addiction. *Good Times* and even *Cooley High* were benign versions of the poverty, crime, and adversity he faced in real life. There was often no food in the house. Like many in his situation, basketball became a salve and later a salvation. He was always small, but he improved his ball-handling and court vision playing against grown men twice his age at courts all over the city. He was bused to St. Joseph's High School—an all-boys, mostly White basketball power ninety minutes from his house—where he led them to the state finals as a junior.

He could've gone anywhere but chose Indiana University because he thought Bob Knight's discipline would be good for him. The autocratic general and his

flashy, city point guard had a few dustups early on. But Isiah bought into the process, and Knight learned how to loosen the reins. They became so close that when Isiah decked an Iowa player and was ejected from a game, Knight never reprimanded him. As a sophomore, Isiah led the Hoosiers to the national championship and was named Most Outstanding Player of the NCAA Tournament. Indiana fans fell for his diminutive frame, easy demeanor, charming smile, and dimples. They called him "Mr. Wonderful." Knight called him "Pee Wee."

In his very first NBA game, he scored 31 points and the Pistons won. By his fifth game, he was yelling at team veterans who weren't committed to playing winning basketball.

"Of all the players I've played with," Bill Laimbeer said, "Isiah was the one I could hitch my wagon to in order to be a success."

Isiah and Laimbeer had just about as different upbringings and paths to the NBA as possible. Yet they bonded over their obsession with winning. Isiah was never a superstar on the level of Magic and Bird. But he was Detroit's star and the single most important draft pick in the history of the franchise. And this was in an era in which it was commonly thought you couldn't build your team around a guard. Especially not a six-foot-one, 180-pound guard.

Jack McCloskey put the team together. Chuck Daly was the coach. And veterans had a voice in the locker room. Still, so many team or organizational decisions were attributed solely to Thomas, rightly or wrongly. He is the face of the rough-and-tumble Bad Boys, though most of the physicality the team is known for was not executed by him. In 1987, trying to defend a not-yet-media savvy Dennis Rodman, Isiah was called a racist for echoing a comment that if Larry Bird was Black, he'd be just another good player. He is still accused, to this day, of engineering the controversial Adrian Dantley trade, though McCloskey's nickname was "Trader Jack" long before Dantley was shipped. And even though it was Laimbeer's idea to walk off the court in 1991, when the Chicago Bulls swept the Bad Boys, ending their reign, there was something about Isiah ducking his head as he went into the tunnel that has forever associated the stunt as his.

But here's the stuff about Isiah that doesn't get remembered enough.

In Game 4 of the 1988 Finals, Isiah led the team in assists and rebounds to secure the home win. This was the day after Isiah's wife, Lynn, gave birth to their son. Isiah had been up for twenty-four straight hours.

In Game 6, leading a fast break, Isiah stepped on Michael Cooper's foot halfway through the third quarter. Joe Dumars saw how big Isiah's right ankle had swollen and wondered how he was even going to get his shoe back on, let alone go out and play. What followed, even Isiah himself can't explain. It was stunning to watch in real time and it is stunning to watch today. Isiah, the smallest guy on the court, shooting off the wrong foot, limping to hustle back after baskets, draining shots that made no sense. His 25 points in the third quarter of Game 6, essentially playing on one leg, is one of the most underrated heroic moments in NBA history. It is as impressive as Jordan's "flu" game or Willis Reed emerging from the tunnel at Madison Square Garden. But Thomas lost by one—the Lakers won after Kareem Abdul-Jabbar made the game-winning free throws after what Lakers coach Pat Riley later deemed a phantom foul—so Isiah's moments got overlooked.

Here is more: Isiah paid the college tuitions of seventy-five people.

He created a basketball league in Chicago to reduce the city's much-discussed gang violence.

He also created another organization, named after his mother, that supports economically challenged families in his old neighborhood.

He has a master's degree from the University of California at Berkeley in education.

He owns a wine company.

If you're going to talk about the Pistons' greatest player, it's only fair to talk about all of him.

When This Dynasty Reigned

- The crack epidemic was taking over inner-city neighborhoods around the nation. This smokable, and potent, form of cocaine was flooded in Black neighborhoods and ravaged communities, exacerbating poverty and leading to a rise in death and crime.

- Reality rap, which morphed into gangsta rap, was born in part as a response to the crack epidemic. The likes of Ice T, Boogie Down Productions, NWA, Too Short, and Public Enemy brought some edge to hip-hop. Their hardcore sounds and graphic illustrations of life in the 'hood produced a rebelliousness that attracted listeners across demographics. One of the seminal moments of the era happened in Detroit when NWA was arrested after defying orders to not play their popular song—"F—ck Tha Police"—at a concert in August 1989, less than two months after the Pistons' first title.

- The lead character of the popular sitcom *Martin* was loosely based on Detroit radio personality John Mason.

Before it debuted in 1992, Mason said the network had people follow him around for forty days, and some of the characters in the show were inspired by characters he'd done in his radio days. Mason would end up becoming the Pistons' public-address announcer and creator of the "Deeeeetroit Basketball" chant that became famous during the Pistons' 2004–05 championship year.

- The Berlin Wall came down in 1989. It was erected in 1961 to keep U.S.-supported, capitalist, and democratic West Berliners and their ideals from entering Soviet Union–controlled, Communist East Berlin. Nearly two hundred people had been killed trying to cross the border. But on November 9, 1989, the East German Communist Party removed the ban on its citizens crossing the border. The decision led to thousands meeting at the wall in an epic display broadcast globally. They drank and sang and used sledgehammers to break chunks out of the wall, which was eventually taken down by cranes and bulldozers. East and West Germany were officially united on October 3, 1990–a month before the Pistons began their title defense.

- The Gulf War started and concluded, all while the Pistons were NBA Champions.

THE CULTURAL IMPACT

The Pistons, one of the original franchises of the NBA, moved to Detroit from Fort Wayne, Indiana, in 1957. They had thirteen straight losing seasons and didn't make the postseason as the Detroit Pistons until 1973. Dave Bing and Bob Lanier–both of whom were selected to the NBA's initial 50 Greatest

Players of All Time list—made them a playoff team in the mid-'70s. But they bottomed out again. They finished 16–66 in 1979–80 and 21–61 the following season. It was baaaaad. The Pistons were a small-market doormat, a blight on the league.

Jack McCloskey, in his first act as the team's new GM, offered to trade his entire roster for Lakers rookie Magic Johnson, which is akin to trading in a jalopy and hoping to come away with a new Mercedes. McCloskey was trying to get a foundation on which to build. The organization had no culture outside of failure. They didn't even have glory years to lean on. The future looked bleak.

Simultaneously, the city of Detroit was struggling. It was once the fourth-largest city in America. It was the home of Motown Records, the most successful African-American-owned business on the planet at the time. But the 1967 riots and subsequent "White flight" decimated the city across the board. Truthfully, though, the city's decline began even earlier.

Black Detroit residents of the 1940s, already forced by law to live in segregated and congested communities, watched helplessly as those neighborhoods were gutted in "urban renewal" projects such as the I-375 and I-94 highways. Auto plants, once the city's main source of pride and income, began to relocate to other regions and countries. The major auto companies that did remain in Detroit were victimized by high gasoline prices and an array of fast-charging international competitors. The tax base fled to the suburbs and with them went resources, leading to a decades-long surge in violent crimes, drug-related murders, and arson. Detroit lost a third of its population between 1960 and 1980. Times were perilous.

In that sense, the basketball team really did represent Detroit.

In 1981, the Pistons landed Indiana University star guard Isiah Thomas. But he didn't want to play for Detroit, a franchise known for its losing. Thomas, a Chicago native who had just won a national title with the legendary coach Bob Knight, sabotaged his own predraft interview with McCloskey in hopes of dropping way down the Pistons' draft board. McCloskey didn't fall for the banana in the tailpipe. He knew a franchise player when he saw one. He drafted Thomas with the No. 2 overall pick and forward Kelly Tripucka, a highly capable scorer out of Notre Dame, with the No. 12 overall pick. The Pistons won eighteen more games than the year before, finishing the 1981–82 season with 39 wins. Those two were the first in a run of good draft picks. With some key trades, the Pistons were back in the playoffs. But the way they did it was different.

Knowing the Pistons needed to be tougher, McCloskey traded for Bill Laimbeer, a seemingly unremarkable young center out of Notre Dame who spent his first two seasons toiling with Cleveland. McCloskey watched Laimbeer battle every single play, even with the Cavaliers down 20 points, and thought, "That's the kind of guy we need." So they got him for a pair of 1982 draft picks along with Phil Hubbard and Paul Mokeski.

McCloskey also traded fan favorite Greg Kelser to Seattle for Vinnie Johnson, a muscular scorer who barely played with Seattle, but McCloskey loved his pull-up jumper and his surprising ability to offensive rebound. The Pistons kept adding guys who'd been overlooked. And dudes known for their willingness to mix it up, get down and dirty to win.

In the 1980s, the NBA was physical. Yes, as irritating as former players might be as they deify their own era, they're right about the comparative softness of modern basketball. Back then, there were no flagrant fouls. Those didn't get instituted until 1990. Before then, clotheslining someone driving the lane was just a hard foul.

Even with that, the darlings of the league weren't exactly popular because of their physicality.

The Lakers were the exciting team from Hollywood who played at a frenetic pace. They had movie stars sitting courtside and a legacy of superstars donning their jersey. In the '80s, Earvin Johnson was the dazzling, smiling magician who attracted eyes with a mastery of finesse. The Celtics were the other darlings. While they were certainly blue-collar, they were the blue bloods in the sport known as much for their innovation. Their king in this era was Larry Bird, who was as slick a player as the game had seen. He was a dead-eye shooter and a clever passer who controlled games with the highest level of expertise. The Lakers and Celtics were at the top of the game because of their skill. They were magnetic marvels because they could put on a show, and you knew you were watching the rarest of talents. Even the star who was clearly coming up next, Michael Jordan, was electrifying because of his athletic ability and grace on the court.

The Pistons did have someone of that ilk in Isiah. But they didn't have that high level of skill throughout the roster, not enough to compete with the Lakers and Celtics. So they pioneered their own way.

The Pistons were good. They had a star. They had talented role players. They

were a quality team. They could hang with the best. But wherever they were less talented, or inadequate, or insufficient, they made up for it with toughness and intimidation. They were good enough on both ends to compete with the top level. But their edge, their difference-making characteristic, was how they made opponents feel them. They countered finesse with force and slowed down skill by cracking skulls. They developed a reputation in the process. They were called dirty. They were accused of trying to hurt opponents. They were told they weren't playing real basketball and they were bad for the sport.

A funny thing happened in all this: They found their identity.

Like their city, they had grown comfortable in the struggle. They developed a hardened mentality. The people of Detroit were tough. They'd been forgotten, disrespected, for so long, they'd grown at peace with the notion of fighting for everything they had. They knew they weren't beloved, so they absorbed the hatred and used it as fuel. So when the Pistons adopted this mindset, the city could recognize it in them. The endearing was sparked.

The branding came on January 18, 1988.

Mahorn was fined and suspended. Isiah was vexed about it.

"If they want to make us out to be a Raiders-type of basketball team," Isiah said, "then we can become a very, very aggressive type of team and let people know this is the game we play."

And with those words, the mission statement of the Pistons' new identity was ratified. The basketball team had done what the people from their community did, what inner cities across the nation had been doing forever: Take what was meant to be a negative and flip it.

"Nobody likes us," Mahorn chimed in. "I don't mind being a Raider of the NBA."

The reference was to the Oakland Raiders, the outlaw NFL team. The franchise moved to Los Angeles in 1982, but the Raiders that Isiah and Mahorn grew up watching built a brand in Oakland as mean and physical with off-the-charts swagger. Safety George Atkinson once knocked Pittsburgh Steelers wide receiver Lynn Swann out cold with a forearm to the back of the head—on a play where Swann wasn't even being thrown the ball. Fellow safeties Jack Tatum and Lester Hayes were regularly known for clotheslining opponents. The Raiders were nasty and proud of it. They not only didn't care if you didn't like them, they preferred it that way. The Pistons were being regarded as dirty and violent like the Silver & Black. Their response? Turn it up then.

The Raiders' owner, Al Davis—whose rebelliousness birthed his team's very culture—was elated to hear of the Pistons' admiration and immediately sent them Raiders hats and sweaters. The Pistons obliged, wearing them during practices and pregame shootarounds.

McCloskey and coach Chuck Daly didn't warm to the connection instantly. The NBA, though, was fully on board. The marketing potential was live. The Pistons' official, NBA-produced 1987–88 team video was called "Bad Boys" and soundtracked to George Thorogood's classic rock anthem "Bad to the Bone."

Still, branding themselves as the "NBA's Raiders" was a bit bootleg. So Billy Berris, a former Detroit high school hoops star, sat down with graphic artist Robin Brant to devise a logo for the "Detroit Bad Boys" that hit the same underdog nerve of the Raiders' pirate logo. Just like that, the NBA had its villain.

It all came full circle at the 1989 championship parade, the Pistons and Detroit. Some two decades after the riots, more than one hundred thousand people of all ages, races, and religions packed downtown Detroit to celebrate their "Bad Boys." Comfortable in their skin, they relished the role of the stepchild. And so did Detroit.

The next wave of Detroit-bred NBA stars—players such as Derrick Coleman, Steve Smith, Chris Webber, and Jalen Rose—competed against Isiah and Dumars in open-court runs at the legendary St. Cecilia's Gym. They then brought that take-no-prisoners attitude to the NCAA and the NBA.

Ironically, it was the city's least winningest pro sports team that brought Detroit back its pride. But no matter where you lived, the Pistons were your team if you felt ignored by the power structure, felt disenfranchised, but refused to be held back by your naysayers. The team became a beacon for underdogs and fighters everywhere.

The NBA had its first rags-to-riches dynasty, and it was denim.

The Bad Boys' demise was met with sadness from those who loved them but mostly self-righteous relief from fans of every other franchise. Teams like the mid-'90s Knicks attempted to use the Bad Boys' blueprint for success. But the NBA eventually abolished hand-checking and cracked down on trash talk and flagrant fouls. These days, if you accidentally hit a player in the head it's a flagrant foul and possible ejection.

The basketball team had done what the people from their community did, what inner cities across the nation had been doing forever: Take what was meant to be a negative and flip it.

The NBA no longer has goons or villains who wear the proverbial black hat quite like the Pistons did. The rivalries don't carry the same venom they did thirty years ago. For those who weren't around back then, it's simple to paint the Bad Boys with a broad stroke and belittle their sustained excellence. It's easy to write them off as a product of that era unable to adjust to, and therefore unworthy of, the modern game. It's often forgotten how they ended the Magic Lakers and the Bird Celtics dynasties, and the Jordan Bulls cut their teeth on the greatness of the Pistons.

But there are still people who remember how good they were, how bad they were, and how they carried a torch for those fighting their way out of the margins. For them, as Will Smith and Martin Lawrence declared, it's Bad Boys for life.

SEE, WHAT HAD HAPPENED WAS . . .

For most, the Pistons' early walk off the court in the waning minutes of the 1991 Eastern Conference Finals against the Bulls is the final mental picture of the Bad Boys. And for those who didn't like them to begin with, it was the most appropriate conclusion of who they were and what they represented. It confirmed they were sore losers and a stain on the game. But, as with most things with this team, it requires a deeper look.

It must be noted, walking off the court during the end of a playoff series was not wholly uncommon in that era.

"Of all the series that I played in all through the '80s," Celtics great Kevin McHale told the Boston Herald, "after a close-out game, unless you were walking with somebody you knew, you almost never said anything. . . . Ninety percent of the series we won, I didn't talk to anybody. They didn't come up to me, and I didn't think they should."

After losing to the Bad Boys for the first time in three series, the Celtics walked off the court with three seconds left in the series-clinching Game 6. There is a famous clip of Isiah slapping hands with McHale at the end of the game, sometimes used as an example of sportsmanship. But the other Celtics were already gone. For all the bad blood shed during the course of the Pistons and Celtics' battles, once the series was over, it was over. No Pistons bad mouthed the Celtics to the media or said they hadn't been great champions. Years later, Larry Bird even hired Isiah Thomas to coach his Indiana Pacers. There was always a baseline of respect between the teams. So when the Celtics walked off the court without congratulating them, the Pistons weren't in their feelings about it. They truly didn't care, which would explain why Thomas had that moment with McHale while they were leaving and while the other Celtics left without shaking hands.

The 1991 Bulls jumped on the Pistons early. With a mentally tougher Scottie Pippen and a hungrier Horace Grant, Chicago had solved the Bad Boys riddle. Before Game 4, Michael Jordan said that the Pistons were "undeserving champions" and "bad for basketball." His coach, Phil Jackson, offered a more delicate but parallel assessment of the situation, telling the *Chicago Tribune*, "We think it's just time to move onto another style of basketball in the NBA."

So, as the clock wound down in Game 4, with the Bulls ahead by a heap inside of five minutes remaining, coach Daly began pulling the starters. The capacity crowd at the Palace of Auburn Hills gave them a nearly three-minute standing ovation, knowing the Bad Boys dynasty had come to a conclusion.

At some point, on the bench, Laimbeer confessed he proposed they walk off the court before the game ended. During a dead ball with eight seconds to go, they did exactly that. Joe Dumars, John Salley, and Vinnie Johnson stayed on the court and congratulated the future champs. Everyone else bailed in a single file line.

This one decision has become a defining moment of the Bad Boys dynasty. But instead of it being a sign of how deeply they disliked the Bulls and how disrespected they felt by Jordan, it became a referendum on the character of those Pistons. Instead of being an indicator of the passion in the rivalry, it became an indictment of the roster. People used it as evidence of the Pistons' unworthiness. Couldn't Detroit have used that moment to show sportsmanship and silence their detractors, give their legacy a good final moment to be remembered by? That wasn't really how it worked for the Bad Boys. If they'd shaken the hands of the Bulls, it wouldn't have registered a blip. They still would've been the tough and dirty Pistons going down, finally defeated by dazzling Jordan and his Bulls. Whatever brownie points they would've gained from the gesture wouldn't have done much to offset their reputation.

PDS—Public Displays of Sportsmanship—are sports' gotcha moments, used to attack character but never to prove its existence. That one gesture likely cost Isiah his spot on the Dream Team, or at least cemented his absence. It perhaps also cost the Bad Boys any hopes they will get their full respect as one of the greatest teams in basketball history. As Isiah said, he would take it back if he'd known it would be such a big deal. But if one final, thoughtless gesture can define an entire era, the Bad Boys probably weren't going to win that battle no matter what they did.

THE VILLAIN

A few characters from the Pistons dynasty were known for being categorically unlikable. But the chief villain? That choice is pretty easy.

Only one Piston was punched and had a ball thrown at his head by Larry Bird.

Only one Piston was two-pieced by Robert Parish.

Only one Piston has been swung on by Michael Jordan and Charles Barkley.

Bill Laimbeer is routinely named among the dirtiest and most hated—if not *the* dirtiest and most hated—NBA players of all time. Unlike Magic, Jordan, or Isiah, he certainly didn't inspire several generations of hoopers to play the game the way he did. He was the prototype of the guy you hated as an opponent but loved as a teammate.

Perhaps the most baffling thing about his origin story is that Laimbeer didn't grow up with the struggle his aggression would seem to suggest. The chip on his shoulder isn't from an absentee father or having to claw his way out of poverty. William Laimbeer Jr. was raised in the suburbs of Chicago and moved to an affluent Southern California city overlooking the Pacific Ocean for high school. His father was a high-ranking executive at Owens-Illinois, a *Fortune* 500 company headquartered in Toledo, Ohio. Laimbeer joked that during his rookie year in the NBA he was probably the only player making less money than his father. He didn't recall wanting for anything growing up or even being in so much as a single fistfight.

One of his first major life adversities, it appears, came in the classroom at Notre Dame, where he had been recruited to play basketball. He flunked out after his freshman year. He joined his father in Toledo and took classes at a local community college to regain his eligibility. He was a reserve his final two seasons at Notre Dame. The team made the Final Four his junior season. He would become a third-round pick of the Cleveland Cavaliers, then basically took a gap year to play in Italy, where he was a star.

He arrived in Cleveland in 1980 and played two decent but unremarkable years there before becoming a Piston. Laimbeer knew he wasn't the most skilled player. But if he could get the more skilled players off their games, he might be able to make an impact. He developed a legion of haters in the process.

In November 1993, a few years after the Pistons dynasty had ended, Laimbeer laid a hard screen on Isiah in practice and broke the point guard's rib. A few weeks later, Laimbeer tried to elbow Isiah in that rib. Incensed, Isiah started swinging and hit Laimbeer hard enough to break his hand. The reactions around the league, gathered by the *Chicago Tribune*, revealed the villainous reputation of Laimbeer.

Jazz forward Karl Malone: "If I ever had to play like Laimbeer, I'd quit first."

Robert Parish: "If you're going to break your hand, then you might as well break it on him."

Magic point guard Scott Skiles: "In my opinion, Isiah couldn't have picked a better guy to punch."

Blazers guard Clyde Drexler: "He's always been a cheap-shot artist and won't change."

One has to wonder if Laimbeer is still paying the price. He can't seem to get an NBA coaching gig to save his life, even as he's succeeded as a WNBA coach, even as his beloved Pistons went through a blundering cycle of coaches while he was winning WNBA titles down the hall for the Detroit Shock. Laimbeer has leaned into not caring how he is remembered. And unlike Isiah, if he had to do it all over again, he would still not shake the Bulls' hands in 1991. Or today.

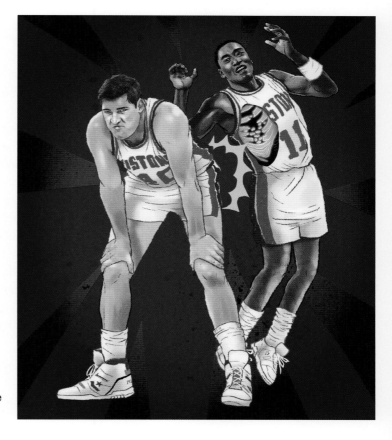

He practices what he inspires.

"I don't like Bill Laimbeer," Larry Bird said in 1987. "Why should I shake his hand?"

HOW THE DYNASTY ALMOST ENDED EARLY

The Pistons went to their first Eastern Conference Finals in team history in 1986–87. The next season, when the expectations were high for them to build on that historic season, they entered the 1987–88 playoffs as the No. 2–seeded Pistons. Few ever remember this, but they almost lost in the first round that year to the 38–44 Washington Bullets. Jeff Malone and Moses Malone are only related by the last name they shared and the problems they gave the Pistons.

Jeff, a sweet shooting six-foot-four guard, went for 33 and 31 in Games 1 and 2—in Detroit. He then went for 35 and 25 in Games 3 and 4 at home, in which the Bullets tied the series with additional help from a rejuvenated Moses Malone and Bernard King. The Bullets got physical right back with the Pistons, and the upstarts from Michigan were up against the wall.

For Game 5, Chuck Daly switched Rodman to guard Jeff Malone. The Pistons pressured, double-teamed, and outwitted the Malones into a combined 3-for-22 shooting that night. King worked hard for his 18 points while battling foul trouble. Joe Dumars emerged from his shooting slump (and repeated Jeff Malone torchings) to lead Detroit with 20 points in the series clincher.

Losing that series could have been catastrophic for the Pistons, completely derailing their trajectory toward a championship. At the time, they were leading the league in attendance and emerging as the only threat in the East to the vaunted Boston Celtics. Losing to an unheralded Bullets team might have led to Trader Jack getting an itchy trigger finger and making panic trades that would have potentially changed everything.

THE FORGOTTEN STAR

On March 27, 1989, Adrian Dantley returned to the Palace—six weeks after the Pistons stunningly traded him to Dallas for Mark Aguirre. Dantley started that night against his old team. According to writer Bill Dow, Dantley walked up to Isiah at the game's opening tip and whispered into his former point guard's ear:

"I know you traded me, asshole."

Dantley was the Pistons' leading scorer in 1987–88, when the Bad Boys were a handful of breaks away from being NBA champions. "The Teacher" was also the oldest member of the team, turning thirty-two in February of that season. He'd been a buckets machine his entire career and, due to his unrivaled gift for drawing fouls, didn't necessarily need to put up a lot of shots to light up a box score. Dantley passed the twenty-thousand-point plateau in 1987–88.

Though his scoring was beyond reproach, his lackluster defense was not. His struggles on that end were a problem for a team trying to change its defensive potency to get over the hump in the East. Dantley was huge for the

Pistons' identity for several years, but two plays illustrate how the relationship had run its course:

One—Game 7 of the 1987 Eastern Conference Finals in Boston. Dantley and Vinnie Johnson bumped heads diving for the ball late in the third quarter. Dantley spent the night in the hospital with a concussion. Johnson's injured neck kept him on the bench the remainder of the game. Down two key guys, the Pistons were unable to compete.

Two—Game 6 of the 1988 NBA Finals. At the very end of Isiah's heroic 43-point performance, the Pistons had one final chance to get the win. But Isiah and Dantley collided during the inbounds pass of the final possession. Dumars was forced into a harried double-clutch jumper that had no chance. Dantley also missed seven of his ten field goal attempts that night.

Neither incident was necessarily all Dantley's fault. But it was emblematic of how change was needed. The Pistons had peaked. Their chemistry was off, they were literally running into each other, and were still not quite at a championship level. They didn't have it.

Rodman was emerging as a defensive and rebounding marvel. Dantley had begun being benched at the end of games when Coach Daly wanted his best defenders on the floor. Daly also believed Dantley's isolation-heavy approach made him too predictable and slowed down their offense. Coach and player had back-to-back shouting matches—once during a game in Boston, the second time behind closed doors in Daly's office.

Also, Dantley had always resented that it was Isiah's team and felt that Isiah's shortcomings were being treated with kid gloves. McCloskey intervened and encouraged Dantley to sit down with Daly and talk out their problems. Dantley declined. Meanwhile, the team sputtered through January 1989, going 8–5.

Because this clearly wasn't complicated enough, Aguirre, a childhood friend of Isiah, was the "Adrian Dantley" of Dallas. He was a high-scoring, defensively ambivalent, moody star who was applauded for his gifts on offense yet criticized for everything else. After seven seasons, his honeymoon in Dallas had also come to an end.

On Valentine's Day, 1989, in the middle of a six-game winning streak, the Pistons traded Dantley and a first-round pick to Dallas for Aguirre. Dantley was a couple weeks shy of thirty-three and Aguirre was twenty-nine. Still, it wasn't a popular move in Detroit, even inside the locker room.

"How could they trade the Teacher? He was my mentor," John Salley told noted Detroit sports writer Mitch Albom. "A lot of the guys felt that way. I like Mark. He's okay, but AD did a lot for us."

Rumors spread that Isiah had engineered the trade due to his own issues with Dantley, which Isiah and McCloskey repeatedly denied. Clearly, Dantley didn't believe the denial.

Aguirre wasn't exactly given the red carpet treatment upon arriving in Detroit. But his experience in Dallas made him hungry to be part of a winning organization. And everything wasn't on his shoulders anymore. The Pistons didn't need a savior. He happily did his damage within the flow of the offense—in fewer minutes and fewer shot attempts than to which he'd grown accustomed. The Pistons watched their scoring average jump by 3 points and went 44–6 for the rest of the season, culminating in their first championship. In their second title season, Aguirre recommended that Rodman start instead of him and embraced his role as a bench assassin. They won twenty-five of their next twenty-six games with Rodman in the starting lineup.

The trade of Dantley for Aguirre could've failed spectacularly. It's a testament to the professionalism of Aguirre and the other Pistons that it went off without a hitch. And as a result, many forget about Dantley, who was essential to getting Detroit to the cusp of greatness.

THE HOME COURT

One of the ironies for a team that came to be identified with the gritty ethos of the city they represented is that none of the Detroit Pistons' glory years actually took place in Detroit. The Pistons played in Cobo Arena in downtown Detroit from 1961 to 1978. Team owner Bill Davidson—who bought the team in 1974—hated Cobo and moved the team thirty-five miles away to the Pontiac Silverdome in 1978. The Silverdome was an eighty-thousand-seat football arena, first and foremost, but regularly seated twenty-two thousand plus for basketball. It was a gigantic building, hosting every major event from WrestleMania III to Super Bowl XVI to Bruce Springsteen

The Pistons became the first NBA team to have a total attendance topping one million fans in a season.

on the Born in the USA Tour. As the team began to improve in the mid-'80s, so did attendance, and by the 1987–88 season, the Pistons became the first NBA team to have a total attendance topping one million fans in a season.

Still, the Silverdome was aging quickly, and Davidson wanted something more modern the Pistons could call their own. In 1989, just in time for the Pistons' first championship season, Davidson unveiled the NBA's first privately financed arena, the $90 million Palace of Auburn Hills, five miles northeast of Pontiac in a wealthy Detroit suburb. The Palace is regarded as the first modern arena, with lower-level luxury suites, club seating, and state-of-the-art practice facilities, none of which were common at the time. It was newer and cozier and easier to get in and out of. It had far better sight lines than the Silverdome and truly represented how the Pistons had arrived.

The Palace remained the team's home until 2017, when owner Tom Gores moved the team back to downtown Detroit and the brand-new Little Caesars Arena.

THE CRAZIEST STAT

The 1986–87 Pistons gave up an average of 122 points per game in the playoffs as they marched to Game 7 of the Eastern Conference Finals. Guess how much they allowed per game the following year: 95 points. That's a 27-point defensive improvement year over year.

8

THE MICHAEL JORDAN BULLS

LaBradford Smith, in his second year out of Louisville, found himself in a premium role as Washington played out the string. With the Bullets' playoff hopes already extinguished, and big man Pervis Ellison out for the rest of the year, Smith ended up in the starting lineup getting all the minutes and shots he could handle.

He had 22 points in a 1-point loss to visiting Orlando. Two games later, he scored 20 in a home loss to Denver. Two games after that, another 20 spot against Cleveland, this time a win. So the six-foot-three guard could score a little bit. Still, he was on no one's radar when Washington visited Chicago. The Bulls and Bullets were playing a home-and-home back-to-back, which is when the teams play each other on consecutive nights, alternating home courts. The Bulls came into the game 43–20, and the Bullets came into the game 18–43. This was a sleepy matchup as the two-time defending champs basically relaxed until the playoffs.

But Smith caught fire. Boy, his jumper was clicking. Baseline. Wing. Free throw. Pull up. Spot up. Curling off screens. He was not missing. He finished with 37 points on 15-for-20 shooting—all career highs. The Bulls still won, 104–99, and Smith was a model of deference in the postgame interviews.

"The shots were just falling for me," Smith told the *Washington Post* after the game. "It happens like that sometimes. Hopefully, it'll happen like that more often. I don't say nothing to [Jordan]. Leave him alone. In the first couple of quarters he was helping out a lot and I was getting a more wide-open shot."

Jordan was incensed. The man he was matched up against scored 37 points and put on a show. In Jordan's house. Making it all even worse, Jordan had a paltry 25 points on 27 shots.

"For whatever reason," Bulls guard B. J. Armstrong said in the documentary *The Last Dance*, "Michael couldn't make a basket."

According to Hall of Fame reporter David Aldridge, who covered the game for the *Washington Post*, Bulls coach Phil Jackson used the occasion to needle his star player.

Jordan shared the story years later: As they were leaving the court, LaBradford Smith told the reigning MVP, "Nice game, Mike." Coming from a second-year player who just got into the starting lineup, this sounded like perfectly deadpanned, high-level trash talk. Jordan heard the sarcasm in Smith's words like one hears a train coming. Oh, you better believe Jordan took this as utmost disrespect. This young punk was trying to belittle him. Him? Michael Jordan! What?!

"He said, 'Tomorrow in the first half, I'm going to have what this kid had in the game,'" Armstrong said in the documentary. "I've never seen a man go after another player the way he did."

LaBradford Smith scored 37 points in the previous game. Jordan scored 36 points in the first half of the next game. The announcers calling the game even pointed out how Jordan was solely focused on Smith.

Remember when Jordan was 9-for-27 for 25 points in the first game? The next night, he was 16-for-27 for 47 points. The Bulls won by 25 this time. The most Michael Jordan component of the entire story? Jordan made up the "Nice game, Mike" part. He just made it up. Years later, reporters asked him if it was true and Jordan copped to the fiction. He needed the extra motivation, so he gave it to himself by concocting a narrative.

"We were talking in the locker room about just, when Michael gets the ball, just get the hell out of the way," Will Perdue said on a podcast. "'Cause he's just gonna go at LaBradford time and time again. And it was kind of like an unwritten rule that everybody knows that Michael has that stat sheet in his back pocket, in his sock. He knows exactly how many points LaBradford scored, and he wants to get that many or more in the first half. He didn't make an announcement to me, nor to the team as a whole. He may have voiced a few things to guys he was closer with on the team. But that's the funny thing, it was known by everybody exactly what was going to happen."

The Bulls were led by a certified basketball assassin. Considered among the most competitive athletes ever, Jordan's killer instincts were off the charts. He was driven to dominate, and the Bulls did it. There is a support group of NBA greats who were denied championship glory because they just happened to play during the era of Jordan's Bulls. No less than twenty Hall of Famers were eliminated from the playoffs by the Bulls, six of them bounced multiple times. Patrick Ewing lost five times to Jordan's team. Charles Barkley lost three times. Karl

Malone and John Stockton have two NBA Finals losses to Jordan. Reggie Miller didn't make the NBA Finals until Jordan retired.

At this point, it's pretty much an objective fact Jordan's Bulls are the greatest dynasty ever, as objective as such a subjective ranking could be. Oddly enough, whatever doubt existed seemed to be erased twenty-two years after the run ended. All it took was a global pandemic and some classic video enhanced to HD.

The NBA suspended its season in March 2020. The COVID-19 pandemic had already prompted the Golden State Warriors to announce it would play the Brooklyn Nets with no fans in attendance, which at the time was an unprecedented decision. But once a player was infected by COVID-19, the whole league was shut down. One by one, professional leagues followed until sports were completely stopped. That's when Jordan came through in the clutch again.

For a year, ESPN had been promoting the June 2020 release of *The Last Dance* to great excitement. But with sports brought to a halt, and fans left with only throwback games, ESPN decided to release it in April. The documentary averaged 5.6 million viewers over ten episodes, making it the most-viewed documentary ever for the network. The undivided attention of basketball fans, casual and die-hard, got to see the dominance of Jordan and the Bulls from their perspective. In addition to never-before-seen footage from behind the scenes of the 1997–98 season, the documentary featured revealing interviews from key figures, including unprecedented access to Jordan. It made for a coronation of the Bulls as the chief among dynasties, in case anyone had forgotten.

It's hard to top two three-peats in the same era, six champions in eight seasons. In the ultimate flex, Jordan got bored enough, or whatever enough, to retire in 1993 and go play minor-league baseball. He played for the Birmingham Barons, the Chicago White Sox Triple-A affiliate. He was performing respectably, too, for a basketball player, giving credence to the idea that if he stuck with it he could make the majors. But the Major League Baseball strike in 1994 shut down minor-league baseball, too. It also gave the opening for Jordan to miss basketball again. So he came back.

And won three more championships.

The only dynasty with a decent argument for such a claim would be Bill Russell's Celtics. But seven of their eleven championships came in an eight-team NBA. For the eleventh championship, the league increased from twelve to fourteen teams. The knock against the Celtics will always be the perceived inferiority of their competition. They also had a problem with exposure. The number of people alive who saw Russell's Celtics keeps dwindling, and the limited footage of that era conspires to keep them out of the public consciousness.

As a result of the pandemic, however, the Bulls were front of mind, in all their glory, reminding the world why they're the greatest.

NBA Finals Appearances

1991 (W)	1992 (W)	1993 (W)
1996 (W)	1997 (W)	1998 (W)

THE FACE OF THE DYNASTY

The highest-grossing movie featuring an athlete is easily *Guardians of the Galaxy*, which garnered $772.78 million at the box office. It costars former WWE star Dave Bautista as Drax.

What? You're saying wrestling doesn't count as a sport because it's scripted?

All right. How about the 1996 *There's Something About Mary* starring Cameron Diaz and Ben Stiller? It features Brett Favre, who was the Green Bay Packers' star quarterback at the time, in a bit more than a cameo role. It grossed $369.88 million.

The highest-grossing movie starring an athlete? Easy. Michael Jordan in *Space Jam*.

That's how big Jordan was—on the same level as Bugs Bunny.

Four years earlier, Jordan was featured in Michael Jackson's video "Jam" from his *Dangerous* album. It was released to a national audience on Fox five days after the Bulls clinched their second title. That's how big Jordan was—he was rolling with the King of Pop.

The website YouGov ranks Jordan as the sixty-ninth most popular person of all time, two spots ahead of Frank Sinatra and ten ahead of William Shakespeare. He's three spots behind Al Pacino and eleven behind Elvis Presley. The only sports figures more popular are Jackie Robinson (45), Babe Ruth (51), and Muhammad Ali (55). The next most popular basketball player is Shaquille O'Neal (107). YouGov's research shows that 95 percent of Americans have heard of Jordan, and that he's equally popular with men and women.

There was something so insanely captivating about the six-foot-six guard from North Carolina. His combination of athleticism, confidence, and style was hypnotizing. And commissioner David Stern, who took over four months before Jordan was drafted, knew what he had on his hands and seized the moment to attach the league to Jordan's wings. He was mailing VHS tapes across the globe, getting the NBA game out to the world.

It was Jordan's skill that made him elite. He averaged more than 30 points for seven consecutive seasons, shooting 48 percent or better in all of them. Jordan was also a hound defensively. He won Defensive Player of the Year in 1988 and made six consecutive first-team All-Defense selections.

It was his athleticism that made him intoxicating. He was so explosive. He moved on the court as if his Nikes had an invisible jetpack, the way he blew past defenders, attacked the basket, hounded ball handlers, and zipped in transition. Even his walk had a springiness. And when he jumped, it was unlike anything basketball had ever seen. He was an evolutionary experience of Julius Erving. No, leapers weren't new. The ABA played an above-the-rim style, highlighted by the likes of Dr. J and Connie Hawkins. But they jumped high. Jordan soared. Maybe it looked that way because he wasn't as tall as his bouncy predecessors. Maybe it was how long he seemed to hang. Perhaps it was how he looked in the air, so cool and graceful, like he was posing. He would take off on one side of the paint and float to the other, spinning the ball off the glass on a reverse layup so pretty it had seemingly every kid in the country trying to mimic it at their local court.

When This Dynasty Reigned

- The U.S. economy grew an average of 4 percent per year between 1992 and 1999. More than 20 million jobs were created in the decade owned by the Bulls, and the GDP grew from $5.5 trillion in 1990 to $9.8 trillion by the end of the decade. The year Michael Jordan won his last championship, the unemployment rate was 4.5 percent. At the turn of the decade it was at 4 percent and didn't get that low again until 2018. A sign of just how well America was doing: The Mall of America, in the greater Minneapolis Area, opened in August 1992.

- Nirvana and Pearl Jam became the faces of the grunge band movement in the widely popular alternative rock scene. Nirvana released its iconic album *Nevermind* in

1991. Pearl Jam's *Ten* rode the wave created by Nirvana, whose frontman Kurt Cobain died from suicide in 1994.

- Founded in 1975 by Bill Gates and Paul Allen, Microsoft gained commercial popularity in 1993 with Windows 3.0 and 3.1. By 1995, 90 percent of the world's desktop computers ran Microsoft's operating system and Microsoft Office products.

- Email blew up. America Online launched in 1995. Hotmail came out in 1996. Yahoo! launched in 1997. Microsoft bought Hotmail in 1997 for $400 million and relaunched it as MSN Hotmail. NetZero launched in 1998.

- Bill Clinton "did not . . . have . . . sexual . . . relations with" Monica Lewinsky between 1995 and 1997.

- Hip-hop went commercial. *The Fresh Prince of Bel-Air*, featuring rapper-turned-actor Will Smith, debuted in 1990 and became a hit. MC Hammer rose to unimaginable heights with his *Too Legit To Quit* album in 1991. The *Billboard* Hot 100 had thirteen rap albums reach number one, starting with MC Hammer's *Please Hammer Don't Hurt 'Em* and ending with the Notorious B.I.G.'s *Born Again*. In between, Lauryn Hill won seven Grammy Awards, and Tupac Shakur and Biggie were killed by gun violence. Tupac released nine albums in the '90s, including three posthumously, and Biggie's *Life After Death* was the highest-selling rap album of the decade. The movie *Boyz N the Hood* was released in 1991 starring NWA rapper Ice Cube, who four years later created the comedy *Friday* and transitioned into movies.

THE ARCHITECT

The man perhaps most responsible for building the Bulls into a juggernaut was a baseball guy. Jerry Krause played catcher for Taft High on the Northwest Side of Chicago. He went to Bradley University in Peoria and got his start in the front-office ranks as a gofer for the Chicago Cubs in 1961. Krause was at a Chicago Zephyrs practice with a friend in 1963. He was taking so many notes, Zephyrs coach Slick Leonard hired Krause as a scout when the franchise moved east to become the Baltimore Bullets. Krause was officially a scout in two sports. He was credited for having a hand in drafting Earl Monroe, Wes Unseld, and Jerry Sloan for the Bullets, and later Alvan Adams, Clifford Ray, Michael Cooper, and Norm Nixon when he left the Bullets to scout for the Suns, 76ers, Lakers, and Bulls in the '70s. He was also still scouting in Major League Baseball. He worked for the Indians, Athletics, Mariners, and White Sox. He was with the White Sox when Bulls and White Sox owner Jerry Reinsdorf came calling.

Reinsdorf said he was warned not to hire Krause, who had developed a reputation for being difficult to work with.

"Everyone I talked to said don't touch the guy," Reinsdorf said in *The Last Dance*. But something about the local guy drew Reinsdorf. He fired Rod Thorn and hired a new general manager in March 1985.

Krause inherited Michael Jordan, whom Thorn had selected with the No. 3 overall pick in 1984. It was obvious almost immediately Jordan was the Bulls' best player as he emerged as one of the league's electric young talents. As a rookie he averaged 28.2 points on 51.5 percent shooting with 6.5 rebounds, 5.9 assists, and 2.4 steals. That would be the best season for most players. A knee injury robbed Jordan of most of his second season.

In 1986, Krause made a drastic move and hired Doug Collins as head coach. Jordan was already healthy and motivated. So Krause gave him a coach who would center the offense around him. Jordan went off. Over his first two seasons in the NBA combined, he took 1,953 shots. In 1986–87, he took 2,279 shots. The result was a scoring average of 37.1 points, which would end up being the highest in his career.

Krause could see that Jordan was revolutionizing the game. Shooting guards were rarely the focus of offenses. There had been great scoring guards before. But the NBA was all about big men. Perimeter players were complementary. Some broke that mold, such as Jerry West, but were usually on teams with star big men, such as Wilt Chamberlain. It was far more common for the small forward, the smallest on the front court, to be an elite scorer. Think George Gervin, Larry Bird, Bernard King, and Dominique Wilkins. They were usually a bit taller and thicker, played closer to the basket, but still had perimeter skills. But Jordan, working from the outside in, made shooting guards all the rage.

In 1987–88, he averaged 35 points on 53.8 percent shooting. Only Jordan and Kareem Abdul-Jabbar have averaged at least 34 points or more and 53 percent shooting or higher. Only twelve players in NBA history averaged 30 points or more on 50 percent shooting or better. Half of the 30–50 Club are centers or power forwards. Another four are small forwards. The two guards? Jordan and Stephen Curry, and Jordan was first.

At the time, it was highly doubted a winning team could be built on a guard. Magic Johnson was an anomaly with the size of a forward, as was Oscar Robertson—but they also won their championships with Kareem. The game was about getting as close to the rim as possible as often as possible. And big men were the most efficient way to do that. But with the way Jordan was scoring, the paradigm of how to carry a team was changing. Krause just needed to capitalize on Jordan by surrounding him with players who were good enough and fit well enough for the Bulls to win.

When Krause hired Collins, he also pulled off a critical trade, acquiring the Knicks first-round pick that would come in handy in the 1987 draft. Krause entered that draft with the No. 8 and No. 10 picks. He was in love with Scottie Pippen out of Central Arkansas. Krause worked a trade the night before the draft, moving the Bulls up to the No. 5 pick while keeping the No. 10 pick. They got Pippen at No. 5 and Horace Grant at No. 10—two core members of their first three-peat. It cost them Jawann Oldham, a second-round pick, and a couple of first-round pick swaps to get Pippen.

The next draft, 1988, he traded away Charles Oakley, who was the Bulls' second-best player when Krause arrived, for a legitimate center in Bill Cartwright. Chicago went from a thirty-win team in Krause's first season to a fifty-win team two years later, to the Eastern Conference Finals in 1989.

Krause's next great move was, against the wishes of Jordan, firing Collins and giving the reins to a coach he discovered in the Continental Basketball Association: Phil Jackson. This was arguably the signature display of Krause's genius.

The year the Bulls won their first championship, in 1991, every player on the roster outside of Jordan was acquired by Krause. He remade the roster around Jordan, and the Bulls grew into a sixty-one-win team in the 1990–91 season. Before they'd won a championship, he drafted what he believed to be a future star in Croatian prodigy Toni Kukoč and stashed him in Europe. Kukoč would end up being a needed boost of talent and freshness when he finally came to the NBA as the Bulls set out to three-peat for the first time.

Krause, whose wizardry—coupled with Reinsdorf's willingness to spend—capitalized on inheriting the greatest player ever. But his own ego, and the style of leadership that had insiders warning Reinsdorf not to hire Krause, would undermine his own creation. Oddly enough, the architect of the Bulls was also central to their destruction.

Krause died in 2017. So when *The Last Dance* documentary resurfaced the demise of the Bulls, he wasn't available to defend himself. Those who were around and knew Krause, who witnessed the Bulls from up close, described Krause as disgruntled about not getting his proper due for his role in building the Bulls. His frustration, coupled with the self-importance of NBA players, created a rift between the locker room and the front office that was seismic enough to break it all up.

The fissures reached a new level when Krause was quoted saying organizations win championships, not players. He contended he actually said "not players alone," but the intention was still received the same. Krause was siphoning some of the praise for the Bulls' success away from the locker room and into the front office. Of course, players weren't enamored.

"We know the team is much bigger than the fifteen players," Jordan said. "Those guys who work in the front office, they were good people. But the most important part of the process is the players. So for him to say that was offensive to the way that I play the game."

The relationship between Krause and Jackson, whom Krause discovered and hired, was what eventually ended the dynasty. Jackson wanted a contract worthy of a coach with five championship rings. Krause didn't consider the head coach to be nearly as integral as Jackson did. The relationship deteriorated. Jackson deemed it irreconcilable. *The Last Dance* was born from a meeting between the two before the final season. Reinsdorf signed Jackson to a one-year deal for $6 million, and Krause told him in no uncertain terms the 1997–98 season would be Jackson's last. Krause, according to Jackson, said it didn't matter if the Bulls went 82–0 and won a championship, Jackson would still be out as the Bulls' head coach. So Jackson used it as a motivational tool for his players, dubbing the season "the Last Dance" and allowing for it to be documented by video.

The big problem with Krause's stance: Michael Jordan was loyal to Jackson and had determined he wouldn't play for a coach other than Jackson. So, essentially, Krause was forcing out Jackson and Jordan.

"If Michael chooses to leave because there is another coach here, then that's his choice, not ours," Krause said. "We would love to have Michael back. But Michael is going to have to play for someone else. It isn't going to be Phil."

Scottie Pippen, Krause's great draft steal, was also on his way out. Unhappy because the Bulls would not rework his original contract, which paid him way beneath his value, Pippen clashed with Bulls management and was known to express his ire by ridiculing Krause. He was being mentioned in trade rumors already before the start of the 1997–98 season, so his departure was inevitable. Jackson left, Jordan retired, and Pippen was traded to Portland.

The Bulls haven't been the same since.

SEE, WHAT HAD HAPPENED WAS . . .

Jordan retired in 1993, after his third straight championship, and went to play baseball. He signed with the Birmingham Barons, the Triple-A affiliate of the Chicago White Sox, pursuing his childhood dream. (Growing up, Jordan wanted to be a baseball player before he was turned on to hoops.) Some two months earlier, his father, James Jordan, was discovered after being murdered while napping in his car along a North Carolina highway.

"It made me realize how short life is, how quickly things can end, how innocently," Jordan said at the news conference announcing his retirement. "And I thought that there are times in one's life when you have to put games aside. I wanted to give more time to my family. I've been very selfish about centering things on my basketball career. Now it's time to be unselfish with them."

Baseball was a bond he and his father shared. So he pursued it. But the 1994 MLB strike stalled his chances of making the big leagues. So Jordan returned to the NBA. He announced his return by sending out a fax—yes, a fax—with two words: "I'm Back."

He switched to No. 45 when he returned, the number he wore in high school. He didn't want to wear 23 anymore because his father was no longer there to watch him. The new number symbolized a new beginning of a career without his dad. He returned March 19, 1995. It was Game 66 for the Bulls, who were hovering just above .500. While he was rusty, and heavier than normal because he bulked up for baseball, the Bulls went 13–4 the rest of the way. He dropped 55 in Madison Square Garden while wearing No. 45. The Bulls earned the No. 5 seed in the Eastern Conference.

They beat the Hornets in the first-round best-of-five series, then faced top-seeded Orlando in the second semifinals. Jordan struggled in Game 1 in Orlando. Up a point in the final seconds, Jordan had the ball stolen from him by Magic guard Nick Anderson, which led to the game-winning fast-break dunk by Jordan's former teammate Horace Grant. After the game, Anderson essentially called Jordan washed up.

"It made me realize how short life is, how quickly things can end, how innocently."

"No. 45 doesn't explode like No. 23 used to," Anderson told reporters after the game. "No. 45 is not No. 23. I couldn't have done that to No. 23."

The next game, Jordan switched back to No. 23, eating the $25,000 fine for the number change, and torched the Magic for 38 points in the Bulls win.

The Magic ended up winning the series in six games. But Jordan—who averaged 31 points, 6.5 rebounds, and 3.7 assists in a series seen as a struggle for him—had all the motivation he needed in the off-season.

THE BEST SIDEKICK EVER?

Jordan said you can't mention him without mentioning Scottie Pippen. And that is perhaps the highest praise of all.

One never won without the other. Pippen is the greatest sidekick of all time. Not because he is the best player to play second fiddle to a star. Magic or Kareem would rank higher in that distinction, depending on who you'd consider second fiddle. Same for Kobe Bryant or Shaquille O'Neal, and Jerry West or Wilt Chamberlain. But no, Pippen is the greatest sidekick because no one has complemented a superstar better. No one has been so great at supporting and maximizing a superstar's talent and window.

Pippen on his own merit is one of the greatest of all time. He was named to the NBA's 50 Greatest Players list in 1996. In most other situations, he would've been the A1 guy. But he was perfect for Jordan, for the era, and Jordan was perfect for him. When the Bulls went from contenders to champions, it was because Jordan began to trust his teammates. He was able to do that because of Pippen.

Pippen was six feet, eight inches tall with a seven-foot-three wingspan. He was a nightmare defensively, so rangy and athletic. He and Jordan made life miserable for opposing guards. But Pippen also served as the point guard. In his best years he was a more than capable scorer. He averaged 20 points or more in four of the six seasons the Bulls won the title. His greatest feat was earning Jordan's trust, being good enough for Jordan to deputize him.

Jordan had to bring that next level out of Pippen, whose legacy will forever have a couple of stains. The first came in Game 7 of the 1990 Eastern Conference Finals against Detroit. Pippen developed a migraine and said he couldn't even see. Most thought, at the time, it was a headache brought on by a fear of the Pistons and a weariness of the aggressive, physical, and relentless defense of Dennis Rodman. It certainly didn't help Pippen's reputation.

The next came four years later when he refused to play the final 1.8 seconds of Game 3 in their 1994 series against the Knicks—because the play was called for Toni Kukoč. Jordan was off playing baseball, and the Bulls belonged to Pippen. When the play was designed for Kukoč, the game tied at 102, Pippen was insulted and declined to go in the game. Kukoč hit the game winner to keep the Bulls alive.

Those two blights, and playing next to Jordan, have made it easy to diminish Pippen's greatness. He was a number one talent with number one production

who played the number two role on the greatest dynasty ever. Very few players in history were as effective and versatile on both ends of the court as Pippen.

THE MASTERMIND

Phil Jackson is known as the "Zen Master." His special gift as a coach isn't so much the Xs and Os. For that, he leaned on Tex Winter, the assistant coach and basketball wizard who created the offensive strategy known as the triangle. Winter's philosophy essentially puts two players on the perimeter and a player on the post all on the same side of the floor, positioned in a triangle. A series of cuts, screens, and movements happen out of that triangle in an effort to create varying options and openings against the defense. The triangle was unique at the time because it highlighted the playmaking ability of perimeter players instead of focusing on the big men, as was the NBA norm. The center, in the triangle offense, was more of a passer.

Undoubtedly, the wrinkles in the triangle and the defense of the Bulls was part of Jackson's entire scheme. But his real talent is getting the talent to be preeminent. The NBA, unlike other professional leagues, had built itself on the superstar. The player-centered focus feeds into the ego of players, which in turn endangers the chemistry of a team. It created a paradox of a situation. It is hard to win a championship without multiple star-level players. But it's incredibly difficult to manage the players and personalities when you have multiple superstars in the same locker room.

$$\frac{x - ut}{1 - (\frac{u}{c})^2}$$

But Jackson was able to do it, at a time where the celebrity of NBA players was reaching new levels. He was flying without a map. His mindfulness approach, his emphasis on self-sacrifice, his attention to even the little-used players, all proved to be strong enough to hold things together. Jackson incorporated yoga into the practices and humor into the film sessions. He made book recommendations personalized to each player. Jordan was given Toni Morrison's *Song of Solomon*. Pippen was given *The Ways of White Folks* by Langston Hughes. Chinua Achebe's *Things Fall Apart* went to Bill Cartwright and Sebastian Junger's *The Perfect Storm* to Luc Longley. B. J. Armstrong? He got *Zen Mind, Beginner's Mind* by Shunryu Suzuki.

With Rodman, Jackson used their shared interest in Native American culture to strengthen their bond. Jackson, a Montana native, would show Rodman some of his artifacts and talk about their history and cultural meaning. Jackson explained to Rodman—who wore a necklace from the Ponca Indian Reservation—that in Native American culture he would be described as Heyoka—"a backward-walking person"—because Rodman was so against the grain. Rodman felt understood and the two grew from there.

Jackson was often knocked as a coach because he had so much talent. The rebuttal to any talk of his greatness would be to suppose any coach could win if they had the talent he coached. But Jackson's task was probably harder. Getting a team loaded with great players to function as a unit is something not many coaches can do. Jackson has proven to be the best at it.

THE CULTURAL IMPACT

Magic Johnson and Larry Bird elevated the NBA into the mainstream. But Jordan lifted the league to pop-culture status. Magic and Bird made people want to see them. Jordan made people want to be him. There was literally a song about it.

> *Sometimes I dream*
> *That he is me.*
> *You've got to see that's what I dream to be.*
> *I dream I move.*
> *I dream I groove.*
> *Like Mike. If I can be like Mike.*

That's the famous Gatorade commercial jingle, which essentially became the theme song for Jordan's rampant success.

The Bulls' era came at a unique time in the country. The 1990s were the decade of peace and prosperity. The country saw tremendous economic growth as the tech era took off. The Dow Jones Industrial Average closed 1990 at 2,633.66. In 1999, it closed at 11,497.12. The financial boom created a certain euphoria in America. People were doing well, feeling good, killing it. The Bulls embodied that spirit and tapped into that commercial success for the NBA. And Jordan was the face of that commercialization as sports' greatest pitchman.

The interesting part: The NBA was making its corporate crossover while simultaneously getting street cred. Hip-hop music and culture had come out

of the boroughs of New York and into the mainstream. Hip-hop began defining what was cool, and even though Jordan wasn't a product of hip-hop himself, hip-hop fell in love with Jordan. Basketball had long been an inner-city pastime, and the way he played was like a revolution. His whole vibe was appealing to the rebellious spirit of the 'hood, which was expressed through hip-hop culture. Jordan was different. He wore baggy shorts when the rest of the league wore essentially high-end boxer briefs. He wore his knee pad on his calf and his wrist band on his forearm. The Air Jordan 1—red, black, and white—debuted at a time when NBA required shoes be mostly white. So Jordan was fined $5,000 every time he wore his first signature shoe. Nike paid the fine, and his clash against the establishment was music to the ears of hip-hop culture. So the inner-city started wearing his shoes as a fashion statement, turning them into a national sensation. LL COOL J, one of the most popular hip-hop artists, wore the first Air Jordans on the back cover of his debut album *Radio* in 1985. The shoes became a window into Jordan's commercial potential.

Corporate America found a cash cow in hip-hop, which led them right to Jordan, who had a cult following in hip-hop.

"He definitely rode the wave of hip-hop and rose to the heights," LL COOL J said. "Hip-hop was definitely some of the wind beneath his wings. Because obviously his talent and charisma did what it did. I think from the beginning there was just a connection between Jordan and hip-hop. Even though a lot of people say—and mind you he was always polite to me—but he wasn't necessarily the biggest hip-hop fan. And you can understand that being his age and where hip-hop was and where he was raised. But we definitely rolled with Mike and helped Mike."

Jordan and the Bulls were occupying stages the NBA had never seen. And then when NBA players were allowed to participate in the 1992 Summer Olympics, the league went global.

The fashion alone from the dynasty was epic. Jordan is still the king of sneakers. His kicks power an entire shoe subculture. The Bulls still have not changed their jerseys or logo, though most teams have updated and upgraded to reenergize their merchandising potential. The Bulls don't need to change anything. They are iconic.

THE FORGOTTEN STAR

Everyone remembers Dennis Rodman, who was the eclectic and yet dominant power forward for the second three-peat. Rightfully so because Rodman is a Hall of Famer. Also, how could you not remember Rodman? His hair regularly looked like a kaleidoscope and he famously wore a wedding dress to promote a book.

But for the first three championships, the third wheel in the Big Three was Horace Grant. The six-foot-ten, 215-pound power forward came into his own at the perfect time for the Bulls. The tenth pick in the 1987 draft, he became a starter his second season and improved every year until he was a core piece for the Bulls. He had some growing pains, for sure. When the Bulls would face the Detroit Pistons, who were known for their bullying style of play, Grant had a difficult time handling the toughness, especially the mental part of it. Michael Jordan used to ride him, trying to get Grant to find that edge. And eventually he did.

In the three title runs, Grant averaged a combined 11.7 points on 55.6 percent shooting with 8.4 rebounds. His production on both ends was critical. In those days, defending the post was paramount, and Grant was the Bulls' best post defender. He was also important on offense because, unlike most teams, the Bulls didn't run their offense through the post. It was run through Jordan and Pippen, and a center was but a cog. Grant, being the weak side valve and screen setter, was needed for his finishing and his midrange jumper.

By the time Jordan returned from baseball, Grant was playing for the Magic. His relationship with the Bulls deteriorated and he signed with Orlando, leaving a huge void in the Bulls roster but also paving the way for a huge signing in Rodman.

Another forgotten piece was Craig Hodges.

With Pippen serving as the de facto point guard, and the offense operating with Jordan as the hub, the point guard in the Bulls offense was primarily a spot-up shooter. The Bulls kept a steady rotation of shooters with Jordan, all little guards who were deadly accurate. Steve Kerr is perhaps the most famous because he filled that role at the height of the Bulls, and went on to do the same for the San Antonio Spurs.

But John Paxson and Craig Hodges were first. Paxson is remembered because he hit the game winner to clinch the 1993 title in Phoenix and because he's stayed around basketball as a front office executive for the Bulls. But Hodges was essentially blackballed from the league and, in 1996, filed a $40 million lawsuit claiming just that.

Paxson was the better overall player and the starter. Hodges was the better shooter who came off the bench. Hodges, most known for his dominance of the Three-Point Shootout during All-Star Weekend, was 35 of 88 in the 1988 playoffs as the Bulls made it to the Eastern Conference Finals. He followed that up by shooting 48 percent from three in the 1989–90 regular season. Paxson didn't take as many three-pointers, but the reliability of his midrange allowed the Bulls to punish teams that put too much attention on Jordan and Pippen.

In the 1991 NBA Finals, Hodges and Jordan carried the three-point load while Paxson struggled. In 1992 it was Jordan and Paxson, while the increasing minutes of B. J. Armstrong cut into Hodges's action.

By 1993, the Bulls had moved on from Hodges but loaded up on shooting. Jordan took and made the most threes in that postseason. Armstrong, Paxson, and Trent Tucker all made double-digit three-pointers during the playoffs. Jordan had the lowest percentage at 38.9 percent. Paxson made 15 of 24. The biggest of his life came in Game 6 of the 1993 NBA Finals, in the final seconds at Phoenix. With the Bulls down 98–96, Paxson hit the game-winning three-pointer, wide-open from the left wing, with 3.9 seconds left to seal the Bulls' first three-peat.

Hodges was waived by the Bulls after the 1992 season, which ended with a championship over Portland. He was thirty-one and a career 43.6 percent three-point shooter, but he never got picked up by another team.

Hodges was an activist behind the scenes, though his profile wasn't large enough to draw the attention he wanted. He solicited Jordan and Magic to strike Game 1 of the 1991 NBA Finals after video surfaced of the police beating Rodney King, but they declined, as detailed in his memoir released in 2017. He partnered with controversial and inflammatory Nation of Islam leader Louis Farrakhan to "curb the breakdown of the African-American family." Hodges publicly criticized Jordan for not being more outspoken against injustice, especially after he essentially declined comment after the LA riots erupted following the acquittal of the officers who beat Rodney King. When the Bulls won the championship, Hodges wore a dashiki to the White House and handed then president George H. W. Bush a handwritten letter criticizing the administration for its treatment of poor people and minorities. He cited all of the above as reasons why he was being blackballed from the NBA and why he was filing a lawsuit, which alleges the owners colluded to prevent him from getting so much as a tryout.

With the Bulls down 98–96, Paxson hit the game-winning three-pointer, wide-open from the left wing, with 3.9 seconds left to seal the Bulls' first three-peat.

Hodges's case was dismissed because the statute of limitations had expired two years before he filed.

HOW THE DYNASTY ALMOST ENDED EARLY

In two alternate universes, the Bulls never got Michael Jordan. A coin flip and a protest nearly prevented the whole dynasty, to say nothing of Portland's draft night choke job.

The first time came in 1979, and before that was a protest.

The Bulls, then in the Western Conference, were 31–51 in 1978–79. The New Orleans Jazz of the East were 26–56. There was no question who would be the No. 1 pick in the draft that year: Michigan State's Earvin Johnson. If the Bulls had won the coin flip, that was who they would've taken. Magic Johnson would've been paired with All-Stars Reggie Theus and Artis Gilmore, an eventual Hall of Famer, under future Hall of Fame coach Jerry Sloan. Their core would have been set for years to come—meaning they likely wouldn't have been 27–55 five years later.

"Life is full of ironies," then–general manager Rod Thorn said, "and so if we had won the coin flip and gotten Magic, we never would have gotten Michael."

The Bulls lost the coin flip and drafted David Greenwood with the No. 2 overall pick. The Lakers, who owned New Orleans' first-round pick that year, got Magic.

The Bulls were back at the bottom of the league in 1983–84. They finished with the third-worst record in the league, second worst in the Eastern Conference. The Bulls lost fourteen of the last fifteen games in the season, the one win was a single-digit victory over the visiting Hawks.

One more win would've taken the Bulls out of their draft spot. The draft order was determined by record, with the worst records getting the highest picks. The NBA draft lottery, which randomized the premium picks, wouldn't be instituted until 1985. They tried to get a win earlier in December of that season. The Bulls lost an overtime game to Houston after Caldwell Jones hit a game-tying three-pointer at the end of regulation. Chicago continued the game under protest, claiming Jones didn't get the shot off before time expired. (Note: This was long before replay review.) The NBA ended up denying the request, and the loss remained a loss. The Bulls had no idea at the time how great of a loss that would be.

Another win would've put the Bulls at 28 victories, tying them with Cleveland. If they ended tied with Cleveland, the No. 3 pick would have been decided by coin flip. The Cavaliers' first-round pick belonged to Dallas that year. So imagine the Bulls won the protest and got to 28 wins. Then they lose the coin flip with Cleveland to determine who gets the No. 3 pick. So the Bulls get pick No. 4 and Dallas would pick No. 3. So in this alternate universe, Jordan is a Maverick.

Of course, then, on the night of the draft, Portland—who acquired the No. 2 pick from Indiana—passed up the chance to draft Michael Jordan in favor of Sam Bowie. So there is another alternate universe where Jordan is a Blazer.

THE VILLAIN

Before an average of nearly six million people spent five consecutive weekends captivated by *The Last Dance* documentary, Michael Jordan was concerned. The behind-the-scenes footage from the 1997–98 season, which must've been in the attic of Phil Jackson's Montana home for twenty-two years, coupled with the honest and vulnerable interviews Jordan gave director Jason Hehir, was going to paint a portrait of Jordan unlike one the nation had seen. And he was worried people would see and think he was "a horrible guy." He feared his legion of cultlike followers would think less of him after they got a glimpse of Jordan without the filters of commercial and corporate marketing. As the documentary unfurled, it was clear why Jordan might have been nervous.

He was petty.

He was demeaning.

He was arrogant.

He was a bully with a forty-six-inch vertical and a god complex who browbeat Scott Burrell, punched Steve Kerr, and belittled the general manager.

He was aggressive.

He was vindictive.

He was maniacal.

And it was epic.

The documentary didn't even reveal the worst of it. Famed NBA journalist Sam Smith, author of the book *The Jordan Rules*, told a story during a radio interview about one of Jordan's coldest acts of bullying.

"Players would come to me over the years and say, 'You know what he did? He took Horace's food away on the plane because Horace had a bad game. He told the stewardesses, 'Don't feed him, he doesn't deserve to eat.' They would tell me stuff like that and they'd say, 'Why don't you write this?' And I would say, 'Well, I can't write it unless you say it.' I don't do 'league sources.' You can't do that kind of stuff on these kind of things. 'If you want to be quoted I've got no problem with that.' 'No, no, no we can't say that about Michael Jordan.'"

None of this ever seems to harm Jordan's reputation. Instead, it may have boosted it. People saw Jordan as unfiltered as ever, and it only enlarged his aura and amped up the devotion of his ardent loyalists.

The worried Jordan miscalculated his hold on the American sports psyche. He misunderstood the reason he leaves us still in awe.

Jordan is approaching sixty years old and is still the biggest name in sports. But that isn't because the globe pegged him as a model citizen who upheld the lofty values of humanity. Maybe early on, as his fame expanded to new levels, his hundred-million-dollar smile in Gatorade commercials gave him wholesome overtones. Maybe he was so thorough in executing his deliberate plan to avoid controversy and tarnishment that his fans attributed the purest of attributes to his blank canvas. But anyone who followed his career had that veil lifted long ago. If his 2009 Hall of Fame speech—when he fired shots at his high school coach for picking Leroy Smith over him—didn't reveal Jordan's biting ways, you just didn't want to see it.

The critical point: This is why we love Jordan. Texture is good. Edge is preferred. The dichotomy of human existence is so much more appealing because it is more authentic. Jordan was inspirational because of how relentless he attacked dominance. We loved his killer instinct, which requires a willingness to kill.

We wanted the legend who talks like our cool uncle after a few drinks, the one who gets loose at Thanksgiving dinner and starts putting family secrets on the table next to the cranberry sauce. Get perfect Jordan out of here. We didn't want him being the ideal role model who our aunts and grandparents could love. We wanted the rebel. We wanted the villain we could live through vicariously. We wanted to imagine our lives with his audacity.

That's why people love villains in general, why we root for them. They're liberated. They're cool. They get to exercise their talents, reap the benefits, and live outside the lines of appeasement. America loves gangsters, from fictional Marlon Brando to actual Al Capone. We're captivated by the legends of Bonnie and Clyde and Billy the Kid because there is a part in us yearning for the bad guy to get away. Heist movies, especially ones based on true stories, will never go out of style. We love Al Pacino because he is so incredible at playing bad guys. Denzel Washington won his first Oscar when he played the dirty cop Alonzo Harris in *Training Day*. Jodie Comer is offing people left and right in the show *Killing Eve* and nobody wants her to go to jail.

So when MJ crossed over from commercial concoction to honest and vulnerable, it only deepened the adoration. There are lines, for sure. Even villains have to have some redeeming quality, some context for their flaws. But being a jerk isn't even close to the line.

His fans ride with him until the wheels fall off precisely because he would not be deterred. Because he set out to destroy everyone and was good enough to actually do it. And he called himself Black Jesus while doing it.

Was he rough on his teammates? Sure. But Jordan was also known for being ready to fight back. He was down for whatever Knicks forward Xavier McDaniel wanted to do in the 1992 playoffs. He mushed Reggie Miller in the face and swung on Bill Laimbeer. Jordan wasn't backing down.

So the fact that twenty years later he still doesn't like Isiah Thomas—whom he refused to play with on the Dream Team—only proves Jordan is just as competitive, vengeful, and singularly bent on eviscerating his foes as ever. And what is more reassuring than knowing you can still count on Jordan to be waging wars and jabbing foes. Most of us can't be so single-minded, so stubborn, so self-sufficient as to not be concerned about mending fences. We probably don't want to be either. But whenever we want a whiff of world dominance, of hypercompetitiveness, and the superiority with which to taunt, we can count on Jordan. Still.

> *His fans ride with him until the wheels fall off precisely because he would not be deterred. Because he set out to destroy everyone and was good enough to actually do it.*

THE HOME COURT

The visiting team, whoever it was, had its starting lineups announced with the backdrop of a murmuring crowd. Public address announcer Ray Clay read off the opponents' names like he was an adjunct taking roll in a community college chemistry class.

Then the United Center would go dark.

The tradition that began at the old Chicago Stadium would raise the hair on the necks of the more than twenty-three thousand in the building and millions more on television. The dark would last for only a few seconds, allowing the cheers of the crowd to crescendo as the dramatic bass reverberated through the arena. Then a spotlight would point toward the championship banners hanging in the rafters. By the time the United Center opened, the Bulls already had three.

The big screen would brighten as a video would play. The distinct electronic keyboard sounds from the 1982 song "Sirius" by The Alan Parsons Project filled the arena as it strummed your soul. Most teams played an organ. But in 1984, Bulls announcer Tommy Davis heard "Sirius" while waiting for a movie to start in the theater. So he started using it to introduce the Bulls and it stuck.

The video on the screen was an animation of a Bull running through the streets of Chicago all the way to the United Center. Laser lighting flashed the Bulls logo on the court. But it was that hypnotic piano sound that became synonymous with the Bulls and hypnotized millions who watched Jordan.

Then Ray Clay would start the Bulls introductions by screaming "ANNNNND NOOOOOWWWWW . . . ," and chills would turn into an adrenaline rush. The guitar would always begin right after Jordan was announced last. By this point the crowd would be so lathered. The energy in the building peaking even before tip-off.

True story: Alan Parsons, a British engineer and producer who worked with the Beatles and Pink Floyd before starting his own band, heard through the grapevine his song had become popular at basketball games. He wasn't a fan. So he had to ask: "Who is Michael Jordan?"

The Bulls introductions became a classic. It was a highlight of the United Center experience and a pioneer for what would become a staple feature of every NBA game: player introductions. They all dim the lights, they all have their chosen song every home game, and they all fill the courts with dancers and lighting. Still, no one has matched the Bulls. They used the same intro for decades. People still go to YouTube just to relive the Bulls intro and that pregame sensation.

THE CRAZIEST STAT

Wilt Chamberlain scored 4,029 points in 1961–62 season. He shot 50.6 percent from the field, making 1,597 shots and 835 free throws. It's even crazier when you realize he missed two games and more than five hundred free throws and still averaged 50.4 points.

What does this have to do with the Bulls dynasty? Good question. Well, only two players in NBA history have scored three thousand points or more in a season: Wilt and MJ. The former was seven foot one, 275 pounds and did it three times. He was 52 points shy of a fourth in another year.

Jordan scored 3,041 points in the 1986–87 season. He only made 12 threes (out of 66 by the way, 18.2 percent).

Only seven players not named Wilt have topped 2,700 points in a season. Only two players from the three-point era have made it into that rarified air: James Harden and Kobe Bryant. Technically, Bryant wasn't from the three-point era. But he made 180 three-pointers in the year he scored 2,832 points in 2005–06, the seventh most ever. Harden, however, is from the three-point era. He made 378 in 2018–19 while finishing with 2,818 points, the tenth most in a season ever.

Outside of Harden, the highest total from the dispensation of three-point proliferation is Kevin Durant's 2,593 points in 2013–14. Even with the shot giving an extra point, no one is coming close to Jordan's 3,0411 points anymore, which illustrates how crazy it is for a guard to score so many points.

And pondering the insanity of Jordan's scoring prowess is but a reminder that WILT CHAMBERLAIN SCORED 4,000 POINTS IN A SEASON.

9

THE SHAQ AND KOBE LAKERS

The NBA fan base was so infatuated with Jordan (and the Bulls). It was a hot romance. It was the kind of intense love that happens only once in a lifetime. Yes, we had been separated before for a spell, but the relationship was even better the second time.

And, just like that, it was over. Jordan broke up with us. It was devastating. He gave the whole "it's not you, it's me" reason. It hurt all the same. Most important, it left a void.

San Antonio won the next championship, in 1999, but the global majority of fans weren't quite smitten with the Spurs. More on them later. David Robinson and rookie Tim Duncan amounted to that first date after a serious relationship. We were still too stuck on our ex, daydreaming about the memories and longing for that excitement.

And then we met these Lakers.

On paper, they looked a whole lot more attractive. Phil Jackson coaching Shaquille O'Neal and Kobe Bryant? Swipe right.

Jordan officially retired in January 1999, giving that relationship some closure. It started as a fun fling when the Lakers won sixteen straight games bridging December 1999 and January 2000. You know, a let-your-hair-down-for-the-new-millennium kind of thing. Things got more serious with the Lakers when they won nineteen straight games in February and March. By May, it was full-on love.

And these Lakers became the greatest rebound team ever. Not rebounding. But rebound. Because they helped the NBA and its fans bounce right back. Two years after experiencing the emptiness from the dismantling of the Bulls, the NBA world was in another serious relationship. These Lakers, in a sense, saved the league.

The 1998 lockout, followed by the second retirement by Jordan, left the future of the NBA uncertain. The quest for the next MJ had been going on for years. In 1992, it was supposed to be University of Southern California star Harold Miner. In 1996, Kobe was the next prophesied heir. But by the time Jordan was gone, the heir apparent wasn't established. Allen Iverson was perhaps the biggest star, but he was an acquired taste. And certainly, his 76ers weren't the dominant team the NBA needed. The potential was there for a major setback following the Jordan era. But the Kobe and Shaq (and Phil) Lakers effectively kept the party going.

It is no small feat following Jordan, who took the Association to heights it never fancied. But the throne didn't go unoccupied for too long. Continuing the legacy of Showtime, these Lakers proved to be quite the spectacle, a magnetic show in their own right.

O'Neal, the behemoth who bullied big men for seven seasons, put it all together—immediate dividends from the hiring of Jackson in 1999. Simultaneously, Bryant came into his own as a superstar, backing up his out-sized ego with domination. And since he was chiseled from the mold of Jordan, watching him play provided some of those old goose bumps.

The 2001 NBA Finals still has the highest average rating (12.1) for a series since the Bulls dynasty ended. The number two market in the country delivered an explosive and charismatic team with drama and an aesthetically pleasing style of play, led by two clear Hall of Fame—bound talents. The Lakers were easy to love and equally easy to loathe, making them the perfect new dynasty for the new millennium.

NBA Finals Appearances

2000 (W)	2001 (W)
2002 (W)	2004 (L)

THE FACE OF THE DYNASTY

According to win shares and box plus-minus and value over replacement player (VORP), Hakeem Olajuwon's best season was 1992–93, when he averaged 26.1 points, 13 rebounds, 4.2 blocks, and 3.5 assists. He shot 52.9 percent from the field in what was his most dominant offensive season. He registered a career-best offensive rating of 114 with a defensive rating of 96. He was so good.

That's about the only season remotely comparable to what Shaq put together in 1999–2000 to get the new Lakers dynasty going. Outside of that, you've got to go all the way back to Kareem Abdul-Jabbar, back when he was Lew Alcindor on the Milwaukee Bucks. Yes, Shaq was that good.

O'Neal was one vote from being the first unanimous MVP in history. He should've been. He's still mad about it.

"He destroyed history being an asshole," Shaq said in 2019 regarding CNN reporter Fred Hickman, who voted Iverson as the MVP in 2000, the only voter to not select Shaq. "It wasn't anybody doing close to what I was doing. And I told the world I was gon' do that. And they saw it in my eyes, they saw it on my face, they saw it every time I played."

Shaq had been on a mission that season. He was motivated to prove he had no equal.

One such display came on his birthday. Shaq turned twenty-eight on March 6, 2000. The Lakers and Clippers were facing off at Staples Center that night, an arena they shared, but it was a Clippers home game. O'Neal requested an allotment of tickets for friends and family to be there for his birthday. Customarily, each player gets a couple of complimentary tickets per game. But when they request more, they are usually accommodated. O'Neal's request for comps, however, was denied. Anything outside of his two freebies, he had to pay.

Shaq was making more than $17 million that season, so money wasn't the issue. It was the principle. He felt disrespected by the Clippers. So he took it out on their big men—Michael Olowokandi, Maurice Taylor, Pete Chilcutt, Anthony Avent—and totaled 61 points and 23 rebounds in forty-five minutes. O'Neal took 35 shots, his most as a Laker.

After a dunk put him over 60 points for the first time in his career, he capped his performance with a lob to Kobe for a reverse dunk.

"He obviously wanted to make a point," Clippers interim coach Jim Todd told the *Los Angeles Times*. "I hoped he would stop at 50."

That was the kind of year Shaq had. Dominance on cue.

Shaq led the league in scoring (29.7 points) and field goal percentage (57.4). He was second in rebounding (13.6) and third in blocks (3.03). His 956 field goals were tops in the league, nearly 200 more than the next highest. It was the most baskets made in the NBA since 1992–93, when Jordan made 992, and it was the most shots made by a big man since Bob McAdoo's 1,096 in 1974–75. O'Neal was a First Team NBA All-Defense selection. He also averaged a career-best 3.8 assists.

His dominance on both ends gave him a player efficiency rating (PER) of 30.6. It was his second consecutive season over 30 and just the tenth such season ever in NBA history. At the time, only Wilt Chamberlain, Michael Jordan, David Robinson, and O'Neal had ever posted seasons with a PER of 30 or better.

When This Dynasty Reigned

- The 2000 presidential election between George W. Bush and Vice President Al Gore was so close it required the Supreme Court to intervene. The count in the decisive state, Florida, was disputed, which led to a recount and "hanging chad" becoming part of the American lexicon. The Supreme Court ruled in favor of Bush, who won the state by 527 votes, leading to a victory in the electoral college 271–266.

- The terrorist attacks of September 11, 2001, rocked America to its core. A pair of hijacked planes took down the World Trade Center in New York, and another crashed into the Pentagon. A fourth plane was crashed into a Pennsylvania cornfield after passengers reclaimed the plane and prevented it from its presumed target in DC, either the White House or the Capitol building. Al-Qaeda took responsibility for the deadliest attack on U.S. soil in American history and has been etched into the psyche of the country since. This was Pearl Harbor for a new generation. A week later, anthrax attacks by mail began.

- The war in Afghanistan began with the U.S. invasion in October 2001, driving out the Taliban and denying Al-Qaeda a safe haven.

- Tiger Woods held all four major golf titles simultaneously, which had never been done before. Having already won the 2000 U.S. Open, the 2000 British Open, and the 2000 PGA Championship, Woods won the 2001 Masters to complete what was dubbed the Tiger Slam.

- In 2000, Netflix, which launched in 1997 mailing rented DVDs, was struggling to survive and approached video rental behemoth Blockbuster Video about a 50-50 partnership. Netflix would run their online brand, and Blockbuster would promote Netflix in its stores. Blockbuster turned them down. Which is good because "Blockbuster and Chill" doesn't quite have the same ring.

- *Survivor* premiered in America in 2000, taking reality TV to another level. *The Bachelor* debuted in 2002.

THE MASTERMIND

It all put Jerry West in the hospital for a few days. Straight exhaustion. The acquisitions of Kobe Bryant and Shaquille O'Neal required every ounce of patience and energy from the legendary general manager.

Bryant entered the 1996 draft after high school, skipping college and going pro from Lower Merion High in Pennsylvania, twenty minutes outside of Philadelphia. In 1995, Kevin Garnett made the same jump, the first to do so in twenty years, and was taken No. 5 overall. While Garnett made the All-Rookie team, drafting high school players with lottery picks was still considered a huge risk. And Bryant was a six-foot-five guard and not a six-foot-eleven power forward like Garnett, at a time when big men were far more coveted. But West watched a seventeen-year-old Kobe Bryant play one-on-one with NBA veteran Michael Cooper in a private workout. West said he'd never seen such a workout. He'd coveted Kobe since.

But the Lakers didn't have a lottery pick, so West had to do some maneuvering. The then New Jersey Nets wanted Bryant with the No. 8 pick. Bryant fell all the way to No. 13 in the draft—thanks to some alleged manipulation by his agent and West, who gamed the process to make teams afraid to draft Bryant—and the Charlotte Hornets selected Bryant so they could trade him to the Lakers. In exchange, the Lakers sent big man Vlade Divac to the Hornets. Divac threatened to retire when the trade talks began, so West had to fix that first.

In the end West got Kobe, and then he cleared up the salary cap space to get the center he wanted: O'Neal.

Shaq wanted out of Orlando because they didn't want to pay him $100 million. To create the cap space to fit O'Neal's salary demands, West had to execute another trade to dump the salaries of George Lynch and Anthony Peeler. The Lakers signed Shaq to the biggest free-agent deal in history: seven years, $120 million.

Yes, 1996 was a great summer for the Lakers. They had the most dominant big man in the game and a premiere perimeter scorer.

But 1999 was when the Lakers put on the finishing touches. In March, they acquired sharp-shooting scorer Glen Rice from Charlotte. Three months later, West hired Jackson, the coach with six championship rings and a reputation for filling a room with his presence. West was well aware of the sour ending to Jackson's relationship with the Bulls, specifically with general manager Jerry Krause, a former Lakers scout whom West knew. He also knew Jackson would command top dollar ($30 million over five years) and that Kurt Rambis, the former Lakers player turned assistant coach, was next in line to be the Lakers head coach. But West still made it happen.

The Lakers added guard Ron Harper, who started for Jackson in Chicago, and guard Brian Shaw, who was with Shaq in Orlando.

West had set the foundation for another Lakers dynasty.

THE CULTURAL IMPACT

The modern NBA has always been about individuals. While sports like the NFL have managed to play up the franchises, the regions, and the rivalries, the genius of late commissioner David Stern, widely regarded as the best the league's ever had and arguably the best in sports, was in the ability to market stars.

The first two stars of the modern NBA were Magic and Bird. Then Jordan built on that. But if the Bulls dynasty ushered the league into people's homes at record numbers, then it was this Lakers dynasty that made the NBA like family. In a very air-dirty-laundry-at-the-repass kind of way.

The marketing of individual stars created an insatiable appetite for access to their person—their lives, their backgrounds, their habits and behaviors. The Lakers had some big personalities who created the kind of drama made for TV. In addition to a three-peat, the Lakers gave the NBA a soap opera vibe. The elements were there for the Bulls, but the media didn't seem nearly as prepared to cover the behind-the-scenes strife. Sam Smith's book *The Jordan Rules*, which details the off-camera Jordan, was considered scandalous for its revelations. But by the time these Lakers took the dynastic baton, the mainstream was ready to soak up the juiciness, and the Lakers fed the beast. They made the intrapersonal relationships just as important as the actual games—especially when those relationships weren't good.

It was this Lakers dynasty that made the NBA like family. In a very air-dirty-laundry-at-the-repass kind of way.

These Lakers were birthed in salaciousness. It began with Kobe.

Bryant was the son of an NBA player. He spent years of his childhood in Italy and could speak multiple languages. He also envisioned himself as a hardcore kid from Philly who doubled as a gangsta rapper. The book *Three-Ring Circus* by Jeff Pearlman tells a story of Kobe in a team meeting during training camp. Everyone introduced themselves. When it was the rookie's turn, he used the moment to warn his teammates that nobody was going to punk him.

He was quiet and kept to himself as a youngster but was also brash as hell and irreverent toward his NBA elders. O'Neal, on the other hand, was a larger-than-life figure on and off the court. He had ambitions beyond basketball—his movie, *Kazaam*, was released in 1996, and he was filming another, *Steel*, in the weeks leading up to his first camp with the Lakers. O'Neal left the Orlando Magic, and his cohort Penny Hardaway, in search of a bigger market and its perks.

Of course, coaches didn't get bigger than Phil Jackson.

Those three figures kept the drama going, and the Lakers became one of the most captivating soap operas in NBA history. Their dominance on the court became secondary in some ways. The shenanigans kept the storylines coming, and the books and documentaries and tales are still being produced.

At the core of the Kobe and Shaq rivalry was Bryant's refusal to submit to O'Neal as the foundation of the offense. The arrogance of Bryant made him feel as if he should be the primary option instead of the dump-it-into-the-post offense. Of course, Shaq was the most dominant figure in the league and was justified in his demand for the ball. Jerry West and Jackson were on his side. O'Neal started calling Kobe "Showboat" because of his flashy style of play. But it was working with the fans as Bryant's jerseys were selling like crazy, which was rumored to irritate Shaq. The two actually scrapped in a two-on-two game during the 1999 lockout, with Shaq slapping Kobe, per accounts in Roland Lazenby's book *The Show*.

When Jackson arrived, he doubled down on the O'Neal-centered offense and even bonded with the Big Fella while Kobe Bryant kept his distance. The Lakers won the 2000 championship and that didn't solve it. Bryant, who was dominant in the NBA Finals, started taking what he thought was his—especially after O'Neal showed up to training camp out of shape. The tension increased.

"I don't even want them in the same room together right now," Jackson told reporters about Kobe and Shaq in 2001.

Not long after he took over as the Lakers coach, Jackson began dating Jeanie Buss, who oversaw the Lakers business operations and happened to be the daughter of owner Jerry Buss. Yes, the coach dated his boss's daughter.

Side note: The boss's daughter ended up owning the team and became the first female owner to win an NBA championship in 2020.

Jerry West, in his autobiography, *West by West*, said he and Jackson never hit it off: "He didn't want me around, and he had absolutely no respect for me—of that, I have no doubt." West left the Lakers after the 2000 championship.

In July 2003, Bryant was arrested on charges of sexual assault. A nineteen-year-old hotel worker accused Kobe of raping her in his hotel room the night before he was scheduled to have surgery. Pretrial hearings began in December. Bryant ended up playing five games, three in the playoffs, after flying in from court. He scored 31 in the first round against Houston, 42 in the second round against San Antonio, and 31 in the Western Conference Finals against Minnesota—all after flying to Los Angeles on a private jet the same day he appeared in court in Eagle, Colorado, figuratively bringing the courtroom and conversations about sexual assault to the playoffs.

In September 2004, the charges against Kobe were dropped after the accuser told prosecutors she was no longer willing to testify. Her name was leaked to the media and she was vehemently harassed. She brought a civil case against Bryant that was settled out of court. Kobe denied the allegations in a press conference, with his wife by his side, calling the sex consensual.

In 2004, Shaq was traded to Miami, and the Lakers became Kobe's team. The NBA, taking full advantage of the eight years of tension between Kobe and Shaq, featured their first game facing off against each other on Christmas Day. It became a tradition. This was the work of Stern, the marketing guru, who turned the league's Christmas Day tradition into the best of dramas, which was ideal for ABC, which replaced NBC as the NBA's national broadcast partner in 2002.

The NBA has grown into a twelve-month sport. The transactions, the relationships, the frictions—they are all part of the never-ending storyline of the NBA. And the league has the Kobe-Shaq Lakers to thank for that.

THE ZEN MASTER

Phil Jackson left Chicago with six championships. When he came to the Lakers, his reputation as a beneficiary of loaded rosters followed him. He had Jordan, Pippen, and Rodman in Chicago. He went from that to Kobe and Shaq.

But the Lakers were another example, a greater example, of his expertise in managing a surplus of top-end talent. The meshing of NBA stars was perhaps harder in Los Angeles because of the dueling egos, unlike in Chicago where the roster was a clear monarchy.

But another shining attribute Jackson brought with him from Chicago was his ability to get the most out of his role players and milk depth. It was his valuing of the supporting cast that made him truly great.

Sometimes that required getting (former) stars to take lesser roles: Ron Harper, Glen Rice, Karl Malone, Rick Fox. Sometimes it required getting the most out of unheralded players, such as Horace Grant, A. C. Green, Brian Shaw. Sometimes it was squeezing production out of players whom no one expected anything from, such as Mark Madsen and Devean George. Derek Fisher was a little-known guard from Arkansas who became a starter for Jackson and went on to play eighteen seasons.

Jackson's championship teams were top-heavy. But he raised the floor by valuing and preparing the end of the bench.

CRAZY 8

His career turned out to be so long, his accomplishments so aplenty, No. 8 tends to get lost in his legacy. The jersey hangs in the rafters of Staples Center, along with No. 24. But the Kobe from this dynasty was an anomaly. As athletic as he was audacious. As skilled as he was stubborn. The origins of Mamba Mentality happened in this jersey.

This version had an afro, full and rugged, and the liberated mentality to go with it. He operated as one whose Hall of Fame bust was already being carved. As much as his audacity made him problematic off the court, it made him electric on it. At that stage of his career, his game still had a streetball flair to it. Plus, the Kobe off the court was searching for his identity. His explosiveness and aggressiveness produced some signature epic performances in the No. 8. Here are eight of them during this dynasty.

1. LOB TO SHAQ

Perhaps the signature moment of this Lakers' dynasty began with a Kobe crossover. Bryant, dribbling at the top, lost Portland's Scottie Pippen with a left-to-right dribble on his way into the paint. Once the defense reacted, he lofted a pass to O'Neal, who slammed it home with one hand. Shaq ran downcourt screaming after securing the Lakers' first trip to the NBA Finals in ten years and gave us an iconic moment.

2. KOBE CLOSES ALONE

Kobe, who patterned his game after Jordan, needed a flu game on his résumé. It came in Game 4 of the 2001 NBA Finals. Kobe sprained his ankle and missed Game 3 and the Pacers won. In overtime of Game 4, Kobe—still visibly limping, Shaq fouled out, and the Lakers nursing a small lead—hit two huge jumpers and tipped in a miss with 5.9 seconds left to stave off the Pacers and take a 3–1 series lead. He wouldn't let the Lakers lose. It was the first of many injuries Kobe would famously play through.

3. SILENCING COWBELLS

In Game 4 of the 2001 Western Conference Semifinals in
Sacramento, Bryant played the entire game and finished with
48 points and 16 rebounds. He scored 15 points in the fourth
quarter, simultaneously frustrating and dazzling the ARCO Arena
crowd with his one-on-everyone drives and creative finishes. He
dropped in a jumper over Doug Christie with a foul and stared at
courtside fans, blowing on his fingers because he was on fire.

4. DOMINANCE AT THE ALAMO

He scored 45 points on an array of jumpers and drives and a
couple of alley-oops in Game 1 of the West final. In what was
expected to be a showdown with the Spurs, Kobe made it clear
who was the best player on the floor. Combining the clincher in

Sacramento and Game 1 vs. the Spurs, Bryant scored 93 points in 95 minutes on 53 percent shooting combined in consecutive games.

"Kobe Bryant right now is playing on a different level," Doug Collins said during the broadcast.

5. REVERSE DUNK IN MINNY

With Minnesota's Kevin Garnett charging toward him, Bryant took off as he entered the paint. Kevin Harlan, the popular play-by-play announcer, knew something was about to happen because he screamed "Buckle up for Kobe Bryant!" as No. 8 jumped.

Bryant went to the Jordan-esque looping reverse layup—the one where he shows the ball one side of the rim, brings it down, and takes it to the other side. But instead of spinning it off the backboard, Kobe dunked it. No. 8 was doing dunk-contest moves on the road in a pivotal Game 5 of a playoff series.

6. BAPTISM OF DWIGHT HOWARD

Bringing the ball up in transition, Bryant lost Orlando's DeShawn Stevenson with a screen and slipped past Pat Garrity like he wasn't even there. The lane was wide open.

Howard was a rookie at the time. He was on the other side of the lane when No. 8 came bearing down. Howard wasn't yet a three-time Defensive Player of the Year, wasn't yet one of the league's great big men. What he was, in this moment, was late getting across the key with the help defense. Kobe took off with one foot inside Orlando's blue-painted key and soared.

Howard, both arms up as he tried to take a charge, was in a perfect pose for the poster. No. 8 slammed it home with one hand, violently crashing against the rim, and shaking for emphasis.

"You dunked on him pretty good," a reporter said.

Kobe smiled without raising his head.

"I baptized him. I baptized him."

Howard said it was the first time he'd ever been dunked on, and his teammates let him hear about it.

7. GAME-WINNING REBOUND

Bryant had the ball in his hands, inside of 30 seconds left, with a chance to win in Game 4 of the 2002 West semis. But he dribbled it off his foot. Point guard Derek Fisher chased the ball down and turned it into a seventeen-foot pull-up for the win. It bricked. But Kobe came out of nowhere, using his jaw-dropping leaping ability to soar for the rebound, snatching the ball out of the air and springing right back up to drop in the game-winner. No. 8 turned a clutch rebound into a highlight.

8. POSTERIZATION OF VINCENT YARBROUGH

Bryant, back in February 2003, caught the outlet pass in stride on the fast break. He changed directions, angling toward the rim by whipping the ball around his back. Yarbrough, a rookie who tried to intercept the outlet pass, hustled to get back in the play and lunged toward the rim where Kobe was headed. Big mistake. Kobe capped the move with a 180-degree reverse dunk over Yarbrough.

NEVER FORGET

The Lakers ended up involved in one of the most memorable NBA Finals moments ever. After winning the first eleven games of the 2001 playoffs, the Lakers ran into Allen Iverson in the Finals. It was a mismatch, but Game 1 turned out to be an epic performance for Iverson. He scored 48 points as the 76ers upset the heavily favored Lakers in overtime.

His Sixers up two in overtime, Iverson hit the biggest shot of the game. A crossover and step-back jumper from the baseline ended with Lakers guard Tyronn Lue on the ground in front of the Lakers bench. So Iverson, after sticking the jumper, stepped right over Lue.

In Game 2, Shaq put the Sixers back in their place. He made 11 of his last 13 shots, bullying Dikembe Mutombo, Todd MacCulloch, and Matt Geiger. He nearly posted the first quadruple-double in NBA Finals history: 28 points, 20 rebounds, 9 assists, and 8 blocks.

And that was the end of the 76ers' hopes. But first, Iverson created one of the coldest, most disrespectful plays in NBA history.

8.24.2

One of the great tragedies in NBA history, in sports history, happened on January 26, 2020, when a helicopter crashed into the side of a mountain in Calabasas, California. The nine people on board—headed to a basketball game at the Mamba Sports Academy in Thousand Oaks—were killed: Kobe Bryant and his thirteen-year-old daughter Gianna; her teammate Payton Chester, thirteen, and her mom, Sarah; Gianna's teammate Alyssa Altobelli, fourteen, and her parents, John and Keri; and assistant coach Christina Mauser; along with the pilot, Ara Zobayan.

Gianna, also known as Gigi, was a rising basketball star with dreams of playing at the University of Connecticut. Bryant, her coach, had become a staunch advocate of women's basketball, even mentoring then Oregon star Sabrina Ionescu.

The NBA has never been rocked like it was with the news of Bryant's death, especially knowing his daughter died with him. He was forty-one.

THE CRAZIEST STAT

Robert Horry has seven championships. Seven. The only players with more are from the Bill Russell era of the Celtics. Horry averaged a championship every 2.57 years of his career.

He will forever be remembered in this Lakers dynasty for the defining shot of his career.

Down 2–1 in the 2002 Western Conference Finals, against the best Kings team they'd faced, the Lakers found themselves trailing 40–20 in the first quarter. The back-to-back champions got down by as much as 24 points at Staples Center and seemed to have finally met their match.

But they started clawing their way back. They turned what was looking like a blowout into a nail-biter. Shaq, a notoriously troubled free throw shooter, made a pair to pull the Lakers within one. Vlade Divac followed by splitting a pair of free throws with 11.8 seconds remaining, putting the Kings up 99–97.

Kobe, tangled with Christie—as he had been for most of the previous three years, it seemed—drove the lane and missed his runner. Shaq got the rebound. He went back up for the bunny, but it rimmed out. With fewer than three seconds left, Divac swatted the ball away from the rim, keeping it away from O'Neal, who was trying for another putback. But Divac's swat proved to be the most perfect bounce pass.

Waiting at the top of the key was Horry. By then, his nickname was already Big Shot Bob. This moment would cement his legacy.

Webber stepped toward the loose ball as if it were meant for him. He caught it on one bounce, went right into his shooting motion, and let it fly. Chris Webber, the Kings star, was defending Horry when the play began but got sucked into the action near the rim. When the ball came out, he was Sacramento's only hope. Webber hauled as fast as his six-foot-nine, 245-pound frame with a surgically repaired knee could get him to the three-point line. He leaped as Horry shot it, flying past Horry's right hand after the ball was released. But he was too late. The shot was gone.

The buzzer sounded just before the three-pointer splashed. Horry did it again.

10

THE TIM DUNCAN SPURS

Ahead of the Spurs' 2003 championship season, third-year forward Stephen Jackson thought Gregg Popovich would kick him off the team because of a sketchy situation involving Tim Duncan and a few paintball guns. Duncan, really, was the true mastermind behind the entire operation. But Duncan, see, was untouchable as the Spurs' new franchise player.

Who in their right mind would even think about pointing a finger at him?
Who would accuse Duncan of straying from his perfect behavior?

Certainly not Jackson, who was still trying to find his footing in the NBA at the time. Jackson spent most of his first season with the Spurs in 2001–02 on injured reserve. So to help make a better impression on the team in Year 2, he decided to stay put in San Antonio throughout the ensuing off-season to get right. He continued to rehab his injury and was constantly in the gym working out with Duncan. And over those summer months, the two built a brotherly bond—one that would eventually lead to a little bit of trouble.

"That's my guy," Jackson said of Duncan on *The Ryen Russillo Show* in 2017. "Tim loved me, and the way he embraced me, it felt like I had my big brother again because I lost my big brother when I was fifteen, sixteen. So Tim Duncan filled that role at the time I was in San Antonio. I have to give him that. That's why I love him to death."

Duncan, who was twenty-seven at the time, took up paintball as a hobby. Imagine a six-foot-eleven, 250-pound man trying to hide in a game of paintball. Oh, the amount of camouflage needed.

Sure, his strong footwork and quick reflexes perhaps came in handy. But it certainly couldn't have been too difficult to spot Duncan, his goggles poking out over a bunker in the midst of a firefight.

Jackson, who grew up in the rugged streets of Port Arthur, Texas, wasn't the type to be easily rattled. In his earlier years, he had been shot at by real guns, with real bullets. So tagging along with Duncan on his paintball excursions was a breeze. Neon blood splatter isn't nearly as scary. At least, that was what he thought.

Popovich told his players they could do whatever they wanted for their team-bonding activity—as long as it didn't involve paintball. Too much of an injury risk. Popovich knew how seriously Duncan took paintball and wanted to kill the idea before it corrupted the rest of the team.

Too late.

Spurs players decided to play paintball anyway along with some friends. Jackson was on Duncan's team, per usual. They were playing capture the flag and, on Duncan's orders, Jackson was making a beeline toward the target.

"I'm running hard, I'm sweating, I'm 007," Jackson told Russillo. "I'm dodging bullets, sliding, I'm just doing all the stuff I see on video games in real life."

Jackson finally arrived at a staircase just a few feet from the flag. He saw an opportunity to grab it without being exposed to a stray Sherwin-Williams bullet. With paintballs still flying in every direction, Jackson ducked down and attempted to reach for the flag, taking advantage of his impressive wingspan. But as he reached, he took a deep breath and his protective mask began to fog up. His vision was obstructed. He continued reaching without realizing he needed to take an extra step on the staircase. It turned out to be a massive miscalculation.

Jackson's mask slid off his face. He lost his balance and hurtled into the staircase mouth first.

"Blood just started to shoot everywhere," Jackson said. "Nobody knows because they can't see me. Nobody knows that I'm about to bleed out."

Jackson, dripping blood, put his mask back on and attempted to walk off the course and end his run. But he should've made his intentions more clear. If only he could have waved a white flag and surrendered. Members of the opposing team had no idea that Jackson was injured. So when he gave up his position, they lit him up.

Jackson took a barrage of paintballs to the back, then turned around to reveal his busted mouth. Stunned, everyone on both teams immediately ran over to make sure he was okay. Duncan was more concerned about how they were going to explain Jackson's injury the following day in practice. They weren't supposed to be playing paintball in the first place. There would be hell to pay.

Popovich told his players they could do whatever they wanted for their team-bonding activity—as long as it didn't involve paintball.

They sat down and started coming up with all sorts of excuses to avoid Popovich's wrath.

Stephen fell down the steps at home.

A ball hit him in the mouth during a workout.

He was out boxing with his friend.

By the time practice rolled around the next day, Jackson thought his fabricated story was solid. But when he walked into the gym and saw Popovich's face, the fierce look in his eyes, he immediately knew he'd have to come clean.

Popovich was hot, ripping everyone involved in the paintball trip, and he was especially upset that Duncan's health was jeopardized. In the middle of Jackson's explanation, Malik Rose walked in and provided some much-needed comedic relief, pointing at Jackson's lip and screaming, "Yo! What is this!" They all burst into uncontrollable laughter. And his reaction did the unthinkable: It made Popovich laugh, too.

Popovich's eventual response to Jackson was right on brand.

"I'm glad it was you and not Tim."

NBA Finals Appearances

1999 (W)	2003 (W)	2005 (W)
2007 (W)	2013 (L)	2014 (W)

THE FACE OF THE DYNASTY

The story goes that Etan Thomas, playing for the Wizards, posted up Duncan. With his back to the basket, he pivoted toward the middle of the lane to go for his reliable jump hook. But Duncan, with his seven-foot-three wingspan, blocked the shot by Thomas. They both ran to the other end of the court after the change of possession. That was when Duncan started talking to Thomas.

"That was a good move," Thomas remembers Duncan saying. "But you have to get more into my body so you can either draw the foul or I can't block it."

Thomas, a Tulsa, Oklahoma, native, was a six-foot-nine power forward who was strong and physical enough to play some center. He was a two-time Big East Defensive Player of the Year at Syracuse before being drafted No. 12 overall in the 2000 NBA Draft. He was by no means on the level of Tim Duncan. But Thomas was no slouch. That was why Duncan's midgame coaching was surprising. He thought Duncan might have been taunting him with condescension. But Duncan was a superstar, and trash talk wasn't really Thomas's style. So the Wizards big man just said, "Okay."

But the next time he had Duncan in the post, he heeded the advice. He pivoted toward the middle again but he leaned his shoulder into Duncan's chest. The blow grounded Duncan long enough for Thomas to get off his skyhook. This time Duncan couldn't block it. Thomas missed, but he wasn't swatted again. So that was a victory.

Duncan chimed in again.

"Much better," he said. Then he continued playing.

Thomas was so caught off guard that even after the game, he had to tell someone. He called his buddy Zee Chilton to tell him about one of the most unique conversations he's had on a basketball court. He realized Duncan wasn't being sarcastic or condescending, but helpful to a big man trying to make his way in the league.

"Tim Duncan is honestly one of the nicest guys in the NBA," Thomas wrote in a Facebook post revealing the encounter, "and one of the best power forwards ever. Respect."

Duncan won't just be remembered for winning five championships, two league MVPs, three Finals MVPs, and fifteen All-NBA and All-Defense selections. He won't just be remembered for scoring more than 26,000 points in his career, more than 15,000 rebounds and 3,000 blocks.

As much as anything, he'll be remembered for how he did it.

The NBA has thrived on the fame and magnetism of its best players, their appeal and larger-than-life aura. But Duncan violated every common characteristic we've come to expect from a superstar athlete. Duncan lacked the desire for attention or the showmanship. He didn't thirst for mogul status and didn't seem to care about taking advantage of all the perks his celebrity afforded him. There was no flash to his game, and he didn't operate like one who knew (and loved when) the cameras were on him. Some of these typical expectations of famous athletes are but tropes, stereotypes affixed to players until they earn them off. There are certainly other humble superstars and Hall of Fame players who didn't covet the spotlight. But Duncan is the poster child for countering the cliché.

Draymond Green, the loquacious Golden State Warriors forward, said he tried to engage Duncan in some competitive banter. Green loves to get in his opponents' heads with his pointed yapping. But it didn't take him long to realize Duncan wasn't the least bit fazed. So Green gave up and never tried again.

Shaquille O'Neal told the *San Antonio Express-News* he had a similar experience.

"The Spurs won because of Tim Duncan, a guy I could never break. I could talk trash to Patrick Ewing, get in David Robinson's face, get a rise out of Alonzo

Mourning. But when I went at Tim he'd look at me like he was bored and then say, 'Hey, Shaq, watch this shot right here off the glass.'"

Duncan was boring compared to his superstar counterparts. He didn't wish to be the center of attention. He didn't dress to impress. He didn't speak often, and when he did, it wasn't very entertaining. He wasn't worried about making headlines. Duncan was an antisuperstar.

All of the glamour that comes with playing in the NBA took a back seat to Duncan's ultimate goal—winning. And despite the massive success he experienced during his legendary career, the calm, simplistic aspects of Duncan's personality never changed. He was genuinely unattracted to the limelight. He wasn't driven by ego or a sense of entitlement. He was true to himself. Always.

Duncan's style of play matched his personality perfectly. While Michael Jordan marveled with his leaping ability and LeBron James with his athleticism, Duncan's signature move was the midrange jumper off the glass. That's so fitting. There was no room for sass in Duncan's game; he preferred a simple approach to offense rather than rim-rattling dunks. He dunked, but he was just as fine, gently dropping the ball over the rim. Mr. It's the Same Two Points.

Incredibly boring or not, Duncan managed to put together a Hall of Fame career and established himself as the greatest power forward of all time. "The Big Fundamental" led the Spurs to five NBA championships while averaging 19 points, 10.8 rebounds, and 3.0 assists per game over his nineteen-year career.

When This Dynasty Reigned

- The Spurs rise coincided with that of rapper Eminem. They were going for their first title when *The Slim Shady LP* peaked at No. 2 on the charts. They were reigning champs when the first single from *The Marshall Mathers LP* dropped.

- Beyoncé and Jay-Z were coupled up at the 2003 All-Star Game for the first time. The two would marry in 2008 and become the First Couple of NBA celebrity fandom.

- Hurricane Katrina made landfall in Mississippi in August 2005. The levees protecting New Orleans failed and the city was devastated by floods, causing a record $170 billion in damages and more than 1,200 deaths. It also forced the New Orleans Hornets to play in Oklahoma City while the city was repaired, paving the way for the Oklahoma City Thunder franchise.

- After June 29, 2007, nothing would ever be the same. The iPhone made its debut.

- Barack Obama was inaugurated as the first African-American president in American history.

- The first generation of the Toyota Prius went on sale in 2000. The millionth Prius was sold in 2008. The car owned the electric vehicle market. But in 2009, a new kid arrived on the block. The first Tesla was sold.

- The Great Recession, triggered by the housing bubble burst, began in December 2007 and lasted eighteen months. It was the worst financial crisis in the United States since the Great Depression of the 1930s.

THE MASTERMIND

Gregg Popovich is the longest-tenured active head coach in the NBA, and he's known for two things: winning without fail and being an authoritarian figure. He psychologically bullies the media in interviews. He curses out even his best players. He routinely derided President Donald Trump and shows no mercy with his verbal assault on racism and injustice.

Popovich has orchestrated five championships with a military-like command. It's his way. Option No. 2 isn't the highway, but humiliation. Option No. 3 is the highway. It's a bit comical. Popovich is seventy-two years old. He's earned the right to be as curmudgeonly as he desires. His rampant success and white hair is license to be blunt and intimidating.

But let's be clear. Popovich has always been a savage. Let's go back.

It was 1996. The season began November 1. Bill Clinton was days from winning his second term in the presidential election. *Independence Day* was still killing it at the box office with *Space Jam* and the first *Toy Story* weeks from hitting theaters. The hip-hop world was still shocked from the recent death of Tupac Shakur and the sports world was still swooning over Michael Johnson's record-breaking performance in the Olympics. This was a long time ago.

The Spurs were coming off a fifty-nine-win season that ended with a disappointing loss in the second round of the playoffs to the Jazz. But Popovich, the general manager, signed Dominique Wilkins and Vernon Maxwell, giving the Spurs more depth and, theoretically, making them even more ready for a sustained postseason run.

But in the preseason, star center David Robinson, the 1995 NBA MVP, injured his back and missed the first eighteen games of the season. The Spurs lost fifteen of them. On December 10, 1996, Robinson was set to return to the lineup. A healthy Robinson would make all the difference. The Spurs were 3–15, so they had a lot of work to do. But they'd had a seventeen-game win streak the season before. Another one of those would've gotten the Spurs back in the hunt. You never know.

So, just in case, Popovich made a move that makes total sense in hindsight. He fired coach Bob Hill the day Robinson returned to the lineup. And guess who Popovich hired as the new coach? Himself.

"I had a pretty strong feeling at that point if he had a chance to fire me, he was going to," Hill said in a 2014 interview with the *Boston Globe*. "I probably should have just resigned and got out of here. I stayed and he got the job. I'm sure he had that in mind all along."

Popovich's coaching career with the Spurs was born with a Godfather move. It only made sense he'd become the don.

The governing style of Popovich wasn't simply for the sake of ego. It worked, in part, because most of his players came to know him as a huge ally in their lives. Most of Popovich's players loved him. His relationship with them as individuals gave him leeway when it came to drawing the hard lines. Pop was executing a philosophy. It dictated how they played and how they remained on top for so long. In an age of superstars, literally at the apex of the Jordan era, Pop was setting the groundwork of an ideology that would elevate the system over the stars. There was no room for attention seekers or stat stuffers. Every player was expected to simply do their job and do it well.

His approach as a coach aligns with his background. He was born and raised in Indiana, where basketball is a religion, where substance is desired over style, and where humility is preferred in the stead of hubris. He also graduated from the air force, which explains the regimented structure and the distinct motivation tactics. So when he took over as coach of the Spurs in December 1996, he began developing what would become the Spurs way. It was movement. It was passing. It was synced team defense. It was making open shots. It was valuing and using players on the back end of the rotation. It was holding every player, regardless of stature and status, to the same standards. To achieve that, Popovich made a habit of laying into his best players. If Duncan was getting the business for missing a minor detail, what would happen to the second-round pick deep in the rotation who has but two jobs to execute?

The strict adherence to the Spurs' principles—sharing the ball, making the simple and available play, sticking to the defensive game plan—seemed to be ideal for developing young talent. There was no ball dominance by any one player. His system was designed to distribute wealth and touches so as to spread the defense thin. Things like making the extra pass, diligently executing rotations, were as much designed to frustrate the opponent as to create camaraderie.

San Antonio seemed to always have players no one had ever heard of somehow producing at levels no one ever expected. Popovich never needed to restock with high-profile free agents or an army of lottery picks to ensure

success, not once they drafted Duncan to follow Robinson. The Spurs seemed to get young and inexperienced players ready faster than any other team. They got the most out of career journeymen or players on the downsides of their careers. Even longtime veterans entering the twilight of their careers, such as Michael Finley, Boris Diaw, and Brent Barry, had success in Popovich's system and extended their NBA life spans. They were part of a solar system of talent and duty orbiting around the Spurs trio of Hall of Famers—Duncan, Tony Parker, and Manu Ginóbili.

Popovich is one of the best at making adjustments. When he took over, Robinson was the man and everything ran through him. Pop used traditional lineups with traditional positions. The Spurs drafted big man Tim Duncan in 1997, the undisputed best player in college and the heir apparent to Robinson. But in the meantime, with them playing together, Pop switched to a twin-towers approach. The Spurs won their first championship in 1999, the lockout-shortened season. When Robinson retired, Pop went back to the one-big-man offense. Eventually, Duncan made the transition from power forward, his natural position, to center so the Spurs could get an extra perimeter player in the lineup.

Popovich's greatest adjustment was arguably to the three-pointer.

He is definitely in the get-off-my-lawn contingency who railed against three-pointers as if they were produced in Area 51. But Popovich still took advantage of them. In the 1996–97 season, the Spurs ranked twenty-sixth in the NBA in three-pointers made per game. By the end of the 2012–13 season, the Spurs ranked seventh. Like other teams, they started spreading the floor and taking advantage of the math of a more valuable shot. The year of their last championship, 2013–14, they finished the regular season tops in the NBA in three-point percentage.

"I hate it, but I always have. I've hated the three for 20 years," he told legendary Bulls reporter Sam Smith in 2018. "If we're going to make it a different game, let's have a four-point play. Because if everybody likes the three, they'll really like the four. People will jump out of their seats if you have a five-point play. It will be great. There's no basketball anymore, there's no beauty in it. It's pretty boring. But it is what it is and you need to work with it."

Not quite his way or the highway.

THE CULTURAL IMPACT

Tim Duncan was a no-brainer when he came out of Wake Forest, so the Spurs don't get much credit for discovering him. But he is from the U.S. Virgin Islands. So, though technically a U.S. citizen, Duncan, in the culture of basketball, is akin to an international player because he comes from outside the American construct of hoops.

In 1999, with the fifty-seventh overall pick, the Spurs drafted a twenty-two-year-old shooting guard from Argentina. He wasn't even ready to come to the NBA yet and spent three more years playing professional ball in Italy before making his NBA debut with the Spurs in 2002.

Manu Ginóbili became the ultimate sixth man with his penetration and passing. He was the architect of the Euro step so popular in today's game. He's one of the great competitors in league history. He broke the reputation of European players being soft and finesse players. Ginóbili earned the respect of legends with his relentlessness, his knack for big performances, and persistent classiness.

In 2001, with the twenty-eighth pick, the Spurs reached for a nineteen-year-old German-born French point guard. It was late in the first round but, still, first-round picks are valuable.

Tony Parker grew into the engine of the offense, his speed and craftiness churning the Spurs along like a hamster providing light with its hustle. Parker didn't look like much: at six foot two, 185 pounds, he was small and frail looking, his jersey too baggy to stay on straight. But he attacked the lane as if he were twice his size. He would drive among the trees and somehow contort himself and scoop it from an odd angle and it would go in.

The Spurs had become basketball's UN.

His impact can't be overstated. He was a six-time All-Star who for stretches carried the Spurs.

In 2002, with the No. 56 pick, the Spurs drafted Ginóbili's teammate from the Argentinian national team: forward Luis Scola.

It wasn't quite clear what the Spurs were doing until the 2002–03 season. Duncan was a certified All-NBA player by this point. Parker made the All-Rookie team the year before and really took a leap in his second season: 15.5 points and 5.3 assists. Ginóbili was a crafty reserve who did a bit of everything when he came in—scored, ran the point, made plays on defense, picked up the pace, and drove Popovich nuts with his unpredictability. San Antonio won the title that year and started a movement. The following season, after a trade and a free-agent signing, the Spurs' top six players in the rotation included Duncan, Parker, Ginóbili, center Rasho Nesterović, and forward Hedo Türkoğlu.

San Antonio drafted Slovenian guard Beno Udrih in 2004, French center Ian Mahinmi in 2005, Brazilian center Tiago Splitter in 2007, and Slovenian guard Goran Dragić in 2007 (though two days later the Spurs traded Dragić to Phoenix). Plus, Australian guard Patty Mills, Latvian forward Davis Bertans, and Italian shooting guard Marco Belinelli thrived in San Antonio.

The Spurs had become basketball's UN.

In the summer of 2004, just how far ahead of the curve the Spurs were became clear. Three Olympics after the Dream Team established America's supremacy in basketball, Argentina illustrated how the rest of the world was catching up. Led by Ginóbili and Scola, both Spurs draft picks (though Scola didn't enter the NBA until 2008 after being traded to Houston), Argentina took the gold medal in the 2004 Summer Olympics, an upset that gave massive credibility to international basketball. Before long, the rest of the league was scrambling to catch up to the Spurs.

Giannis Antetokounmpo and Luka Dončić are two of the transcendent young stars of the league. The NBA draft is increasingly international at the top. Every team now has international scouting and spots on their roster for developing young talent, often from overseas. And much of the credit is due to the Spurs' commitment to and success at tapping into the global pool of players. If San Antonio has done nothing else, it has made international players respectable. The Spurs unlocked the paradigms of how good non-American players can be and how a team can be built with them, even around them.

Several positive outcomes have stemmed, at least in part, from the Spurs' investment in international players. For one, basketball has grown into such a global game. The Spurs winning titles with Ginóbili and Parker, coupled with the success of Dirk Nowitzki and others, has inspired a new generation of NBA talent. But also, San Antonio raised the bar on scouting. Any team sticking exclusively to NCAA talent is simply limiting its potential. Finding the gems overseas can make the difference between a championship or not. Meager international scouting plans simply won't cut it.

Another good outcome: The basketball fan is much more internationally savvy because of the influx of international players. Their success promotes a desire to understand the homelands and culture of players from abroad. People at least take the time to know where they are from instead of just calling them Europeans or Africans. Their talent garners respect where there once was doubt. The Spurs have led the charge in globalizing the NBA and its American fans. That was so vivid during the 2020 NBA restart. When NBA players used the bubble as a way to participate in the country's reckoning with racial injustice, they were joined by players like Dončić (Slovenian), Jusuf Nurkić (Bosnian), and Steven Adams (New Zealander) plastering statements of equality in their native tongues on their jerseys.

We know *Respectez Biso* is French for "Respect Us" because Serge Ibaka—a Republic of the Congo–born big man who lived in France before becoming a naturalized citizen in Spain, where he played basketball—wore it on his Toronto Raptors jersey.

As much as titles, international inclusion is what San Antonio has given the culture of basketball.

THE VILLAIN

Easy. The no-BBQ-having, phony, Hollywood diva, celebrity-obsessed, mocha-Frappuccino-sipping, always with the AirPods in the ear, bleeping Lakers of Los Angeles.

They had just hired legendary Bulls coach Phil Jackson in 1999 following the lockout-shortened season in which the Spurs captured their first NBA championship. Shortly after he accepted the job, Jackson did an interview with ESPN where he shared his thoughts about the lockout year.

Essentially, Jackson told reporters a fifty-game regular season wasn't enough to validate a true champion, boldly proclaiming the league should put an asterisk next to San Antonio's 1998–99 title. He didn't think they deserved the same status as regular champions. Spurs players immediately put a target on his back.

"It completely ignores all the hard work we put in that season," former Spurs guard Avery Johnson told Jackie MacMullan of ESPN.

Jackson was already throwing shots at the defending champs before he even coached a game for the Lakers. In retrospect, his words were the catalyst for one of the league's best rivalries of the early 2000s. But the Zen Master had won six NBA championships during his tenure with the Bulls, between 1987 and 1998, establishing himself as one of the greatest coaches of all time. He threw verbal jabs because he could back them up. The Spurs eliminated Los Angeles in the second round of the playoffs in 1999, which prompted Jackson's hiring. So, clearly, his intentions were meant to give his new team a competitive edge. He knew San Antonio was the team to beat out West, and discrediting them publicly was psychological warfare. And in Jackson's first season as head coach, his Lakers were dominant.

Later that season, in February 2000, David Robinson made his tenth and final All-Star game appearance. During Western Conference player introductions, he stepped through a glowing stage prop of the San Francisco–Oakland Bay Bridge, shrouded by smoke and with a wide smile on his face. Robinson approached the handshake line comprising coaches, league executives, and his fellow All-Star players. As the Western Conference coach, Jackson was first in the pecking order. He reached his hand out to Robinson for a handshake. Robinson ignored him.

Not even All-Star weekend camaraderie could douse the flames of the blooming Spurs and Lakers rivalry. As for the All-Star game itself, O'Neal and

Tim Duncan were named co-MVPs. And after the game, O'Neal snatched the MVP trophy from Duncan and said, "You already have one of those rings, so I'm taking the trophy."

This was war.

Los Angeles, led by their superstar duo in Kobe Bryant and Shaquille O'Neal, won 67 games (compared to the Spurs' 53). O'Neal was MVP after and the Lakers took down the Indiana Pacers to capture their twelfth NBA Championship, Jackson's seventh title. The Spurs, on the other hand, were eliminated in the first round of the playoffs by the Phoenix Suns.

"My mom told me when I was little not to use the term 'hate,'" said guard Antonio Daniels, who played four seasons with San Antonio and won a title. "It's just you didn't want to see the Lakers win. It wasn't a hate thing by any stretch of the imagination. You don't hate anybody you competed against. It's just the fact that you really wanted to beat them. If somebody else was playing them, you really wanted that somebody else to beat them. You know? That's what a rivalry is. If you had a chance to beat them, you wanted to beat them. I think that was the big thing. I don't think there was hate there, at least from the San Antonio side. It's just the fact that you wanted to beat the Lakers at all costs."

The Lakers and Spurs would meet again in the 2001 Western Conference Finals.

Despite the Spurs' home-court advantage, they proved to be no match for Jackson's Lakers. Los Angeles swept San Antonio. The average margin of victory was a staggering 22 points, which was essentially the Lakers twisting the proverbial knife and assuredly leaving an asterisk-shaped hole in the Spurs' flesh.

The Lakers went on to defeat Philadelphia for back-to-back titles. The next season, San Antonio was eliminated by the Lakers again, this time in the Western Conference Semifinals. Los Angeles went on to three-peat.

So if you ever wonder why the Spurs and their fans get a special kind of joy out of beating the Lakers, that's why. They got to feel the tingling sense of revenge in 2002–03. San Antonio knocked the Lakers out of the playoffs in the second round on its way to another championship.

When the teams met in 2004, David Robinson was retired, Phil Jackson had left the game, and the Lakers had assembled a super team featuring Bryant,

O'Neal, Gary Payton, and Karl Malone. In Game 5, with the series tied 2–2, Duncan hit a long improbable fadeaway jumper—OVER SHAQ!—to give the Spurs a 73–72 lead with 0.4 seconds left in regulation. Victory was assured. The players celebrated. The fans went their special kind of San Antonio crazy. Spurs Nation was salivating over eliminating the Lakers again.

Then Derek Fisher.

Payton inbounded the ball to Fisher. Running toward the sideline with his back to the rim, he caught the pass, turned, and shot it, all in one motion. Incredibly, stunningly, it went in. Fisher sped off the court and straight into the locker room. Didn't even stick around for replay.

If you ever want to get chased out of the Alamo, say you believe Fisher did all of that in less than four-tenths of a second. Replay shows the ball was out of

his hands when the clock hit zero. But even Fisher later acknowledged he might have benefited from the clock starting a hair late.

"A prayer was answered," Payton said of Fisher's game winner.

Not one from the Spurs.

During the 2000s, the Spurs and Lakers combined for seven titles and nine Finals appearances, and they faced each other five times. Two teams constantly battling for NBA supremacy, both with vastly different ideologies. The Spurs were a small-market icon all about team basketball, led by their humble superstar in Duncan. While the Lakers were typically associated with glamour and flash, were in the second largest market in the nation, and were leaning heavily on their star power.

They were polar opposites, attracting each other in clashes that bolstered both squads.

"The talent, the coaching, everything in San Antonio was kind of a perfect storm," Bryant said on a podcast. "If they weren't in the picture we probably would have run ten [championships] in a row."

THE CRAZIEST STAT

Someone in America was born in April 1998, the same year the Spurs made the playoffs for the first time under Popovich. Some twenty-two years later, that person owned an undergraduate degree and was a year into their career. Or perhaps that person just finished one of those five-year programs to earn a bachelor's and a master's degree. And in August 2020, in the restart bubble in Orlando, was the first time in this person's life the NBA playoffs started and the Spurs were not in them.

Twenty-two years. That's tied for the longest streak of consecutive play-off appearances in NBA history (Philadelphia 76ers, 1950–1971). Over this twenty-two-year span, San Antonio won a league-best 69.9 percent of its games (1228–528) with 170 playoff victories, six conference titles, and five championships.

11

THE KING DYNASTY

He's been to ten NBA Finals in his career, including eight straight. Only Bill Russell has been to as many Finals or eight straight of them. He's won four titles, one more than Larry Bird. He won three titles in a span of five years, a feat accomplished by Magic Johnson and Stephen Curry. He reigned over a league, in a way reminiscent of Michael Jordan. He's spent the better part of two decades contending for a title, a la Tim Duncan. He's lost six times in Finals, two fewer than Jerry West. If he stays healthy, he will break Kareem Abdul-Jabbar's all-time scoring record.

No, LeBron James may have never played for a dynasty. The Miami Heat were close and in the most favorable of lights could be deemed one. But giving those teams the status of a dynasty wouldn't even do LeBron the greatest service. His four-year stint with the Heat was but a segment in a career held up as the standard for the NBA. He has put three franchises on his back, including the Cavaliers twice, and rendered a few otherwise legitimate championship contenders without hope.

"If you can find somebody to stop LeBron in these moments, I'll give you $100," then Toronto guard DeMar DeRozan told reporters after Game 2 of the 2017 Eastern Conference Finals. Then after the Cavaliers finished the sweep of the Raptors, DeRozan added:

"If we had LeBron on our team, too, we woulda won."

He has outdueled three future Hall of Famers in his three championship victories (a young Kevin Durant, Duncan, and Curry). And, of course, he made history by being the first to come back from a 3–1 lead in the Finals.

LeBron James is a dynasty unto his own.

One of the biggest figures in all of sports, LeBron has been the center of everything that happens in the NBA over at least the last decade. The balance of the league's power shifts when he moves. He is the ruler with which modern stars are measured. His greatness has bridged generations. He ushered in a new era of player empowerment. And after seventeen seasons, he keeps piling up records and eye-popping numbers.

The 2020 NBA playoffs, held at Disney World in Orlando because of the pandemic, was a historic battle of attrition and mental resilience. He left July 9 to quarantine and enter the NBA bubble—a confined premises isolated for the NBA on the Disney World complex—where twenty-two teams finished the 2019–20 regular season and the entire playoffs were held. Players were tested every day. Leaving required another round of quarantine before returning. They wore bracelets to track their oxygen levels and keep integrity with social distancing. They had no physical contact with the outside world. Couldn't even DoorDash. No nightclubs. No family time. No mind-clearing drives. No marching in protests. Their families and friends weren't allowed until the second round of the playoffs, which began two months after they arrived. At the end of it all, three months later in October, LeBron James was hoisting another trophy. He was thirty-five years old.

Four-time MVP (and probably should have at least one more). Four-time champion. Four-time Finals MVP. A thirteen-time first-team All-NBA selection. A five-time first-team All-Defense selection. He has a scoring title (in 2008) and an assist title (in 2020), one of only six players ever to finish tops in both categories in his career.

He is the NBA all-time leader in playoff wins, games, minutes, points, field goals, free throws, steals, and win shares. He is second in playoff triple-doubles, as well as second in NBA Finals history in total points, assists, three-point field goals, and steals.

But the accolades aren't why he is a dynasty unto himself. It's more about the longevity of his reign and the uniqueness of his impact. Even when he loses, he's the story. The 2007 NBA Finals was less about San Antonio winning again and more about whether LeBron James would ever have a real shot at getting his first title. When he lost the 2015 championship to the Warriors, the dominant discussion was whether he should be the Finals MVP even in defeat. Because of his ardent supporters and diligent detractors, LeBron shapes the dialogue like no other player. The NBA universe has a way of orbiting around him.

It doesn't mean he is perfection personified. Criticism finds fertile ground on his name. But this era of basketball cannot be told without the successes and failures of LeBron James.

Every player who has a credible stake in the theoretical and unanswerable Greatest of All Time debate has been part of a dynasty. LeBron is without question in that conversation.

Part of the allure of LeBron is that the public has watched him grow up. A dynasty in the traditional sense usually features a succession of people from the same family who play a prominent role in the business or government. From the Kennedys to the Kardashians to the Ewings and even the Roys—the appeal is the transition of power and how it unfolds. LeBron has been on a journey from promising youth to sovereign empire, and it has all played out like a drama series. The only comparable player is Kobe Bryant, who entered the NBA as a phenom at eighteen. Because of Kobe, the nation's interest skewed younger. While Kobe wasn't a household name until he got to the Lakers, LeBron was at sixteen years old. He's been the heir apparent since he was deemed "the Chosen One" on a 2002 cover of *Sports Illustrated* at seventeen years old.

Ruler of the NBA is a mighty legacy. The face of the league is a royal position in the landscape of sports. The search for a successor after Michael Jordan's dynasty led directly to Kobe Bryant, who felt like the most natural evolution from His Airness. But the entire time, the reign of LeBron looked to be a wholly unique empire because he was a player unlike any the sport has ever seen.

LeBron became all that his potential suggested and more. He exceeded the expectations set so high above him. In the process, after twenty years of tracking his every move, he now has a legion. There are many massive, passionate, and loyal fan bases in sports that fervently, and obnoxiously, ride for their team. Celtics fans, Lakers fans, Warriors fans are the NBA's best examples of such. These fan bases have been known to take over opposing arenas and war on social media as if it were a sworn duty to their republic. If the Knicks and Bulls ever produce a winner again, they'd make this list, too. But they haven't produced one, in part, because of LeBron. His dominance over the Eastern Conference for so long snuffed out the viability of most franchises and, in the process, created his own cult following that rivals the followings of whole teams. They are loyal to LeBron. His team is their team. His journey is their journey. From Cleveland to Miami, back to Cleveland, and now in Los Angeles.

Because when you are the dynasty, then the dynasty is wherever you are.

NBA Finals Appearances

2007 (L)	2011 (L)	2012 (W)
2013 (W)	2014 (L)	2015 (L)
2016 (W)	2017 (L)	2018 (L)

THE CULTURAL IMPACT

LeBron James might end up as the NBA's all-time leading scorer. He is on pace to eclipse Kareem Abdul-Jabbar's record of 38,387 career points in the 2022–23 season.

But even if he does, that still may not be the most defining part of his legacy. His exceptionalism already has him in the conversation with Michael Jordan as the greatest of all time. But perhaps his most lasting impact is the era of player empowerment he ushered in and championed. What LeBron has done with his own career has served as a blueprint for the star athlete who wants to maximize his earning potential, his influence, and his power. LeBron has combined a commercial success similar to Jordan, an off-the-court business success akin to Magic, and the narrative control of Kobe Bryant. He has aptly wielded it all, accruing enough cache to change the industry.

LeBron has done what no athlete has done before by being at the absolute top of the game, on the court and off, and assuming complete control of his enterprise. While the history of athletes has been corporations and companies profiting from them and kicking them back a portion, LeBron flipped it by dictating to the machine and making it work for him. And he can do so because there is no bigger name in the NBA. He has shown players how to leverage their own celebrity and influence instead of being leveraged.

He turned his high school teammate into a renowned business partner. He made a friend he met in the airport one of the most powerful agents in the league. They started their own production company, management agency, and even HBO show. His sovereignty as a megastar set a precedent others could follow.

Another example is his activism. His proclamations and statements became more than a PR stunt and a hashtag. He was at the forefront of the modern athlete's involvement in social activism and racial justice. At a time when elders were calling for more professional athletes to use their platform, LeBron did.

He used his name and clout to start a school: I Promise School in his home-town of Akron, Ohio. It serves hundreds of kids, who all receive dedicated educational and emotional support and whose parents can receive free GED classes or visit the school's stocked food and clothing center. Uniforms are pro-vided for free, as are bicycles and helmets for every student. Taco Tuesday meal packs began rolling out to I Promise families in March 2020 amid the onset of the coronavirus pandemic. And the I Promise Program supports more than one thousand students throughout Akron, Ohio's public school district. Years before, upon its founding in 2004, the LeBron James Family Foundation began pouring money into Akron and beyond. Both the program and the school, which opened its doors in 2018, are literal embodiments of the declaration, "Black lives matter."

LeBron's activism didn't begin as a rebuttal to Fox News host Laura Ingraham's "shut up and dribble" remark in 2018.

In 2012, while playing for the Miami Heat, LeBron donned a hoodie with his teammates as a solemn nod to the fatal shooting of seventeen-year-old Trayvon Martin. In 2014, he wore an "I Can't Breathe" T-shirt, the final words of Eric Garner, a forty-seven-year-old father of six who was killed by a police officer using an illegal chokehold. With his following, he brought massive awareness.

The fatal shooting of a relative baby in Cleveland, twelve-year-old Tamir Rice, in 2015 prompted LeBron to call for stronger gun control, which also addresses so-called "Black-on-Black" violence, which is, in other words, gun violence plaguing Black communities that are overwhelmed by poverty and often over-looked by local, state, and national leaders.

A pair of LeBron 15s that don the word EQUALITY across the back now belong to the Smithsonian's National Museum of African American History and Culture, where a Muhammad Ali exhibit exists partly because of a multi-million-dollar donation fueled by LeBron's foundation. When asked about those black-and-white shoes, which he wore in 2017 while playing against the Washington Wizards in the nation's capital, LeBron responded, "Us as Americans, no matter the skin color, no matter the race, no matter who you are,

I think we all have to understand having equal rights and being able to stand for something and speak for something and keeping the conversation going."

It was also 2017 when someone spray-painted the N-word across one of his homes, just ahead of the NBA Finals. In a press conference, LeBron was not without words.

"Hate in America, especially for African-Americans, is living every day. No matter how much money you have, no matter how famous you are, no matter how many people admire you, you know being Black in America is tough. And we got a long way to go, for us as a society and for us as African-Americans, until we feel equal in America."

In a 2018 interview with CNN's Don Lemon, LeBron said Trayvon's death marked a moment when he knew his voice and platform "had to be used for more than just sports." And then there were his words to the Class of 2020.

"Most importantly, building your community is how you change the world. Unfortunately, the system does not solve the real problem. Education, violence, racism—they must be solved in the street," LeBron said to pandemic-trapped high school seniors watching online. "Class of 2020, the world has changed. You will determine how we rebuild, and I ask that you make your community your priority."

His activism hasn't created a mold. But it has set the standard for the current generation of athletes. Many others don't need LeBron's example. But because of his magnitude, the spotlight was on him, just as it was on Jordan, and James didn't shy away. When NBA players were determined to maintain their activism in the 2020 bubble, "more than an athlete" went from a declaration to a grass-roots platform. The entire league was using the 2020 NBA restart as a call for justice and equality.

Before Game 5 of first round series between Milwaukee and Orlando, on August 26, 2020, George Hill was so broken up about the shooting of Jacob Blake by Kenosha, Wisconsin, police that he decided he wasn't going to play. It was another example of an unarmed Black man being shot by the police, and Blake wound up paralyzed from the waist down after he was shot seven times in the back by officer Rusten Sheskey, which Blake's three sons witnessed from the back seat of his car. When Hill decided not to play, his teammates joined him, and the Bucks, opting to forfeit the game, did not come out of the locker room for Game 5. The Magic declined to accept the forfeit and the game became a joint walkout. The players from Houston and Oklahoma City, sched-uled to play later, jointly decided not to play as well. Before long, the entire slate of games for three days were postponed. The NBA players' walkout triggered protests and walkouts in other sports. It also sparked a closed-door meeting with players on what to do next.

James, one of the most outspoken proponents of joining the bubble, was ready to abandon the entire postseason and go home. He had his teammates with the Lakers and the Los Angeles Clippers roster on board with him. But after some passionate debate among the players—several players wanted to stay in the bubble and use the platform—it was determined either way they needed a plan. So James reached out to his friend, someone with experience handling crises and coming up with a course of action: former president Barack Obama. The players emerged unified.

LeBron, in his own way, has picked up the baton once held by Muhammad Ali, Bill Russell, Kareem Abdul-Jabbar, Jim Brown, and even Colin Kaepernick. His involvements are carefully curated, calculated, and relatively low risk com-pared to his ancestors in sports activism. He has no shortage of dissenters and people who have grown weary of his antics and forays into politics and race relations. But he's been dealing with a segment of fan disapproval for years and it couldn't stop the growth of his empire. Seriously, what's anybody going to do to LeBron?

Within his brand of activism lies a boldness that increases with age, business savvy, and unconditional support from loyalists. He isn't afraid to call others to the carpet, as he did former president Donald Trump, Drew Brees, and Donald Sterling. Nor was he quiet about attempts of voter suppression, which was a hot topic ahead of the 2020 presidential election. His collaborative non-profit organization, More Than a Vote, was an answer to that, aiming to recruit poll workers in Black electoral districts, among other initiatives. Staples Center was a voting center for the 2020 election.

"More than an athlete" went from a declaration to a grassroots platform. The entire league was using the 2020 NBA restart as a call for justice and equality.

LeBron and his business partner, Maverick Carter, raised $100 million to launch the SpringHill Company, a media company with an unapologetic agenda—content maker and distributor bent on giving voices to creators with something impactful to say.

That's on top of his media company, Uninterrupted, which grew into an "athlete empowerment brand" that has adopted the "more than an athlete" mentality. The phrase has been commodified into sold-out sweatshirts and T-shirts. Sales from customizable tees bearing the question, "DO YOU UNDERSTAND NOW?" went to the NAACP's Legal Defense Fund.

Those tees were on sale for eight days, four hours, and six minutes—an ominous nod to the eight minutes and forty-six seconds the Minneapolis police officer knelt on the neck of George Floyd, a forty-six-year-old father of five who died while in police custody. A video that plays on the website flashes a series of phrases that all begin with, "Shut up and . . . " as a basketball dribbles at an uneasy staccato that, at times, echoes of gunshots. That video also lives on LeBron's Instagram, where he's amassed more than 70 million followers and counting.

Others have followed a similar playbook, beginning to define for themselves what it means to be more than an athlete. Players like Stephen Curry, Kevin Durant, and Carmelo Anthony have used their enormous platforms to bring awareness to injustices and promote change. LeBron's teammate Kyle Kuzma and his activism within his hometown of Flint, Michigan, is just one example of the era of activism LeBron has led. And it's hardly a coincidence the very league LeBron has redefined over the years decided to support its players in their desire to contribute to the racial justice movement. The NBA even emblazoned the courts with "Black Lives Matter" when the games reconvened in the bubble.

LeBron isn't the only one, and there is a new generation of even younger athletes getting involved and speaking out. But they do so on roads paved by James. From endorsing candidates to speaking out against the governmental powers, to maintaining leverage over franchises, to owning the rights to his story and his voice instead of leasing it out, LeBron has shown the players just how much power they have.

THE DECISION

It began as the first blight on what was a pristine résumé. But history has shown it to be the opening salvo of a revolution.

When LeBron lost the 2007 NBA Finals, concluding his fourth season, it certainly felt like the beginning of his arrival. He averaged a career-high 31.4 points in 2005–06, his third season, but lost a grueling seven-game series to Detroit. The next season, he scaled Mt. Pistons in six games, including an epic performance in Game 5 when he closed the game with 25 straight points.

But when the Spurs easily swept the Cavaliers in the 2007 Finals, the clock started ticking. Cleveland was so overmatched by the Western Conference power, it underscored his meager supporting cast. He lost a seven-game series to the eventual champion Celtics in 2008. Then 2009 ended with an Eastern Conference Finals loss to Orlando. After another early exit at the hands of the Celtics in 2010, LeBron passed on the handshakes and hugs that have become tradition at the end of a series. He ripped off his jersey as he headed to the locker room, and into free agency.

Just shy of two months later, LeBron was on national television declaring he was "taking his talents to South Beach."

He was ridiculed for how he handled his announcement—even though it raised $6 million for charity—and was attacked for leaving Cleveland. He became a villain. But what hindsight reveals was how he changed the NBA, perhaps forever.

First, he orchestrated his own free agency. Such matters were normally left up to general managers and agents. Players have historically been pawns in an NBA off-season that is more like a high-stakes fantasy draft. But LeBron partnered with his friends, Dwyane Wade and Chris Bosh, and they plotted out their own plan. He became the unofficial general manager, manipulating who would be his costar and where they would play.

Joining the Heat with Wade and Bosh was a huge turning point in LeBron's career. Instead of waiting for the Cavaliers to surround him with the help he needed, he left to make his own way. He wound up with teammates much closer to his talent level, giving him a much better chance to take down the powers of the league.

He paid a price for it as the move nearly destroyed his legacy. For a time he was everything wrong with the NBA, selfish for making it all about him, weak for teaming up with superstars, a diva for choosing glamourous South Beach over the Midwest grind. And when they lost to Dallas in the 2011 NBA Finals, it only turned up the vitriol.

But LeBron bounced back, winning back-to-back titles, including an epic seven-game revenge win over San Antonio in 2013. After the Heat lost in 2014, the second chip in his revolutionary decision came into play.

While dictating his new team and new situation, LeBron didn't sacrifice his leverage. He signed a six-year, $110 million contract when he went to Miami. But he had an early termination option (ETO) in his contract for the final two years. He exercised it in 2014, becoming a free agent again.

Security is usually the priority for NBA players. A player in LeBron's situation, with eleven years of service, would normally want the longest contract possible at the highest rate to extend his financial prime. But James exchanged long-term security for freedom. Salaries are suppressed anyway by contract maximums. LeBron knew he could command the most possible, and he made so much money off the court he could afford to settle for a little less.

The short-term contracts he preferred made his tenure more like a presidential term where the reelection efforts begin right after inauguration. Except it wasn't LeBron campaigning. The threat of his pending departure kept his employer always campaigning. His team couldn't afford to not put the best roster together, or not focus on winning immediately, or do what it took to please him, because LeBron was always a year or two from leaving.

In 2014, when he signed with Cleveland, returning to the franchise owner who berated him when he left the first time, LeBron doubled down on his freedom-over-stability stance. He signed a two-year, $42.2 million contract with the Cavaliers, including another ETO. Knowing any team would have him, LeBron used the threat of his departure to keep Cleveland in the palm of his hand. He opted out after one year and signed another two-year deal with an ETO. He opted out again in 2016 and re-signed a new deal. This time, it was for $100 million over three years. Yes, with another ETO.

This blueprint would be used by maximum-contract worthy players moving forward. Kevin Durant was the biggest name to do so, keeping an opt-out for all three years he spent with the Warriors. Kawhi Leonard signed a three-year deal with the Clippers in 2019 that included an opt-out after the second year.

COMING HOME

It was the moment that will be remembered forever, the exclamation point in a legendary career.

"I set out a goal—two years—when I came back to bring a championship to this city. I gave everything that I had. I poured my heart, my blood, my sweat, my tears into this game. Against all odds. Against all odds."

LeBron surprised many when he announced he was leaving Miami and going back to the Cavaliers. He announced it in an article on the cover of *Sports Illustrated* that read, simply:

I'm Coming Home.

This was the purpose, to make this kind of history, to create this moment, this feeling. The kid from Akron delivered the long-awaited championship to his hometown team. And like a lion declaring dominion over his pride, calling out his supremacy, LeBron roared.

"CLEVELAAAAAND. THIS IS FOR YOOOUUUUUU!"

Winning back-to-back championships with Miami puts him in a select group of consecutive championship winners. But the most dynastic accomplishment he ever pulled off was coming back from a 3–1 deficit in the Finals against Golden State. The Warriors had won a record 73 games and were going for a second consecutive title. They'd blown out Cleveland the first two games and eked out a win in Game 4, putting the series seemingly out of reach.

Undoubtedly, LeBron had some major luck fall his way. Draymond Green was suspended for Game 5 after racking up too many flagrant foul points. Andrew Bogut, the Warriors' starting center, was injured in Game 5 and knocked out of the series. And Curry, who sprained his MCL earlier in the playoffs, was less than 100 percent on the court. The perfect storm set up LeBron to make history. But he still had to seize it.

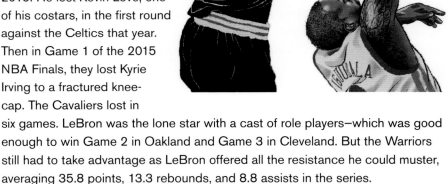

On top of that, it was he who had the bad injury luck in 2015. He lost Kevin Love, one of his costars, in the first round against the Celtics that year. Then in Game 1 of the 2015 NBA Finals, they lost Kyrie Irving to a fractured knee-cap. The Cavaliers lost in six games. LeBron was the lone star with a cast of role players—which was good enough to win Game 2 in Oakland and Game 3 in Cleveland. But the Warriors still had to take advantage as LeBron offered all the resistance he could muster, averaging 35.8 points, 13.3 rebounds, and 8.8 assists in the series.

In 2016, it was LeBron's turn to take advantage. Golden State jumped out to a commanding 3–1 advantage in the series, a deficit the Warriors had just overcome in the Western Conference Finals. But no one had done it in the Finals before.

"He looked around and said, 'You know what guys? It's written,'" Kevin Love said, recalling LeBron's locker-room pep talk. "'We're going to win tomorrow night. We're going to have a huge game. It's going to be tough. It's going to come down to the last few minutes. We're not losing at home. Game 7, anything can happen.' That's how it played out. It still gives me chills thinking about it."

It played out almost as LeBron predicted. The Cavaliers switched to their black, sleeved jerseys for the rest of the series, becoming the first team to ever wear sleeved jerseys in the Finals. And he pulled off the feat that would set him apart and make him dynastic.

THE RISING TIDE

ESPN's Dave McMenamin told the behind-the-scenes story of when LeBron decided to return to Cleveland and the conversation he had with his teammate James Jones. When LeBron was plotting his exit from Miami, he broke the news to Jones, whom he calls his favorite teammate of all time. Jones is a Miami native, who arrived to the Heat before LeBron, so the local team losing the King stung a little for Jones. But his local ties to Miami meant he also understood why LeBron was going home.

But then LeBron hit him with the plot twist: He wanted Jones to join him. LeBron was planning to bring a title home to Cleveland, and he needed someone to help him transform the culture of the Cavaliers. So after six years with his beloved Heat, to which LeBron blessed two more rings and a status they never imagined, Jones went to Cleveland to help his friend do something similar in his home.

"I told J.J., as long as I'm playing, he's going to be around," LeBron told ESPN in 2015. "He's not allowed to stop playing basketball. So, I'm going to make sure I got a roster spot for him. I love him. He's the greatest teammate I've ever had."

Jones retired from the NBA in 2017, years after it was clear his best days were on the horizon behind him. After his first season with LeBron, in Miami, Jones's minutes dropped noticeably. He was in the Cavaliers' rotation for the 2014–15 playoffs. Outside of that, he was mostly a bit player and a strong locker room influence.

But he went to seven consecutive NBA Finals and won three championships. In 2019, he was hired as general manager of the Phoenix Suns.

Jones was the personification of arguably the most telling evidence of LeBron's greatness. He is one of the most technically sound, physically gifted, and most durable athletes to ever play in the NBA. But in basketball, a barometer of eliteness is how much better a player makes his teammates, and LeBron has a list of players who have tasted glory simply because they played with him.

LeBron, because of his clout, popularized the pattern of superteam building. Technically, it has been going on since the beginning of the NBA. The modern era of basketball saw Kevin Garnett and Ray Allen join Paul Pierce in Boston in 2007 and win a title. But those three, at best, were on the back end of their primes. When LeBron joined Miami, three All-NBA players in the peak of their powers created a new era of collaborations. But it was in response to earlier in his career when Cleveland surrounded him with role players, most of whom he needed to prop up with his own ability. Before playing with Dwyane Wade, the only time LeBron played with a Hall of Famer was the year before with Shaquille O'Neal, who was in his twentieth season and well past his prime.

Because of LeBron, players often find themselves playing at a level, and on stages, that belies their ability. Some players have been so boosted by LeBron they parlayed it into contracts they never lived up to. Some were never quite as good once they left his side, even a few fell out of the league. But many got paid.

Daniel Gibson, Matthew Dellavedova, Sasha Pavlović, Timofey Mozgoz, Norris Cole—they all received national prominence playing next to LeBron and disappeared into oblivion after leaving his side. Add them to the likes of Jones, Tristan Thompson, and Anderson Varejão, and you could directly trace more than $313 million of new contracts earned from playing with LeBron.

And what about the players who extended the relevance of their careers next to LeBron? Ben Wallace, Wally Szczerbiak, Mike Bibby, Eddie House, Rashard Lewis, Chris Andersen, Shane Battier, Channing Frye, Kyle Korver, Mike Miller, Richard Jefferson, Deron Williams, Shawn Marion, Dwight Howard, J. R. Smith. Even Ray Allen transitioned from superstar into an ideal role player next to LeBron with the Heat, and Allen hit one of the most clutch shots in NBA history in Game 6 of the 2013 Finals.

But in basketball a barometer of eliteness is how much better a player makes his teammates, and LeBron has a list of players who have tasted glory simply because they played with him.

Kyrie Irving and Anthony Davis became champions and shined on the biggest stage—a stage they never reached when they had the chance to lead their own teams, because their greatness merged with LeBron's.

THE VILLAIN

If we're looking at the player who would be his greatest adversary, an easy choice would be Stephen Curry. Or maybe it's Tim Duncan, or Kevin Durant, both of whom beat LeBron twice in the Finals. But Duncan never got the buzz Curry achieved and Durant did it when he joined Curry's team. Curry was the one most juxtaposed with LeBron, the one who seemed most poised to take LeBron's crown because of how dominant the Warriors were. LeBron went from having Curry as a pupil in his basketball camp, to supporting Curry while he was starring at Davidson College, to duking it out with Curry in the NBA Finals. No player in his career has threatened LeBron's supremacy as much as Curry, who has more wins over LeBron in the Finals than any other player, who emerged from almost nowhere to create a juggernaut that threatened LeBron's reign.

But Curry was good for LeBron. Curry was the motivation LeBron needed to reassert his supremacy. With Kobe and Duncan faded from elite levels, Curry gave LeBron a new foe, a new era to conquer, a new style of play to adjust to and adopt. So yeah, many LeBron supporters saw, and still see, Curry as a villain in the story line of the King.

But the reality is, LeBron is the greatest villain in his own story.

He's had his jersey burned. Cavaliers' owner Dan Gilbert turned a basic font, Comic Sans, into vindictive calligraphy. James has been attacked for years—for being so hyped, for getting a $90 million shoe deal before he played a game, for not winning a title, for not having a killer instinct, for not shaking hands after a series, for leaving in free agency, for how he left, for his balding hair, for not being able to shoot, for not shooting, for not entering the dunk contest, for complaining to officials too much, for his free throws, for bowling over players, for never getting called for fouls, for disrespecting coaches, for his treatment of teammates. Despite his supreme athleticism, LeBron has always been a stationary target for vitriol.

Some of it is indeed his own doing, for sure. He can be passive-aggressive. He has been known to skirt responsibility publicly while making power moves privately. He can be stubborn. He does belittle his teammates sometimes, even if inadvertently or justified. Yeah, he can come off as arrogant, purporting himself as the epicenter of whatever space he's in. He's also been known to go with the woe-is-me posture, playing the underdog card a little too strongly for a guy who has it all. He even once belittled fans for being miserable in their lives. To be sure, some of these slights are merely perceived, born of speculation, which is also partly his fault because he isn't the most transparent. He keeps things so close to the vest, sometimes speculation is all there is.

But in the grand scheme of villaindom, James has been a model citizen. An acceptable villain, worthy to root against, even dislike, but certainly not to paint with the brush of a really bad dude. For a player who has been in the public eye since he was a sophomore, for a kid who has grown into a man under the scrutiny of people waiting for him to fail, his public persona is impressively clean. His personality quirks and intrapersonal conflicts only prove he's human. The discipline and focus he's shown to keep his nose clean and avoid the pitfalls that have beset so many others should be enough to excuse other stuff off as texture to his personality.

The real reason LeBron is a villain is not about what he's done, but where he is and when. His reign has come in the social media era. His personal dynasty has coincided with the proliferation of Twitter and Instagram and memes and cyberbullying and virtue signaling and keyboard gangsters. Being at the top of the game simply comes with a percentage of acrimony aimed at your feet. It's baked into the position. Curry was a beloved darling until he started winning MVPs and competing for titles. Then he had to pay his popularity tax. Kevin Durant, James Harden, Russell Westbrook—they all pay it.

LeBron is the one-percenter in that class, so he's contributed more skin to the game than anybody. He's been on top so long, his detractors have grown roots in their position. Pundits and talking heads have spent so much time, garnered so many eyes, picking him apart that it has essentially become part of their job description. The LeBron hate has metastasized. The same is true with the LeBron love. For some, he can do no wrong. Many of them pledged their loyalty long ago, back when it was cool to pounce on LeBron. NBA Twitter is often LeBron supporters and LeBron detractors arguing with each other, seeing only what they want while cherry-picking data and anecdotes to fit their entrenchment. A Culled War, if you will.

That's why LeBron is his own dynasty. The presence of love and hate is the truest sign of impact.

12

THE STEPH CURRY
WARRIORS

When Prince walks in, you know it's different. A new stratosphere.

The Warriors had already won the 2014–15 championship. They started the following season with a 24-game win streak, captivating the nation. And they kept going. The buzz was growing as the Bulls' regular season record of 72 wins was in reach.

The Warriors were chasing 73 wins. Stephen Curry was piecing together his unanimous MVP season. Golden State was all the rage.

On February 24, 2016, Prince announced the first dates on his Piano and a Microphone Tour would be at the Paramount Theatre in Oakland. His former girlfriend Denise Matthews, known to the world as Vanity, had died on February 15 and was going to be funeralized on the morning of February 27. When his tour dates were announced, the funeral was switched from public to private because Prince was going to be there. The night of the funeral, Curry scored 46 points in Oklahoma City, in the NBA's first prime-time Saturday night game, and he capped it with an epic thirty-seven-foot three-pointer to beat the buzzer. The next night, while performing at the Paramount Theatre, with Draymond Green in the crowd, Prince shouted out Curry.

"What can you truly count on besides Steph Curry? And you can count on Steph Curry."

Two nights later, Prince added another date in Oakland, this time at the twenty-thousand-seat Oracle Arena on March 4, 2016. He also contacted the Warriors. Golden State owner Joe Lacob and his wife, Nicole, gave Prince the two tickets next to them courtside. In honor of Prince's appearance, the Warriors changed the decoration at the player and VIP entrance of the arena to all purple.

The Warriors were 54–5 when Oklahoma City came to town on March 3, 2016. Just as players were lining up at half court for the opening tip, the legend appeared seemingly out of nowhere. In shimmering blue pants with a matching top pulled over a black hoodie. With black sunglasses under his picked-out afro, he strolled to his courtside seat as if the soles of his shiny blue boots were made of clouds. Wearing black gloves featuring his symbol on the backhands, he clutched a chrome cane encrusted with diamonds and gold.

"I was digging the outfit," Curry said. "And the cane."

This wasn't like Jay-Z and Beyoncé showing up. This was Prince. He stands five foot three and weighed 112 pounds of cotton candy. But his presence was large enough to fill Oracle. And the global icon brought his renowned aura to the Warriors. A Minneapolis native and basketball diehard, Prince was spotted in the suites when the Minnesota Lynx clinched the 2015 WNBA Championship, and he threw a party for the team afterward. He used to sit courtside at Timberwolves games, back when Kevin Garnett had the franchise near the top of the Western Conference. But over the years, he became less visible on the NBA scene. Even when he did go to T'Wolves games later, he did so unannounced and nobody would even know. But he made his return to courtside this night in Oakland. Because he had to see the Warriors.

The next night, at his concert in the same building, Prince shouted out Curry again during his performance.

Eight weeks later, on April 21, 2016, Prince died from a fentanyl overdose. One of his final acts on Earth was to confirm the Warriors' elevation from a basketball team to a pop-culture staple. This team was transcendent, and the stamp of approval came from Mr. Purple Rain himself.

NBA Finals Appearances

2015 (W)	2016 (L)	2017 (W)
2018 (W)		2019 (L)

THE FACE OF THE DYNASTY

One of the perks of attending Warriors games, a limited bonus for an exclusive portion of the fans, required being at the arena some two hours before tipoff. That was when the crowds would gather. Even on the road, even fans wearing the opposing team's jersey made it a point to be there and take in the phenomenon.

Stephen Curry warming up.

Before every game, Curry goes through a routine that doubles as a sideshow. He starts with two balls, getting warm with a series of dribbling drills revealing the quality of his ball handling and the work that goes into it. Then he works on shots near the rim: floaters, high-arching flip shots, finger rolls. It looks like he's messing around but he's not. For Curry, the goal is for every shot he takes in the game to be one he's already worked on, and that includes tricky layups.

Then the real show starts. Curry gets out behind the three-point line and starts working his way around the arc. He takes threes off the dribble, on the move, going left, going right, off balance, spotting up. He even simulates running around to get open before receiving the pass and getting up a quick shot. He makes his way out to the deep threes. The thirty-footers. The thirty-five-footers. The half-court shots. The crowd gasps when he makes those. He then goes into the midrange, with assistant coach Bruce Fraser simulating a physical defender. He focuses on footwork and the angling to get his shot off while crowded.

This became such a spectacle, the Arena started opening earlier so some fans with tickets in certain sections could get in to watch. The regional sports network that broadcasts Warriors games, NBC Sports Bay Area, started airing Curry's warm-ups as part of their pregame show. Opposing teams also started letting select fans in the arena early and even marketed Curry's warm-ups as a perk for upgrading the ticket.

The way Curry plays the game simply captivates. He brought the marvel to shooting in a way the NBA hadn't seen before. He was Larry Bird, Reggie Miller, and Steve Nash rolled into one six-foot-three point guard with the creative mind of a filmmaker crafting a narrative. And because he was relatively small and young in the face, especially in a league of giants, the way he played was inspiring. His version of excellence seemed more attainable. Jordan had a nation of hoopers doing reverse layups trying to hang in the air as long as possible. But you had to have some athleticism for that, and not everybody has leaping ability. Curry had a nation of hoopers shooting from long range. And while his skill is probably even more unique and unattainable than leaping ability, it felt all-inclusive. If you practiced hard enough, if you tried enough times, you could shoot like Stephen Curry. Most people would never know what it feels like to soar for a tomahawk dunk, looking down on the rim like LeBron. But with Curry, on the chance you made one deep three, you got to feel what he feels, to share in his euphoria of seeing your bomb swish the net even if you couldn't fathom his efficiency. In that way, so many people could connect with Curry, including young people, including women and girls.

Curry was so inspirational, his former coach Mark Jackson pointed out the ramifications of his widespread impact.

"Steph Curry's great. Steph Curry's the MVP. He's a champion," Jackson said while broadcasting the 2015 Christmas Day game between the Warriors and Cavaliers. "Understand what I'm saying when I say this. To a degree, he's hurt the game. And what I mean by that is, I go into high school gyms, I watch these kids, and the first thing they do is run to the three-point line. You are not Steph Curry. Work on the other aspects of the game. People think that he's just a knock-down shooter. That's not why he's the MVP. He's a complete basketball player."

Jackson received backlash for his comments, but his point underscored how Curry changed basketball. He shifted the focus from getting as close to the rim as possible for the highest-percentage shot available to getting behind the three-point line and taking advantage of the extra point. The Warriors have him and Klay Thompson, also an all-time great three-point shooter, and they put extreme pressure on defenses with their deep shooting.

It wasn't just on playgrounds where players fell in love with the three-pointer. The entire league followed Curry's lead. The use of the three-point shot skyrocketed. At the end of the 2014–15 season, the NBA as a league averaged 22.4 attempts from behind the arc per game. At the end of the 2019–20 season, it was up to 34.1. Players find it hard to get on the court if they can't shoot the three-pointer, and the center position, long the most coveted of them all, has been marginalized by the demand for distance shooting. Because defenders have to now extend out farther than ever, because players shoot from so far, bigger and slower players are at a disadvantage on defense. If they are giving up open three-pointers because they can't defend on the perimeter, going back on the other end to score two points in the paint just isn't going to cut it. As a result, players who were traditionally considered power forwards—not quite as big as centers, more agile, more skilled typically—are now playing center to allow teams to get more shooters on the court and be able to defend more of the court.

These days, in large part because of Curry and the Warriors, even centers are expected to shoot threes, and seven-footers are stepping behind the arc with regularity.

Curry also had the underdog story—and America loves underdogs—even though his story was atypical to the hard-luck tale of many NBA stars. Curry's father, Dell Curry, was a noted NBA player, a sharpshooter in the days of Jordan. His three kids grew up wealthy in an idyllic nuclear family. Still, Curry had to claw his way to the top. He was small—tiny by basketball standards—as he came up in the game. His frail frame and boyish face were an instant invitation to underrate him. He played high school ball at a small private school in Charlotte. While he was good, he was too small to warrant a top-level Division I scholarship. In his neck of the woods, if you had basketball aspirations they included attending Duke, North Carolina, or even Wake Forest. Curry was recruited by neither. Virginia Tech, the school where his father starred, only offered him to walk on. Curry chose Davidson College, a small private school about an hour from Charlotte, for its academic prowess. But he dominated in the 2008 NCAA Tournament as Davidson College became one of the most memorable Cinderella teams ever, and Curry captivated the nation as this little guy who could shoot the lights out and was taking down powerhouse programs.

He was drafted No. 7 overall by the Warriors in 2009. Even then, he wasn't expected to be a megastar. A few general managers who saw some of Steve Nash in him suspected All-Star potential. But repeated ankle injuries the first few years of his career seemed to rob him of even that. And playing for the lowly Warriors was an easy way to become irrelevant.

Curry didn't really hit the national radar, outside of his fun NCAA tournament run, until 2013 when the Warriors made the playoffs and people outside the Bay Area got to see his shooting. But it wasn't until the 2014–15 season, when he became an MVP candidate as the Warriors surged to the top of the Western Conference, that Curry's popularity went nuclear.

Per NBA standards, especially in this millennium, that's practically out of nowhere. Most NBA stars we see coming. They come from big colleges where they dominate and are expected to be stars because of their size and talent. In the era of high school players going pro, sparked by Kevin Garnett and Kobe Bryant, the basketball public began learning about players even earlier than college. LeBron was a sophomore in high school when the buzz began about him. Middle schoolers are now getting future-star attention, such as Kyree Walker, who was a known commodity in the eighth grade and is now expected to enter the 2021 NBA draft. Most of the players who become superstars had long been prophesied to do so. Curry took a nontraditional route and in a few years had a popularity on par with LeBron James.

When This Dynasty Reigned

- The sports activism that mirrored the national movement for racial justice in 2020, in the middle of the pandemic, actually began in the backyard of the Warriors. While they were gearing up for a third straight trip to the Finals, 49ers quarterback Colin Kaepernick took a knee in protest of police brutality during the national anthem at a preseason game at Levi's Stadium in Santa Clara. Kaepernick was the first athlete to take a knee for racial justice and sparked a movement the NBA helped spread.

- Donald Trump became the forty-fifth president of the United States.

- Tarana Burke coined the phrase #MeToo back in 2006, but the movement took off in 2017 after a *New York Times* expose about Hollywood producer Harvey Weinstein and allegations of sexual harassment and assault.

- Not even two weeks after the Warriors won their first championship, in June 2015, the U.S. Supreme Court ruled the Fourteenth Amendment required all states to grant and recognize same-sex marriages. The White House lit up in the colors of the gay pride flag to celebrate the ruling.

- The Impossible Burger made its commercial debut in restaurants in 2016 and was pretty much everywhere by 2018, taking the plant-based meat substitute into the mainstream.

- Drake dropped the album *Scorpion* in 2018, which turned the Canadian rapper into the streaming music king.

THE ARCHITECT

Oddly, the Warriors don't have exactly one architect. This dynasty was pieced together organically with a series of fortunate events. Maybe the architect was fate, reparations for the forty years the Warriors spent in NBA wilderness. A lot had to happen for this dynasty to come together. A lot of fortuitous breaks, a lot of moves that worked so well. Owner Joe Lacob became famous for saying the Warriors were "light years ahead" of the rest of the league.

June 25, 2009: This dynasty began when the Minnesota Timberwolves shocked the world and drafted Syracuse point guard Jonny Flynn with the No. 6 overall pick in the draft. The Warriors' war room celebrated because Stephen Curry was theirs, the deal they had with Phoenix for that pick be damned. No one knew at the time—save for perhaps the grandiose delusions of general manager Larry Riley and head coach Don Nelson, who were elated Curry fell to them in the draft—but this was where hindsight points as the beginning of the Warriors. It was crazy to think at the time, but Golden State laid a foundation in a twenty-one-year-old with a middle school yearbook face Photoshopped onto his body.

July 15, 2010: Joe Lacob and Peter Guber officially beat out Larry Ellison in the silent auction to buy the Warriors. The winning bid of $450 million set an NBA record for a sale price at the time. According to Ethan Strauss of *The Athletic*, Lacob and Guber won by circumventing the silent auction process and meeting then Golden State owner Chris Cohan in person. The face-to-face negotiation included an exploding offer that denied Ellison, a vastly wealthier figure, a chance to submit a higher bid. That power move put the franchise in the hands of Lacob and Guber, which would prove to be a monumental change in the vision and aggressiveness of the franchise.

May 20, 2011: The Warriors made Jerry West an executive board member and consultant. They now had one of the all-time-great executives in the room, bringing instant credibility to the newly formed front office.

June 6, 2011: The Warriors hired Mark Jackson as coach, who said during his introduction: "You might as well hitch on to the bandwagon because things gon' be a-changing."

June 23, 2011: The Warriors drafted the perfect sidekick for Curry. During the draft process, West threw his immense weight behind Klay Thompson, the Washington State shooting guard who was a prolific scorer but had some question marks. One of them was maturity after, in March, he was arrested for marijuana possession. The Washington Wizards and Sacramento Kings were both reported to have interest in Thompson, but both passed him up. The Warriors, they listened to West.

March 13, 2012: Monta Ellis was traded to the Milwaukee Bucks, along with Kwame Brown and Ekpe Udoh. In return, the Warriors finally got what they had been in search of for decades: a center. Andrew Bogut was in many ways a perfect fit—legit seven feet tall, defensive minded, an excellent passer who didn't command post ups, ideal to put in an offense centered on two shooters.

April 25, 2012: Curry has his second surgery on his right ankle in as many off-seasons. Doctors went in not sure if he would need reconstruction, but the problem wound up being just scar tissue and debris needing removal. After more than two dozen ankle sprains in two years, his ankle would finally be structurally solid.

June 28, 2012: The first draft with Bob Myers as the general manager was the greatest of his tenure and one of the most important in Warriors history. They selected Harrison Barnes with the No. 7 pick, Festus Ezili with the No. 30 pick, and Draymond Green with the No. 35 pick. This draft would eventually give the Warriors two starting forwards—with Green turning out to be one of the greatest draft steals of all time—and a backup center who filled in as a starter. That's three more rotation players on rookie contacts, to add with Curry and Thompson. With Bogut at center, the Warriors had their core.

October 31, 2012: Curry, coming off ankle surgery, opted to sign the Warriors' final offer for a contract extension—four years, $44 million. He could have turned it down. He would have become a free agent at the end of the 2012–13 season. If he played well, he'd be in line for a bigger contract. But whether his ankle would hold up was a big question mark, even for Curry. He blinked and took the guaranteed contract, opting for the security in front of him over possible higher pay later. He wound up grossly outplaying his contract, but having him on a bargain set the Warriors up to stock their roster and surround Curry with good players.

February 27, 2013: Stephen Curry. Fifty-four points. Madison Square Garden. A star was born.

July 5, 2013: While the Warriors were surprisingly in the mix for the biggest free agent on the market, Dwight Howard, the player they most wanted and needed, was quietly trying to work his way to Golden State. Andre Iguodala, who played for the same Denver team the Warriors had just upset in the playoffs, spurned the Nuggets and Kings to take less money with the Warriors. And it was his doing.

"We had become a destination where other NBA players—really good NBA players—wanted to play. That was huge for our organization and helped solidify our arrival," Lacob said.

May, 19, 2014: The Warriors fired Mark Jackson after the first-round loss to the Clippers in the 2014 playoffs. After passing on Stan Van Gundy's request for head coach and team president, the Warriors set their sights on Steve Kerr, who had already verbally agreed to become the head coach of the Knicks. But with the Warriors calling, Kerr backed out of the New York opportunity and chose instead to inherit the 51-win Warriors. Kerr brought with him a scheme and philosophy that would unlock the offensive potential the Warriors had under the hood.

July, 11, 2014: The Warriors signed Shaun Livingston, who would become the ideal backup point guard and bolster their one-of-a-kind bench.

July 4, 2016: KD

THE HAMPTONS 5

It all began in a $10,000-a-day house on Long Island. Kevin Durant, the prize of free agency in 2016, rented a renovated old mafia mansion in the Hamptons for ten days while he listened to pitches from teams hoping to land him. The contingent for the Warriors' meeting included four players: Curry, Klay Thompson, Draymond Green, and Andre Iguodala. Others were there, but the focus was all about the players. They went off to private quarters and talked basketball, leaving the executives behind. They talked about basketball, philosophy, and how they'd fit together. But it all came down to two men, the two stars who would have to share a kingdom.

Durant asked Curry if he wanted him on the Warriors. Curry convinced Durant he did. And so was born one of the most talented teams ever.

The best shooting backcourt ever in Curry and Thompson. A defensive wizard and secondary playmaker in Draymond Green. Andre Iguodala was the sixth man who served as a backup point guard, a defensive stopper, a spot-up

shooter, and an ultimate leader. Livingston was another ball-handling wing with the size and length to keep the defensive pressure up. And the piece that put them over the top was Durant—who was all of those things plus arguably the greatest scorer ever. He was the supercharge the Warriors wanted after losing the 2016 NBA Finals.

With four All-Stars—Curry, Durant, Green, and Thompson—the Warriors were too loaded for LeBron James.

Boston put together a Big Three in 2007 by trading for Kevin Garnett and Ray Allen to put with Paul Pierce. It got the Celtics another title. In 2010, LeBron James and Chris Bosh joined Dwyane Wade in Miami, creating another Big Three, with Ray Allen as a luxurious option off the bench. They twice faced a San Antonio Spurs squad that featured Tim Duncan, Tony Parker, and Manu Ginóbili.

But the Warriors had one-upped the trend. And their abundance drew the ire of fans around the league.

THE PEAK SEASON

There was a moment there where it looked as if the Warriors would dethrone the Bulls as the greatest dynasty ever. They'd won the 2014–15 championship, practically coming out of nowhere to win their first title in forty years. They followed with a record-breaking 2015–16 season, winning 73 games to break the Bulls' record of 72, and Curry had arguably the greatest offensive season in NBA history. Certainly the most unique.

Curry finished the year at 30.1 points on 50.4 percent shooting. Only twelve players in NBA history have averaged at least 30 points on 50 percent shooting. But he did so with a true shooting percentage of .669—easily the highest of the bunch—and an offensive rating of 125 points per possession, tied for second with 1990–91 Michael Jordan. Of the twelve players, only Adrian Dantley had a higher rating of 126, in 1983–84. And Curry became a member of the 30–50 Club in a way no one had ever seen before. He made 402 three-pointers, dramatically altering the landscape of basketball. His long-range shooting stretched the floor as it had never been stretched and ushered in a new paradigm of offensive.

Curry was injured in the playoffs that year. He missed two games with a foot injury in the first round, and another four after spraining his right knee on his first game back. The Warriors dragged themselves to the 2016 NBA Finals, where they proved to be the perfect foil in LeBron James's dream signature moment.

When Kyrie Irving drilled that game-winning shot in Game 7, over the out-stretched hand of Curry, culminating one of the most dramatic win-or-go-home games in NBA history, the Warriors' case for the greatest ever went out the window. Winning the championship was a prerequisite. And many fans—and members of the NBA fraternity—were elated the Warriors didn't finish the job.

But the failure set up perhaps the biggest coup in NBA free-agent history. It landed them Kevin Durant. Here is why it was checkmate for the NBA.

The Warriors overcame a 2–1 deficit in the 2015 NBA Finals by inserting sixth man Andre Iguodala into the starting lineup. The following season birthed what NBA writer Vincent Goodwill coined the Death Lineup. Warriors coach Steve Kerr, who returned Iguodala back to sixth man duties following the first title, would close games with a smaller lineup. The starting center would be benched, and power forward Draymond Green would shift to center. Traditional small forwards Iguodala and Harrison Barnes became the forwards along with guards Curry and Klay Thompson in the backcourt. It created an agile, swarming, skilled quintet. They sacrificed size for speed, and strength for playmaking. The Death Lineup was the secret weapon on the road to 73 wins, eviscerating opponents right at the moment they expected to win.

Thompson, Green, Barnes, Iguodala, and Livingston gave the Warriors five players who were at least six feet, six inches tall with above-average wingspan and excellent defensive instincts. The Warriors' defensive scheme? Switch everything. The NBA ethos prided itself on man-to-man defense. There is something macho about a defender sticking with his man. But in a league dominated by the pick-and-roll and spot-up shooters, the Warriors instituted their switching scheme. Instead of fighting through the screen, they just swapped defensive assignments. It required a rhythmic sync, a cohesion that allowed them to operate on a string. But the secret to its success was having a collection of tall perimeter players. With their shooting, and unique defense, the Warriors were potent on both ends.

But the Death Lineup met its match in Oklahoma City, which had a brutal lineup of its own. Serge Ibaka at center and Durant at forward, both of whom were taller and more athletic than their Warriors counterparts, neutralized the speed and skill advantage the Warriors usually enjoyed. It took everything Golden State had to survive the Thunder. They rallied from a 3–1 series deficit with championship mettle. But Cleveland had a small-ball lineup, too, and theirs featured LeBron and Kyrie playing at historic levels.

Durant ended up being the ultimate upgrade for the Warriors. He was the perfect fit as he had everything: height, shooting, ball handling, passing, rebounding, shot blocking, ball pressure. And on top of all that, he was good enough to dominate games. With Durant on the Warriors, it was a perfection rivaled only by the likes of the *Purple Rain* album.

Durant gave the Warriors the Death Lineup 2.0. Barnes was good on defense, but Durant made them otherworldly. With Curry and Thompson as the guards, and with Green and center Zaza Pachulia joining Durant in the frontcourt, the Warriors' starting lineup had an incredible balance of offense and defense. In 2016–17, they outscored opponents by 23.7 points when they were on the floor together. When the Warriors wanted to turn up the pressure and speed, they replaced Pachulia with Iguodala and became more versatile. The switching scheme was even more overwhelming because Durant added shot-blocking ability.

He gave the Warriors five dynamic wing players who could defend pretty much every dominant scoring guard or forward in the league. Thompson's wingspan is six foot nine. Iguodala and Livingston each have a wingspan of six foot eleven. Green has a seven-foot-one wingspan. Durant's was seven foot five. The Warriors had a seemingly endless lineup of long, athletic, and intelligent players who could stick with quick guards on the perimeter and could hold their own in the paint. It freed up Curry to do what he does best on defense, pressure the ball without fear of getting beat, serve as a roaming helper, and jump into passing lanes. They were a switching, swiping, savvy fivesome.

The Warriors started a trend the league would copy. Teams started to mimic their wing-heavy approach and switch-everything scheme. Because of the Warriors, all teams now have a version of a centerless lineup. Small forwards, shooting guards with great size, and power forwards who are especially quick and athletic—they became a premium and are still in high demand.

In 2016–17, Durant's first year in the Bay Area, the Warriors set an NBA record with an offensive rating of 115.6. It was the most potent offense ever—bested only by the same team two years later.

There have been twenty-three teams in NBA history to register an offensive rating of 114 or better, making them the greatest offensive juggernauts the league has ever seen. Ten of them made the Finals. Seven of them won the title.

> *The Warriors had a seemingly endless lineup of long, athletic, and intelligent players who could stick with quick guards on the perimeter and could hold their own in the paint.*

Five of the twenty-three teams registered a defensive rating below 105, making them a rare combination of explosive offense and dominant defense.

Of those five? Three of them were Jordan's Bulls teams. Two of them were the Warriors with Durant.

The two Warriors teams had effective field goal percentages—which factor in three-point shooting—above 56 percent, the only one of the twenty-three teams to shoot the ball so well from distance. The previous high was the Showtime Lakers at 55.1 percent.

But the best case for the 2017 Warriors, in a showdown with the 72-win Bulls for the greatest season ever, came in the playoffs. They won 15 straight playoff games and were on the cusp of a perfect postseason before the

Cavaliers made 24 three-pointers in Game 4 to avoid a sweep. During the playoff run, the Warriors outscored opponents by 27 points per 100 possessions.

The numbers don't paint the full picture, not as much as how defeated they made opponents look, or how dynamic they were together. Once Durant got in rhythm with his new teammates, they were a quartet of stars unlike any other. They were arguably the greatest shooting team ever with Curry, Thompson, and Durant. They were even more defensively potent with Durant because of his wingspan and athleticism.

The 2015–16 Warriors were on the brink of challenging the Bulls for single-season supremacy. While they came up short, getting Durant supercharged them and made an ever better case for the greatest team ever.

THE DYNAMIC DUO(S)

It usually takes three All-Star caliber players to be a true championship contender in the NBA. But NBA lore has a special place for duos. Something about there being only five players on the court really accentuates duets. The third star often has to take a bit of a back seat. Not enough ball to go around, usually. Plus there is a flow to the NBA tandems. They roll off the tongue.

Jordan and Pippen. Penny and Shaq. Kobe and Shaq. Magic and Kareem. Russell and Cousy. Stockton and Malone. Wilt and West. Lew and Oscar. Reed and Frazier. LeBron and Kyrie.

For just three years, the Warriors had such a duo, a one-two punch that belongs in the pantheon of legendary tag teams. Curry and Durant.

They don't have the luxury of longevity together. And they don't have the inside-outside scoring balance that is most common. But this might have been the most offensively explosive duo in NBA history.

For three straight years, they had the highest offensive rating of any two players together in the NBA who played at least a thousand minutes. Over their three seasons combined, the Warriors averaged 121 points per 100 possessions when Curry and Durant were on the court together. Every year they played together, they registered the highest offensive rating of any duo that year that played at least fifteen games together.

In their three years together, Curry and Durant combined to average 52 points on 50 percent shooting. In the playoffs, they combined for 57 points on 48.4 percent shooting.

Matching up in a two-on-two would be tough for them. Their combined weight is less than Shaq's thighs. Imagine Durant trying to defend Kareem while Curry locked up with Magic. But what they lack in size they compensate for with range. Incredible range. Curry and Durant each have the ability to shoot, handle the ball, pass, and finish. It makes them interchangeable. They both can create offense, and they both can lock in and become scorers. Because they were both so good, it became an issue who would serve as the primary playmaker. They mostly alternated who controlled the offense. Perhaps more time could have produced even better chemistry between the two. But the high-end brilliance of the pair made them a deuce for the ages.

HOW THE DYNASTY ALMOST ENDED EARLY

The Warriors had won two championships, but they didn't have that *it* element yet. They entered the 2018 playoffs seeking to become back-to-back champions. That would put the Warriors in rarified air. But they ran into a hungry and talented Houston team, one that had already lost twice to the Warriors in the postseason and had added Chris Paul. Golden State was on the brink of elimination after losing Game 5 in Houston. Paul pulled his hamstring in the final minute of the fourth quarter and wound up out for the rest of the series.

In the locker room after Game 5, coach Steve Kerr went from player to player and told them they were going to win the series despite being down 3–2 and Houston having home-court advantage. They'd just lost and were on the verge of having their entire legacy tarnished, and Andre Iguodala was out with a knee injury. Yet Kerr was confident.

The Warriors won Game 6 in Oakland handily, thanks to a combined 87 points from Curry, Thompson, and Durant. But in Game 7, they were down 15 points on the road in the second quarter with just under five minutes to play in the half. Steve Kerr called a time-out, and the Warriors looked defeated. But in that huddle, something happened. Whatever issues were prompting their lackluster play, which was usually marked by a rash of turnovers, seemed to be scared off by the imminent threat of being eliminated. With a raucous crowd at the Toyota Center smelling Golden State blood, the Warriors decided to win. They banded together and decided to go down swinging.

"I wouldn't even say it was a conversation," Durant said of the locker room at halftime. "It was more an energy. You know how you kind of just know? It was, 'All right Steph. C'mon. Let's go. We're down 11.' It was on us. We just had to figure it out."

The Warriors came out of halftime and outscored Houston by 18 points in the third quarter. The Rockets famously missed 27 straight three-pointers, and the Warriors survived.

COMING UP SIXES

Who knew way back then, in 2013, a magical trend was starting. The Warriors were on the verge of their first playoff series win since 2007. They were up 88–79 with less than two minutes left. Oracle Arena was rumbling. And then something happened. The Warriors started falling apart. The Denver Nuggets, minutes from elimination, got desperate and started pressing. And the Warriors looked rickety. Oracle got nervous. They had five turnovers and a missed three-pointer over the final two minutes. The only thing that saved them was two trips to the free throw line as they could barely get the ball over half court. But the Warriors survived and won their first playoff series in the Curry era.

Their Game 6 drama was born.

The next series, they lost in Game 6 to the Spurs in Oakland, ending their season.

Two years later, in 2015, they were in Memphis. Curry picked up a loose ball and heaved it before the third-quarter buzzer sounded. He drilled it from seventy-five feet, driving the dagger into the Grizzlies. The Warriors had been down 2–1 in the series, getting beaten up by a bigger and more physical Grizzlies squad. But they rallied back, shifting the tide of the series with their quickness on defense and transition game. Eventually, they crested the hill, getting past their toughest foe to date. It was Game 6.

Two series later, the Warriors clinched their first title since 1975 in Cleveland. In Game 6.

Game 6 Klay was born in 2016. The Warriors were down 3–2 in the Western Conference Finals and on the road in Oklahoma City. Golden State was in desperate need of something special. The Warriors had been dominated by the Thunder—then led by Durant and Russell Westbrook—and got down 3–1 in the series. The Warriors won Game 5 in Oakland and returned to Oklahoma City, where they were demolished in Games 3 and 4. Klay Thompson delivered one of the most epic performances in playoff history. Thompson made 11 of 18 from three-point range and scored 41 points to save the Warriors. He almost single-handedly kept the Warriors in the game with his shooting, catching fire and reinvigorating the champions.

The next series, in Game 6 of the 2016 NBA Finals, Curry famously fouled out and threw his mouthpiece, hitting a courtside fan. And his wife, Ayesha, took to Twitter to say the game was rigged.

The Warriors never made it to a Game 6 in their 2017 title run.

The next big Game 6 came in 2018. This time it was at home. Facing elimination to the Rockets, Game 6 Klay showed up again: 35 points including 9 of 14 from three.

In 2019, the Warriors put away the feisty Clippers in the first round of the playoffs on a 50-spot by Durant, a performance so dominant that two of the Clippers' best players spent the postgame drooling over KD.

Patrick Beverley: "I mean, he's Kevin Durant."

Lou Williams: "I promise we tried."

Beverley: "We didn't roll over. We didn't just say, 'Come on, man, you know what? Just give us 50 tonight.' Of course not. He's a hell of a player. The shots he took, he made some tough shots. If you was a coach, what would you tell us to do? Thank you."

Williams: "We tried everything. So we tried everything. We had several different coverages for KD, and . . . "

Beverley: "It didn't work."

Williams: "Like sometimes, you come across special people and it doesn't matter what you send to them. There's no scheme. There's no defense, there's no nothing that you can do with special people. He's one of them. And he showed it tonight. He put them guys on his shoulders."

Durant injured his calf in the next series, in the third quarter of Game 5. The Warriors hung on to win but faced a daunting task in the next game against James Harden and Chris Paul, facing elimination. It was Game 6, and they were a win from clinching a fifth-straight trip to the Finals, so they needed some drama. And Curry gave it to them with one of the worst first halves of his career. He went to the locker room scoreless at halftime. But in the second half, he exploded for 33 points and put the Rockets out of their misery. Game 6 Curry.

In the 2019 Finals, they lost the final game at Oracle Arena in Game 6, and they lost Klay Thompson to a torn ACL. Before he went down, he was on fire. He had 30 points in thirty-one minutes and was in one of his grooves. Game 6 Klay was in the building.

THE CULTURAL IMPACT

The record price for an NBA Finals ticket is $69,287.21.

An unknown fan bought two of the courtside seats for Game 6 of the 2019 NBA Finals at Oracle Arena. It was the final NBA game in Oakland before the

Warriors moved to San Francisco. So that bit of history totaled $138,574.42, or the price of a nice two-bedroom flat in several states.

And that's not even the most spent for a game.

In Game 4 of the same series, a fan bought four tickets in the second row. The total damage: $181,740. That'll definitely get three bedrooms. But for this dynasty, that's petty cash.

What the Warriors did, building a dynasty in the heart of the Bay Area, was invite Silicon Valley into the NBA circle. The tech boom in the late 1990s and early 2000s flooded the Bay with money and created a West Coast epicenter for capital. But the second tech boom began shortly before the Warriors took off. While Mark Jackson and Stephen Curry were turning the Warriors into contenders, the high-tech surge was being fueled by cloud services and the social-media revolution. The money was reaching astronomical levels. In 2017, the Bay Area had fourteen individuals reach billionaire status, pushing San Francisco to number three on the list of regions with the most billionaires. It still ranks number three with seventy-seven billionaires, according to the 2020 Billionaire Census by Wealth-X.

Oracle Arena became their hangout spot. As the Warriors rose to another stratosphere, their games became the ultimate flex, the place to be seen. The courtside section at Warriors games was like a tech convention with millionaires wearing free gold T-shirts over their shirts and ties. Pop star Rihanna showed up for Game 1 of the NBA Finals courtside to cheer on LeBron James against the Warriors in Oakland. Apple senior executive Eddy Cue could be seen on video telling her to sit down, which drew the ire of Rihanna fans on social media. It had long been common for actors and rappers to show up at NBA games. The Warriors created the trend of attracting CEOs, angel investors, and product engineers.

Some recognizable billionaires might show up at a Warriors game. Oracle cofounder Larry Ellison. WhatsApp cofounder Jack Koum. Salesforce founder Marc Benioff. Twitter and Square founder Jack Dorsey. AirBnB cofounder Brian Chesky. Even the Warriors are owned by a venture capitalist in Joe Lacob, who landed tech giants like Chamath Palihapitiya, an early Facebook executive, and YouTube cofounder Chad Hurley as minority owners of the Warriors.

The Silicon Valley presence became a draw for the Warriors. Players interested in off-the-court business interests were drawn to the tech industry. Andre Iguodala—who invested in Zoom, a play that proved immensely profitable when the country went virtual during the pandemic—and Kevin Durant came to the Warriors in part because Silicon Valley was a cherry on top. Curry and Draymond Green are heavy into the tech sector. Curry and Iguodala created a Tech Summit specifically, and exclusively, for athletes to learn about and network in that space.

They all use their fame and panache to get in the door, and they have the capital to invest. Meanwhile, the tech bros get to rub elbows with superstars.

These days, the NBA is entangled with the tech sector. The Clippers, Kings, Grizzlies, and Hawks were all bought by tech tycoons in the last decade. Players are becoming investors, pitchmen, and disruptors. The Warriors' contribution to the culture was marrying the NBA with Silicon Valley and giving tech culture some swag.

THE VILLAIN

Draymond Green took the court for pregame warm-ups on the floor of Quicken Loans Arena on February 1, 2020. The teams had a combined 23–75 record at the time, a long cry from the historic clashes between the Warriors and Cavaliers in the NBA Finals. LeBron James had already gone to the Lakers and Kyrie Irving to Brooklyn (after a stint in Boston). Curry and Thompson were on the injured list. Andre Iguodala was on hiatus in Memphis. All that was left was Green and memories. Yet when he took the court, they booed as if it was Game 4 all over again.

"When they booed him pregame, I saw him smiling," Steve Kerr said. "He loves to be the villain. Sometimes that's what it takes to get him going."

Green wears the black hat like Johnny Depp wears a fedora or Samuel Jackson a Kangol. It fits Green like he was born with it. He relishes the role of the hated. He feeds off it.

Green is a savant on defense, the way he swarms ball handlers, reads the floor, instinctually reacts in angles, and quarterbacks the scheme. At six foot seven, 230 pounds, he can dribble well and he passes like a guard. He rebounds with a noted hunger. But his secret weapon is the fire in his belly. Green plays with such an intense energy. He has a competitive drive that has carried him from an overweight high school star to a game-changing NBA champion. And nothing gets his fire burning hotter than when he's got an enemy to

vanquish. He loves the art of trash talking, of getting beneath the skin of his foe, of humiliating. His aunt, Annette Babers, who played at Michigan State, taught him how to talk trash. And Green is now one of the NBA's greatest of all time—which makes him an easy villain.

"I want to punch him in the face so bad," Charles Barkley said. "I'm just telling you. I want to punch his ass in the face. I do."

Green's most epic moment came in 2017. In late February, with the Clippers visiting town, Green lit into Paul Pierce, who announced the 2016–17 season would be his last. Paul, a future Hall of Famer, wasn't playing that night when the Clippers came to Oakland. But Green heard Pierce talking from the bench.

Green was defending Blake Griffin, who drew a foul and was headed to the free throw line. That's when Pierce started barking.

"I'm not even preparing to hear a word from Paul Pierce," Green said in an interview with *E:60*, recalling the incident. "And then he starts talking from the gate.

"BG he can't guard you! He can't guard you, BG! He's too little."

The game was forty-one seconds old. But that lathered Green. Griffin made the first free throw, and Green used the break in the action to respond. He was lined up on the low block shouting toward the Clippers bench. Since he was right under the basket, the microphone on the rim picked up his commentary.

"Chasing that farewell tour! They don't love you like that! You can't get no farewell tour! They don't love you like that! You ain't got that type of love. You thought you was Kobe?!"

It was the perfect illustration of Green's mentality. He goes for the jugular. He is trying to rip out hearts. And he never stops talking.

Many, many fans despise him for his verbosity. Assuredly, the referees do as well. Green lays into them every game. He finished tied for second in the NBA for most technical fouls five times in a six-season stretch.

On top of that, the postseason has produced the most fervent Green disdain. During five consecutive trips to the NBA Finals, the Warriors played multiple series against Houston, Portland, San Antonio, New Orleans, and Cleveland. They had multiple opportunities for Green to grate on them.

Plus, a few incidents feed into his bad-guy persona. In the 2016 playoffs, he kicked Oklahoma City center Steven Adams in the groin. Twice. The second time warranted a fine from the league, which was mercy because a suspension would have been acceptable. In the next series, the NBA Finals, a clash with LeBron James—in what the league deemed a swing at James's groin—wound up getting him suspended for Game 5 of the Finals. It opened the door for the Cavaliers to complete a comeback from a 3–1 series hole.

Nobody is safe from the wrath of Draymond. Even his teammates get it. He got into infamous verbal altercations with Steve Kerr and Kevin Durant. He's known for letting his teammates have it in practices and on the sidelines. And they all put up with it. Well, not Durant, who acknowledged publicly his confrontation with Green contributed to his departure from the Warriors in 2019 for Brooklyn. But most put up with it because Green happily wears the black hat for them. He willingly, pridefully, takes the heat for them. He uses the same fire to defend them, to attack the opposing stars. He draws all the venom his way, absorbs it as a fuel, and uses it to accentuate his powers.

Many people can't stand Draymond Green. And that's just the way he likes it.

THE HOME COURT

In 2019, the Warriors moved into their new $1.4 billion privately financed arena in San Francisco. Chase Center is a state-of-the-art, high-tech facility on the shores of San Francisco Bay—on land purchased from tech giant Salesforce— and a shimmering beacon that points to the financial might of Silicon Valley. It is a luxurious marvel befitting of one of the most valuable franchises in sports. In July 2020, *Forbes* listed the Warriors number five on its most valuable sports team list with a valuation of $4.3 billion—behind the Cowboys, Yankees, Knicks, and Lakers, and just ahead of the Spanish pro soccer club Real Madrid—which is a meteoric climb in a decade.

But before they moved into their fancy new digs, they built their dynasty across the Bay Bridge in Oakland. The Warriors turned a concrete edifice befitting of the grassroots, blue-collar city where it dwelled, into a national gem. For years, when the Warriors were a lowly franchise disappointing its base annually, Oracle Arena was still far more full than the franchise deserved. It came to life during the era of the Run TMC Warriors, when Tim Hardaway, Mitch Richmond, and Chris Mullin anchored Don Nelson's frenetic offense, the original small-ball experience.

Oracle gained national prominence during the Warriors' historic upset of the Dallas Mavericks in 2007, becoming the first No. 8 seed to beat a No. 1 seed in a seven-game series. The arena was so loud the energy could be felt through the television.

Oracle gained its nickname in 2013 when Curry led the Warriors back to national prominence. Again, the scene in the arena was so raucous and loud, it was dubbed Roaracle. It became its own entity. It would be ignited by a barrage of Curry and Thompson three-pointers, and opponents would crumble under its weight. Like that time Thompson found the zone and couldn't miss, making nine three-pointers and scoring 37 points in a single quarter.

But Oracle was old. Opened in 1966, it was one of the oldest in the nation. The Warriors moved to Oakland full time in 1971 and played there every year save for 1996–97, when the arena underwent renovations. It had seen mostly losing over its years. The Warriors won the championship in 1975, sweeping the Washington Bullets, but their home games in that series were played in the Cow Palace because the arena, owned by local municipalities, was unavailable.

The Warriors finally brought glory to Oracle, making five straight NBA Finals.

Lacob and Guber had visions for a new arena when they bought the team. The lure of greater financial gain had their eye on San Francisco the entire way. Oracle was located in East Oakland, an industrial part of the city that grew dilapidated over time and had yet to experience the upgrades of gentrification. It was homey, a bit grungy. It had a texture to it. Ownership's vision for the Warriors, however, was far more exquisite. The Silicon Valley influence on the Warriors desired a much more modern and progressive venue. So they moved the Warriors across the Bay, ending the era of a basketball relic.

13

THE NEAR DYNASTIES

If only George McGinnis, a six-foot-eight forward known as "Baby Bull," had gotten a little more arc on the leaning pull-up he took from thirteen feet to beat the buzzer in Game 6 of the 1977 NBA Finals. The 76ers would have sent the game to overtime, won, and forced a Game 7 on their home floor at the Spectrum.

If only after Kareem Abdul-Jabbar didn't return to action after spraining his ankle in Game 5 of the 1980 NBA Finals, and didn't score fourteen points in the fourth quarter. Or if Henry Bibby didn't step out of bounds to squander Philadelphia's last chance. Or the 76ers, who went into Game 6 with a chance to clinch, didn't become victims of the historic performance of rookie Magic Johnson in place of injured Abdul-Jabbar.

If only Philadelphia didn't give up a 40–9 run, on a barrage of Lakers fast breaks, between the third and fourth quarters of Game 1 of the 1982 NBA Finals. They wouldn't have blown a 15-point second-half lead and cost themselves home-court advantage. Then maybe the series wouldn't have ended with another Game 6 loss in Los Angeles.

If any one of those things had happened and the Sixers won the series, Philadelphia would have a strong case for a dynasty. If two of those happened, they'd be a lock.

But dynasties are often exceptional because of the competition they overcome. In the wake of the NBA's best teams lies some squads that were on the cusp of a similar greatness if not for the wrong bounce or two. Some even have good cases for being considered in that ilk.

While lionizing the most epic teams, don't forget about the ones on their heels.

DR. J'S PHILADELPHIA 76ERS

The 76ers had just about everything, starting with the star of stars: Julius "the Doctor" Erving.

Dr. J is one of the reasons the merger happened in the first place.

After he averaged 26.3 points and 20.5 rebounds at University of Massachusetts, one of only six ever to do so in college basketball, he used the so-called hardship rule to enter pro basketball early. He signed with the Virginia Squires in the ABA in 1971 for four years and $500,000. He averaged 27.3 points and 15.7 rebounds as a rookie with the Squires. He was already a star and one of the most exciting players in basketball.

The Milwaukee Bucks still selected Erving in the 1972 NBA Draft, No. 12 overall, while Erving's Squires were preparing for the ABA Eastern Division Finals. A day later, Erving agreed to a $2 million deal with the Atlanta Hawks. This started the first of several legal battles involving Dr. J.

The Bucks believed they held Erving's NBA rights since they drafted him. The Hawks believed he wasn't subject to the draft because he was already playing professional ball in the ABA. A judge ruled Erving had to return to the Squires until the dispute was arbitrated.

In his second season with the Squires, he averaged 31.9 points, 12.2 rebounds, 4.2 assists, 2.5 steals, and 1.8 blocks. This only raised the interest in Dr. J.

It was finally resolved in August 1973, and the New York Nets of the ABA paid the ransom. In a $4 million deal, the Nets paid $750,000 to the Squires to buy Erving out of the remainder of his contract. Another $425,000 payment went to the Hawks, who thought they had signed Erving and reportedly gave him a $250,000 signing bonus. And then another $2.8 million went to Erving—eight years, $350,000—to bring him to New York.

The Nets won two of the next three ABA championships. The ABA had a reputation for being the league of fun and excitement, juxtaposed to the rigid NBA. The ABA had the red, white, and blue ball and many of the good African-American players. It played a fast pace, with what was called a playground style, thanks to incredible athletes who ran, soared, and dunked. And the cherry on top was the three-point shot. ABA Commissioner George Mikan instituted it, and the three grew to be basketball's version of the home run, adding a layer of excitement to the league's high level of entertainment.

Dr. J was the face of the league. On Valentine's Day in 1975, he scored 63 points in the Nets' 176–166 loss to the San Diego Conquistadors. In 1976, he won the inaugural Slam Dunk Contest, defeating Artis Gilmore by taking off from behind the free throw line and dunking. Well, not quite from behind the free throw line.

When the ABA merged with the NBA, in August of 1976, Erving's Nets were one of the four teams to join the league. But Nets owner Roy Boe had a problem. Not only did Dr. J want a new contract after leading the Nets to two ABA titles, but the NBA was requiring a buy-in of more than $3 million from each new franchise. That prompted Boe to sell his best player to the 76ers. Philadelphia signed Dr. J to a six-year, $3.5 million contract and paid the 76ers $2.1 million, which helped the Nets owner offset the indemnification fee.

In his first year with the 76ers, Dr. J led the 76ers to the Finals. They lost to Portland, but it seemed like the beginning of a dynasty, a near miss that promised more.

They had no shortage of noteworthy stars. The Erving era of the 76ers started in 1976 with Julius Erving, George McGinnis, Doug Collins, World B. Free, and a young Darryl Dawkins, who came out of high school.

By the time they got back to the Finals in 1980, after losing to the Blazers in 1977, the 76ers had added future Hall of Famer Bobby Jones, Dawkins had become a key presence inside, and Maurice Cheeks was a talented young point guard. The next season, they added Andrew Toney, who would become a prolific scorer. They almost made the NBA Finals again in 1981 but blew a 3–1 series lead in an Eastern Conference Finals. The same squad lost the Finals in 1982.

The breakthrough came in 1983. After falling short for years, the 76ers acquired Moses Malone. He was a five-time All-Star who averaged 31.1 points and 14.7 rebounds the year before. At six foot ten, 215 pounds, Malone was a bruising big man who was a load to handle and an upgrade over Dawkins. He famously predicted the 76ers would sweep through the three playoff series. "Fo', Fo', Fo'," he said when asked how they would do.

With Malone leading the way, and thirty-two-year-old Erving playing costar, the Sixers nearly did it. They won the first seven games before Milwaukee got rolling in the fourth quarter and surprised the 76ers for Game 4. But Philadelphia ended the series in five games and then swept the Lakers in the Finals.

A rookie named Charles Barkley out of Auburn gave the 76ers another jolt in talent in 1984–85. But their one last run ended at the 1985 Eastern Conference Finals.

In the end, they made four trips to the NBA Finals, including two losses to the Lakers, and three other trips to the Eastern Conference Finals, including two losses to the Celtics. The Dr. J 76ers were one of the best teams of all time. They just happened to exist during the era of two dynasties.

Dr. J and the 76ers represent a flaw in the dynastic model. The G.O.A.T. teams of the NBA tend to have an unfair monopoly on reverence. Their exceptionalism has a way of obscuring the greatness of their competitors. When the Magic and Bird wars are discussed, the 76ers teams they also warred with get forgotten. The dominance of dynasties on the court and in the hearts of NBA fans has a way of minimizing some of the other stellar teams who should be remembered.

THE HAKEEM OLAJUWON ROCKETS

How in the world are the Rockets not a dynasty?

They won back-to-back championships in 1993 and 1994.

They had a superstar, one of the greatest centers ever, in Hakeem Olajuwon. University of Houston coach Guy Lewis had a contact who told them about the big man from Lagos, Nigeria. Before he even played a game in college, they were calling him "Akeem the Dream" as the hype came with him. (Note: In the pros, he added the H to his name, which is how it was in Nigeria. In college and early in his pro career, it was translated "Akeem" by Americans and he just went with it.) He ended up the No. 1 pick in the 1984 draft—he would've been Rookie of the Year had it not been for some guy named Michael Jordan. Together, the seven-foot Olajuwon paired with the seven-foot-four Ralph Sampson made up the famed "Twin Towers" of the Rockets, and they combined for 42.7 points, 22.3 rebounds, and 4.7 blocks.

They made the NBA Finals in 1985. Oddly enough, the Twin Towers were outplayed by a smaller frontcourt tandem, Larry Bird and Kevin McHale, who averaged 25.8 points on 57.3 percent shooting. In the Game 6 clincher, McHale and Larry Bird each had 29 points while the Twin Towers combined for 27.

In December 1987, the Rockets traded Sampson to Golden State, breaking up the Twin Towers and centering the franchise on Olajuwon. He was even better as the lone center in the lineup. Known for his incredible footwork and craftiness in the post, Olajuwon was a marvel among big men. He could turn to either shoulder, hit fadeaway jumpers, and was a good passer. He developed what was called the Dream Shake, a favorite move of his where he would freeze the defender by faking both directions rapidly enough that it looked like a shake.

He made history in the 1993–94 regular season. The Dream was the first player ever to win the NBA MVP, the NBA Defensive Player of the Year, and the NBA Finals MVP—outplaying Knicks Hall of Fame center Patrick Ewing, including in the decisive Game 7 win in Houston. The following year, Olajuwon outperformed another future Hall of Famer. Third-year center Shaquille O'Neal averaged 28 points, 12.8 rebounds, and 6.3 assists—which is a phenomenal series. But Olajuwon was just better—32.8 points, 11.5 rebounds, 5.5 assists—as the Rockets swept the young O'Neal and Penny Hardaway.

> *[Olajuwon] developed what was called the Dream Shake, a favorite move of his where he would freeze the defender by faking both directions rapidly enough that it looked like a shake.*

These Rockets titles were also the coronation for Clyde Drexler, the longtime superstar with the Blazers who finally got a ring, and the coming-out party of Robert Horry, who would go on to win five more rings and become one of the best, and most decorated, reserves in NBA history.

So how does this not qualify as a dynasty? Back-to-back championships. A major superstar. Even another trip to the 1997 Western Conference Finals?

The answer is actually pretty simple: Michael Jordan.

The Rockets won their titles while Michael Jordan was on a break from basketball. Well, technically, they won the first title while Jordan was playing baseball. For the second, Jordan returned a month before the playoffs and lost to the same Orlando team Houston swept. But it was clear Jordan was not fully back to himself yet. Plus, once Jordan returned, the Rockets never even proved to be an adversary. Houston couldn't get past Seattle and Utah to even meet the Bulls in the Finals.

Because of that, the Rockets are regarded as the substitute teachers of dynasties. As great as they were, their impact had a ceiling because they didn't beat the best of the era.

THE JERRY WEST LAKERS

A mob of fans stormed the court and lifted Wilt Chamberlain in the air. The organist played Barbra Streisand's "Happy Days Are Here Again." Pat Riley, then a Lakers reserve, poured a bottle of champagne on his own head. Jerry West, though, he was a bit shell-shocked. As Lakers owner Jack Kent Cooke, and players from the Knicks, even then TV broadcaster Bill Russell, came to congratulate him in the Lakers locker room, he kept responding to them with how he couldn't believe it.

The Lakers were finally champions—after twelve seasons since moving to Los Angeles from Minneapolis, after seven losses in the NBA Finals, six to the Boston Celtics, and even a crushing loss to the Milwaukee Bucks in the conference finals (after the Celtics had finally faded). West, one of the original Los Angeles Lakers, was there for all the heartbreak.

"Just to go over to that bench and sit down knowing you've won," he told reporters inside the celebration in the Lakers locker room. "What a gratifying feeling. In the past, I've said teams we beat were lucky. But I know that's not it now . . . because I know how we won it. This is the greatest team I've ever played on."

Indeed it was. The 1972 Lakers were sooooooo loaded on paper. Wilt Chamberlain. Elgin Baylor. Jerry West. Gail Goodrich. Four Hall of Famers.

They set an NBA record with a thirty-three-game winning streak, which still exists today, because they were so much better than everyone else. They won 69 games, and the only real resistance was a rematch against the Bucks in the West Finals, which the Lakers won in six games.

However, save for Goodrich, they were all on the downsides of their careers. Chamberlain was thirty-five and averaged 14.8 points and 19.2 rebounds in the regular season, and about the same in the playoffs. His career averages: 30.1 points and 22.9 rebounds.

Jerry West was thirty-three and had contemplated retiring before the season. He came back and was still an All-Star, including All-Star game MVP in '72. New coach Bill Sharman made West the team's primary playmaker, and he registered a career-high 9.7 assists. He averaged 25.8 points, but it was a decline from his previous year. West's scoring average dropped every year from 1969–70, when he averaged 31.2 points at thirty years old.

And thirty-seven-year-old Elgin Baylor? He played nine games that season. He tore his Achilles in 1970 and was never the same. He didn't play at all during the postseason.

The only youngster was Goodrich, who was twenty-eight that year and six years into his career. His role increased under Sharman as well, and his average jumped 8 points to a career-high 25.9 as he and West made up what was at the time the best shooting backcourt even before the three-pointer.

Had this collection of players been together earlier? Definite dynasty. But they all had the Boston Celtics problem.

Baylor and West were an incredible duo in their primes. In the 1961–62 season, they combined to average 69.1 points, 26.5 rebounds, and 10.0 assists per game. In the 1966 Finals, their fourth time in five years, they rallied from a 3–1 deficit to force a Game 7. West got hot in the fourth quarter, and the Lakers nearly erased a 16-point fourth-quarter lead. West averaged 33.9 points, and Baylor averaged 25 points and 16.4 rebounds.

It was Wilt Chamberlain who broke the Celtics' hold on the championship. He had lost to Russell's Celtics four times since he entered the NBA in 1959 and did so on three teams: the Philadelphia Warriors, the San Francisco Warriors, and the Philadelphia 76ers. But in 1967, after Boston had run off eight straight championships, Chamberlain finally beat Russell in the Eastern Division Finals.

That 76ers team was also stocked. Hal Greer actually led the Sixers in scoring in that five-game series. Only John Havlicek's 150 total points topped Greer's 146. Chamberlain averaged 21.6 points and 32 rebounds. The 76ers also got a combined 40 points per game from Wali Jones and future Hall of Famer Chet Walker.

Boston and Philly teams met again the following year in the East finals. Russell and Sam Jones—still highly productive—were thirty-three and thirty-four, respectively. Chamberlain and Greer were each thirty-one. The young buck among the stars was Havlicek, and he emerged as the best player. He averaged 25.6 points, 9.3 rebounds, and 8.6 assists, the new head of the Celtics' snake that saw five players average double figures. Russell did just enough to contain Chamberlain, and the Celtics took their title back. A win by the 76ers, and maybe they're a dynasty.

But after the season, Alex Hannum left the Sixers to coach the Oakland Oaks of the ABA. Earlier Rick Barry, who became the star of the San Francisco Warriors after Chamberlain was traded to Philadelphia, had a dispute over salary with the Warriors and signed with the Oaks. A judge ruled he had to sit out a year, but the door was opened for players to leave their NBA teams and go to the ABA. Hannum joined Barry in 1968. When the 76ers didn't find a coach Chamberlain wanted, he demanded a trade. Wilt didn't have an agent and he did only one-year deals, so he was adept at wielding his leverage as the game's biggest star. Eventually, the 76ers traded him to the only team he would play for: the Lakers.

A new big three was formed: Wilt, West, and Elgin.

All three of them averaged more than 20 points and 4.5 assists as the Lakers won the West and made it to the 1969 NBA Finals against, guess who, the Celtics.

This was Bill Russell's last hurrah. He was thirty-four years old, and his offense had disintegrated mightily. But he was still a defensive wizard, a force on the boards, and a championship leader in his third year as player-coach. Russell held Chamberlain to an average of 11.7 points in 47.3 minutes, the fewest he'd ever averaged in the Finals at that point. The series was tied 3–3 after each team won on their own court. All of the first six games were single digits save for Game 6 with the Lakers pulled away at the end. It set up a Game 7 final show-down in Los Angeles at the Forum.

Jerry West—who had 42 points, 13 rebounds, and 12 assists in Game 7 and was named Finals MVP—led the Lakers on a furious rally from down 15 points to give the Lakers a chance. But Don Nelson hit a famous lucky shot, a pull-up from the free throw line that bounced off the rim and way above the backboard before dropping in, to resettle the Celtics, and they held on to win Game 7.

And another dynasty was prevented.

THE MIAMI HEATLES

It's Shawn Marion's fault. And Jason Terry's. And Jason Kidd's. And, of course, Dirk Nowitzki's.

If there is a reason the Miami Heat with LeBron James, Dwyane Wade, and Chris Bosh aren't considered a dynasty, it is because those long-in-the-tooth NBA stars from Dallas got together and thwarted the most hyped collection of stars ever.

When LeBron announced he was leaving Cleveland to join Wade in Miami, and Bosh was also leaving the Toronto Raptors to join them, it was instant hysteria. It was simultaneously the greatest thing ever and the worst thing that could happen. This era of Heat basketball had all the makings of a dynasty.

They were riveting. They had massive star power. They were culturally iconic. They were polarizing. They were insanely memorable. They went to four consecutive NBA Finals and won back-to-back championships.

But when NBA dynasties are mentioned, you won't hear about these Heat because of the one thing they didn't have: decisive dominance. Two out of four titles is not bad by any means. Their record of accomplishment is on par with the Detroit Pistons. It just wasn't on par with their hype.

And now, as good as they were, and as entertaining as they were, the whole endeavor in hindsight seems a bit underwhelming.

"Not two. Not three. Not four. Not five. Not six. Not seven. Hey, and when I say that, I really believe it."

That was LeBron's famous quote about how many championships the Heat would win with their Big Three. And it came after an introductory press conference that rivaled a WWE event. They had a band, dancers, a stage, smoke machines, a DJ, and a packed AmericanAirlines Arena to welcome the biggest free-agent coup of all time. The expectations for this trio of All-NBA players joining forces in their prime were stratospheric.

Which was why the 2011 NBA Finals were such a letdown. The Heat won 58 games and breezed through the Eastern Conference. Miami beat the Boston Celtics—featuring the Big Three of Kevin Garnett, Paul Pierce, and Ray Allen that LeBron couldn't overcome while in Cleveland—in five games. But then they met the Dallas Mavericks in the Finals, which was an upset on its own as the Tim Duncan–led Spurs and the Kobe Bryant–led Lakers figured to be the favorites from the West. But San Antonio was upset in the first round, and the Mavericks swept the aging Lakers.

Dallas figured to be easy work for the Heat stars. But the Mavericks had so much experience, and the Heat had little together. Of the seven players who averaged double-digit minutes for the Mavericks in the Finals, four of them were at least thirty. The average age of those seven players was thirty-one, and their average years of experience was 12.4. Conversely, five of Miami's top seven in minutes were under thirty and their average age was 27.9.

The expectations for this trio of All-NBA players joining forces in their prime were stratospheric.

But the advantage of youth and talent did not win out for the Heat in one of the greatest Finals upsets in NBA history.

LeBron, who was vilified for leaving Cleveland, and for creating a behemoth of a three-headed monster, was arguably the third-best player on the Heat in the Finals. The defense of Shawn Marion, and the limitations of LeBron's game (which he would work on) led to James averaging just 17.8 points in the Finals. He had averaged more than 24 points in each of the three series leading up to the Finals.

The Heat rebounded in the lockout-shortened 2011–12 season. After grinding through two tough series against Indiana and Boston again, they made easy work of Oklahoma City, an upstart team featuring three future league MVPs in Kevin Durant, Russell Westbrook, and James Harden. The Heat simply had more experience and outclassed the young Thunder.

The 2013 NBA Finals was the highlight of the era. Miami won an epic seven-game series over the Spurs, with LeBron exorcising demons from 2007, when he was swept by the Spurs, and 2011, when he disappointed against Dallas. It didn't seem like the peak at the time, more like the Heat had finally gotten into a groove. But in the 2014 NBA Finals, Miami was outclassed by the Spurs, who needed just five games to eliminate the Heat. Wade, who had been struggling with injuries, wasn't the same. The hype and attention they rightfully garnered seemed to exhaust their potency and unison. After they lost, James returned to Cleveland as a free agent.

The era began with disappointment and ended with it. The real reason keeping the Heat from the elite levels of NBA's G.O.A.T. teams is because they were victims of their own hype.

THE LEW ALCINDOR BUCKS

In a 1968 expansion, the NBA rewarded Milwaukee with a franchise. It was the return of the NBA after the Milwaukee Hawks moved to St. Louis in 1955 (and eventually to Atlanta in 1968).

After posting the worst record in the East in their inaugural season, and winning a coin flip, the Bucks received the No. 1 draft pick for 1969. This just so happened to be the year the best big man anyone had seen since George Mikan and Bill Russell was leaving college. The seven-foot-one Lew Alcindor from the UCLA juggernaut was the consensus top pick after his third All-American nod. But the New York native and his famed skyhook also drew major interest from the competing ABA. Mikan, the commissioner, wooed Alcindor hard. Eventually, Alcindor asked each team to submit their best offer: the NBA's Milwaukee Bucks and ABA's New York Nets. He chose the Bucks offer. The Nets countered with five years, $3.25 million—more than the $1.4 million the Bucks offered—but Alcindor opted to keep his word since he'd given a verbal commitment to the Bucks.

The next year, Alcindor was named the 1970 Rookie of the Year after averaging 28.8 points and 14.5 rebounds and Milwaukee made the Eastern Division Finals. Because of Alcindor, they were an instant contender.

In April 1970, the Bucks made a trade to get some help for their dominant center. Milwaukee acquired Oscar Robertson from the Cincinnati Royals. Robertson was a six-foot-five point guard who did it all, and with ten years of experience he also brought veteran leadership. After averaging more than 30 points in six of his first seven years, Robertson had to slow down his scoring a bit. But he and Alcindor were a dynamic duo that formed practically out of nowhere.

They won the newly formed Western Conference by beating the San Francisco Warriors and the Los Angeles Lakers, who were without injured Elgin Baylor and Jerry West. The Bucks then swept the Baltimore Bullets in the Finals.

The day after the Bucks clinched the title, Alcindor announced he converted to Islam and changed his name to Kareem Abdul-Jabbar. A dynasty was in the offing.

A healthier Lakers team, with a thirty-five-year-old Chamberlain, in his final postseason, beat the Bucks with Abdul-Jabbar, Robertson, and a four-time All-Star in Bob Dandridge.

The year after that, the Bucks were upset in the first round by the Rick Barry–led Golden State Warriors.

The year after that, they made it all the way to the Finals riding the greatness of Abdul-Jabbar, as Father Time caught up with Robertson. The Bucks went into Boston Garden facing elimination for Game 6 and played a thriller that went into overtime. Abdul-Jabbar's skyhook in the final seconds proved to be the game winner and forced a Game 7. But the Celtics' depth outlasted the Bucks. Though it was in Milwaukee, it was the Bucks who struggled. Abdul-Jabbar was 10-for-21 and was outplayed by future Hall of Famer Dave Cowens.

With Robertson going 2-for-13, the Celtics had the better supporting cast and cruised in Game 7.

Robertson retired, the Bucks failed to make the playoffs, and Abdul-Jabbar wanted out. Increasingly conscious and hailing from the bustling metropolis of New York, he'd never quite bonded with Milwaukee. He wanted to go home to New York, or Los Angeles, or DC. He had one year left on his contract and made it clear he would not re-sign. So instead of losing him for nothing, Milwaukee traded their franchise center to Los Angeles.

And the Bucks never matured into a dynasty.

THE WALT FRAZIER KNICKS

In a span of five years, the Knickerbockers won two championships, lost another NBA Finals, and reached two Eastern Conference Finals. They gave us swag personified in the form of Walt Frazier. They gave us one of the most iconic moments ever—when Willis Reed ran out of the tunnel despite his injured hip.

Why don't the Knicks get more dynasty love? It was an issue of parity.

The end of the Celtics era created a power vacuum. The forefathers of the NBA were old. The stars were fading. The NBA was transitioning into a new era.

There were ten championships between Russell's last title in 1969 and the start of the Magic Johnson–led Lakers dynasty in 1980. Eight teams won in that span, including the Knicks and Celtics winning twice with a couple years in between.

No one team dominated. It was the first era of NBA parity where several good teams vied for supremacy and most of them got their day of glory.

Also a factor: the ABA. Birthed in 1967, at the back end of the Celtics dynasty, the American Basketball Association grew into a rival. With players like Dr. J, Charlie Scott, Dan Issel, Spencer Haywood, George McGinnis, Rick Barry, Connie Hawkins, Artis Gilmore—it was hard to be unanimously dominant in the way a dynasty needs to be with a competing league full of obviously great players. The dominance had to be so overwhelming.

While the Knicks might not have met that standard, they were perhaps the most successful of the parity era. Certainly the most interesting.

In 1969–70, the Knicks won 60 games as Frazier took a sophomore leap. The Atlanta fella with all the style one man can withstand. He had the epic mutton chops with the big hats and fancy suits. They called him Mr. Cool. The six-foot-four point guard was up to 20.9 points and a career-best 8.2 assists with 6.0 rebounds in his third season. And the Knicks ascended with him.

Willis Reed, the six-foot-nine center, was already the established Knicks star. But Frazier gave the Knicks a No. 2 they needed, a playmaker who could score and run the show. Dave DeBusschere, who came over from Detroit, solidified his Hall of Fame status by giving the Knicks his last remaining good years. And Bill Bradley, the former Princeton star and Rhodes Scholar who played in Italy his first two years out of college, was just coming into his own.

The top-seeded Knicks survived a seven-game first-round scare against the Bullets. But they beat the Bucks handily in the next round and wound up in another dogfight against the Lakers. In a pivotal Game 5, Reed was knocked out of the game in the first quarter with a hip injury as the Knicks got down early. But the Knicks rallied from a double-digit deficit in the fourth quarter. The Madison Square Garden crowd

They gave us one of the most iconic moments ever—when Willis Reed ran out of the tunnel despite his injured hip.

of more than nineteen thousand was engulfed in the drama as the Knicks survived. They lost in Game 6 as Reed was still out with an injury, setting up a Game 7 at the Garden.

The game was delayed while Reed was receiving treatment in the locker room. No one knew what was up, but he was getting a cortisone shot so he could play. And when he emerged from the tunnel before the game, the Garden went crazy. His presence energized the team, in addition to giving Wilt Chamberlain some resistance. The most inspired: Frazier. He was magnificent with 36 points, 19 assists, and harassing defense all over the court.

The front cover of the New York *Daily News* read KNICKS WIN IT! in what seemed like the biggest font possible. It was the first championship for a franchise that was there from the beginning. The Knicks were one of the original franchises in the Basketball Association of America in 1946.

Three years after their first, the Knicks won again in 1973. Reed was on the downside, but Frazier arguably had a better team around him. Earl "the Pearl" Monroe joined Frazier for one of the most dazzling backcourts in history. Bradley and DeBusschere were still really good. Phil Jackson, longtime vet and future Hall of Famer Jerry Lucas, and Dean Meminger rounded out a rotation of the best defense in the NBA. They kept the Celtics 10 points below their season average in the second round of the playoffs, outlasting Boston in a seven-game series.

The elderly Lakers—Wilt, thirty-six; West, thirty-four; Goodrich, twenty-nine; Baylor, retired—were easy work for the Knicks in the Finals. Los Angeles managed just 96.8 points per game, 15 points below their regular-season average.

The Knicks ran it back again the following year with the same core. This was their chance to really separate themselves from the rest of the pack. But after nearly getting upset by Elvin Hayes's Bullets, they lost in five games to the Celtics in the Eastern Conference Finals.

Still, a formidable five-year run, especially in light of what the franchise has done since.

ACKNOWLEDGMENTS

One of my good friends, who I've known for decades now, did this animated short about the time he met Dennis Rodman in the airport and, because of his mother, choked and didn't get an autograph. Filmmaker Jason Gilmore executed this funny piece of storytelling in *Me, My Mom and Dennis Rodman* that is light-hearted and cute. He's practically laughing as he tells the story. Jason and I know it's funny now, but it wasn't funny then. Because he was that big of a Pistons fan.

So when I got to the Bad Boys section of this book, I knew exactly who to call. As we do from time to time, we talked Pistons basketball. Sometimes I like to get him started on Michael Jordan and the Bulls for my own entertainment. No, the rivalry isn't dead in his heart. But it was great to visit with him about the Pistons dynasty, especially the impact the Bad Boys had on the culture, what they meant to diehard teenagers like himself, and the context of how that team fit into its society.

It was so fun geeking out on these historical, philosophical, and even existential conversations about basketball with people who find the same pleasure. It reminded me of the perks of traveling the land covering the NBA, as I did for ten years as a beat writer and another five or so partially as a columnist: connecting with fellow hoop heads. Sure, you get to see family and old friends on the road. But then there are those people who know why you're in town, think what we do is cool, and are appreciative when you can find them a couple of tickets. Yes, it's a bit of a flex. But there is some meaning there, too—a joy of basketball being shared, a kinship of people who were seized in their youth by the NBA and still care more than they probably should. Especially in the playoffs, it was a habit of mine to hang out near the arena before the game, catch the vibe, and have lunch with a local who wanted to experience it, too. Such benefits are usually taken for granted, but the pandemic created an appreciation for even the simple things, like good basketball conversation.

That's what this book was—a good basketball conversation. I had many of them with people I know who care deeply about these teams, and with old sports writers through their old stories chronicling the classic and profound moments that made these teams great. So many hours just flew by reading the *Minneapolis Star Tribune* archives from the days of George Mikan or *Boston Globe* articles from sixty-something years ago to uncover the meaning those Celtics had in those times. Reading the books, watching the documentaries, poring over the stats, it was like a graduate course in basketball. I couldn't do this without those conversations, without those previous works, and definitely not without Newspapers.com!

But the most critical acknowledgment, the one that trumps them all, belongs to my wife. My sanity would slip through my fingers if not for her presence and love. Three books in now, I am still a complete mess writing them. She is the one who gets better at this process.

INDEX